GIVE REFUGE TO THE STRANGER

GIVE REFUGE TO THE STRANGER

THE PAST, PRESENT, AND FUTURE OF SANCTUARY

Linda Rabben

Walnut Creek, California

Left Coast Press is committed to preserving ancient forests and natural resources. We elected to print this title on 30% post consumer recycled paper, processed chlorine free. As a result, for this printing, we have saved:

3 Trees (40' tall and 6-8" diameter)
1 Million BTUs of Total Energy
239 Pounds of Greenhouse Gases
1,152 Gallons of Wastewater
70 Pounds of Solid Waste

Left Coast Press made this paper choice because our printer, Thomson-Shore, Inc., is a member of Green Press Initiative, a nonprofit program dedicated to supporting authors, publishers, and suppliers in their efforts to reduce their use of fiber obtained from endangered forests.

For more information, visit www.greenpressinitiative.org

Environmental impact estimates were made using the Environmental Defense Paper Calculator. For more information visit: www.papercalculator.org.

LEFT COAST PRESS, INC.
1630 North Main Street, #400
Walnut Creek, CA 94596
http://www.LCoastPress.com

ISBN   978-1-61132-029-9 hardcover
ISBN   978-1-61132-030-5 paperback
eISBN 978-1-61132-031-2

Library of Congress Cataloging-in-Publication Data:

Rabben, Linda, 1947-
Give refuge to the stranger : the past, present and future of sanctuary / Linda Rabben.
    p. cm.
ISBN 978-1-61132-029-9 (hardcover : alk. paper)—ISBN 978-1-61132-030-5 (pbk. : alk. paper)
1. Asylum, Right of. I. Title.
    K3268.3.R33 2011
    342.08'3--dc22

2010051477

Printed in the United States of America

⊗™ The paper used in this publication meets the minimum requirements of American National Standard for Information Sciences—Permanence of Paper for Printed Library Materials, ANSI/NISO Z39.48–1992.

Cover Photo: Jim Corbett helps Guatemalan refugee climb a border fence into Arizona, 1984. Ron Medvescek/*Arizona Daily Star*.

In memory of Miep Gies, 1909–2010, sanctuarian,

and Howard Zinn, 1922–2010, social historian;

and with thanks to JE, for being there.

CONTENTS

ACKNOWLEDGMENTS

Many people in several countries gave me various kinds of help—and refuge—during the four years I spent researching and writing this book.

At home in the sanctuary city of Takoma Park, Maryland, Rev. Phil Wheaton and Michael McConnell gave me informative interviews about their work for the 1980s Sanctuary Movement. Zelda Bell provided practical assistance that made it possible for me to do research in the UK and France, and Alice Haddix helped arrange my visit to Tucson. Maura Polli read Chapter Two and made helpful suggestions for changes. Imam Daoud Nassimi and Professor Steven Caton kindly provided information about sanctuary in Islam.

In Tucson sanctuarians Rev. Ricardo Elford, Rosemary and Bill Hallinan, Rev. Robin Hoover, Mike Humphrey, John Miles, Sebastian Quinac, Rachel Wilson, and others kindly gave me interviews; Abby Root offered hospitality and a listening ear. Linda Green, Kathryn Rodriguez, and Kent Walker helped in other ways.

In El Paso Joe Heyman was tremendously helpful during my visit; afterward he read Chapter Two, made useful suggestions for changes, and became a friend. Also in El Paso and environs, sanctuarians Kathleen Erickson, Delia Gomez, Fernando Garcia, Ruben Garcia, and Rev. Peter Hinde gave inspiring interviews that increased my understanding of old and new sanctuary movements. In Juarez, Mexico, Sr. Betty Campbell and Sr. Mary Alice shared their experiences with me.

In St. Paul, MN, the matchless Nelly Trocmé Hewett shared her encyclopedic knowledge of her parents André and Magda Trocmé and of Le Chambon-sur-Lignon and the surrounding region; she also read Chapter Six and corrected many errors, small and large.

In Le Chambon-sur-Lignon, France, Annik Flaud and Gérard Bollon graciously provided a great deal of information in a very short time. Thanks also to my friend John Graney, M.D., who drove me to Le Chambon with dizzying proficiency along the winding back roads of the Haute Loire.

I am grateful to interviewees, such as "Mary," who requested anonymity. They are heroes whose courage and persistence continue to impress and encourage me.

In Britain Mahamad Al-Shagra, Rev. John Arnold, Sally Daghlian, Bob Deffee, Emma Ginn, Jim Gomersall, Eveline Louden, Roger Norris, Dele Olawanle, Kate Roberts, Jan Shaw, Debora Singer, Ahlam Souidi, Chris Williams, and Jean Wilson gave me interviews and inspiration. Conor Gearty was a gracious and encouraging host at London School of Economics' Centre for the Study of Human Rights, where I was a visiting fellow in 2007–08. My colleague at CSHR, Michael Welch, was helpful to me in London and after. The Scottish Refugee Council in Glasgow gave me shelter for a week and taught me much about integration. My special thanks go to John Campbell and his family, Gary Christie, Celia Clarke (who read Chapter Nine), Jonathan Cox (who read Chapters Nine and Ten), Mike Kaye, Moyna McGlynn (who read Chapter One), and Rev. Nicholas Sagovsky, who were especially encouraging. Zoe Stevens and Rev. Patrick Wright kindly facilitated visits to detention centers. Moyra Ashford, Sue and Patrick Cunningham, Catherine Kimmel, Pauline Moon, John and Elizabeth Nurser, Jan Rocha, Patti Whaley, and Rob Wheeler provided indispensable hospitality and friendship.

Librarians and archivists, such as Wendy Chmielewski, curator of the Swarthmore College Peace Collection, gave me valuable assistance. Thanks also to employers and colleagues who gave practical help: Juan Mendez of the International Center for Transitional Justice, Robert Goodland, Marie Marr Jackson (my supervisor at the United States Institute of Peace, who allowed me to work from the UK in 2007), and Virginia Bouvier, also of USIP, who made me aware of Colombian peace communities. My editor at Left Coast Press, Jennifer Collier, encouraged me with her enthusiasm, understanding, and good advice. I am grateful to copyright holders who gave me permission to reproduce images of their work.

Patchouli did not live to see me finish the book, but she was a devoted companion during the research. John Eckenrode's stalwart moral support has made all the difference.

If I have forgotten anyone who helped, I beg pardon. The mistakes in this book are my own, and I ask forgiveness for them, too.

Fleeing the threat of genital mutilation 17-year-old Fauziya Kassindja left her home in the West African country of Togo in late 1994. Unlike many girls in her ethnic group she had avoided "cutting," because her father did not approve of the practice. But after he died his kin decided to marry her off to a 45-year-old local leader who insisted that she undergo the procedure (Kassindja and Bashir 1998).

With the help of her mother and sister Fauziya fled Togo on the first plane she could board, to Germany. After a short stay there she acquired a false passport and came to the United States, where she had relatives. She requested asylum on arrival. Despite the fact that she was a minor who should not have been detained, the Immigration and Naturalization Service sent her to various jails and prisons for 17 months. During her incarceration she was kept with convicted felons although she had not committed any crime. She fell ill, suffered from suicidal depression, and was prevented from practicing her religion. Fauziya was lucky, however. Unlike most detained asylum seekers in the United States, she had pro bono legal representation and moral support from human rights organizations and activists.

I read about Fauziya's plight in a *Washington Post* op-ed article early in 1996. As a human rights activist working on Brazil for Amnesty International (AI), I found the story of her ordeal difficult to believe. Could the United States' asylum system really be so unjust, so cruel? I started writing to Fauziya in prison and sent her "care packages" of toiletries and (at her request) Islamic literature. By this time *The New York Times* was covering her case in the Metro section of the paper, because she was detained in northern New Jersey. I contacted her pro bono lawyers and asked for the case records, where I found many details not mentioned in the *Times* articles. AIUSA could not take up her case but suggested that I write a letter to the editor of the *Times* urging her release. The newspaper published my letter across from an editorial calling for her to be paroled while her case was adjudicated. About a week later she was paroled, and six weeks later she was granted asylum. The decision in her case set an important precedent, making it possible for young women threatened with genital mutilation to gain asylum in the United States.

That was how my involvement in asylum began. I started attending meetings of a group of Washington organizations that work on these issues, represent asylum seekers, do public outreach and advocacy, and educate Congress and policymakers. As an anthropologist and a non-lawyer, I found the intricacies of U.S. immigration law daunting. Focusing on Brazil and writing books on human rights took most of my time and energy in the late 1990s and early 2000s. But I could not let go of the asylum issue. Too many heartrending stories of detained asylum seekers kept grabbing my attention. As a human rights activist I was encountering torture survivors and other victims of human rights abuses who struggled against great obstacles to gain refuge in the United States.

After 9/11 the situation for asylum seekers in the United States became even worse. I also became aware of the draconian laws against them that were passed and implemented in European countries. After finishing a book on Brazil in 2005—10 years after I first heard about Fauziya Kassindja—I was looking for a new subject to write about. I found an article I had published back in 1997 about detention conditions for asylum seekers. Almost a decade later those conditions had changed little. Despite the concerted pressure of human rights organizations over the years, the immigration service (now known as Immigration and Customs Enforcement, or ICE) was still mistreating thousands of asylum seekers and other immigration detainees. As the immigration issue acquired greater political visibility in 2006, I started doing research for this book. I soon found out that sanctuary's roots go deep into human history. As a result my research ranged widely, over thousands of years of giving refuge to strangers around the world. It took me to archives, libraries, detention centers, courtrooms, offices, and communities in the United States, United Kingdom, and France. I interviewed asylum seekers and refugees and acquired more knowledge along the way by working for a refugee agency and volunteering at a center for torture survivors.

As an anthropologist I wondered where the idea of asylum came from, how it evolved, and whether it was a "human universal." To try to answer these questions I did research in a wide variety of disciplines and periods. First I wanted to find out if my own discipline could provide a framework for analyzing and interpreting the phenomena of asylum and sanctuary in many cultures. It was not difficult to find numerous works on the human distaste for, hostility toward, and avoidance of "the Other"; but studies of cooperation and sociability among humans of different groups were much less common.

My hypothesis was that sanctuary might have begun to help females to avoid incest and to diversify the gene pool of receiving communities. But subjects I had thought important to look into, such as endogamy and exogamy (marriage inside and outside one's group or community), are no longer in fashion among anthropologists. As a result I could find very few modern publications on those topics. Late 19th- and early 20th-century anthropologists such as Edward Westermarck seemed to be the last people to have been interested in them. The most useful studies of sanctuary that I found were written in 1887 and 1911 by classical or church scholars. One of the academic readers who reviewed my manuscript doubted that such antique sources could be acceptable in this day and age. (Because they were very carefully documented, I think they are still relevant, and so I have cited them.) Even the Human Relations Area Files, which contain ethnographic studies on hundreds of subjects, contained nothing on sanctuary more recent than the 1980s.

Studies of chimpanzees and bonobos, our primate cousins, seemed more germane and promising. Primatologists have done important research on altruistic behavior within and among communities of those species. Their sophisticated studies have found that "aiding others at a cost or risk to oneself is widespread in the animal world" and "helpful acts that are costly in the short run may produce long-term benefits if recipients return the favor" (de Waal 1996: 12). De Waal also has not shied away from pointing out similarities between primate and human behavior. He and other primatologists have gone beyond the debate over rigidly deterministic (and to my mind, reductionist) theories of the "selfish gene," which could not explain altruism, by studying primates' behavior over time, in captivity and in the wild.[1] Their observations have shown that primates give refuge to strangers, especially females fleeing to other communities from incestuous approaches or violent attacks by male kin. These findings seemed to reinforce my own interpretation of sanctuary as rooted in primordial rules of exogamy and the incest taboo (which Westermarck correctly analyzed a century ago). My approach takes into account sanctuary's apparent universality in our species, as well as its altruistic character. I could not find any other account of sanctuary among humans that interprets the phenomenon in this way.

A number of anthropologists have tried to apply primatological findings to human behavior. A useful book called *Missing the Revolution: Darwinism for Social Scientists* helped me understand both the advantages and dangers of extrapolating from one species to another and of using Darwinian theories to explain human behavior. As a result I have been very careful in Chapter Two. I hope that interested researchers will build on my modest attempt to develop an interpretation of sanctuary behavior that takes both biological and cultural evolution into account.

Discussing sanctuary and asylum comparatively, across thousands of years and many societies, is a bold exercise. Several reviewers wanted me to give more attention to the "social and cultural factors that shape people's actions and national policy and practice," the "social, economic or other conditions [that] promote positive responses to the asylum seeker" and the "factors [that] turn people against refugees." But I found I could not take a conventional approach to social causation by pointing to abstract "factors" or "forces" in the face of a richly contradictory reality. Risking their lives and livelihoods to help despised strangers, the sanctuarians whose stories I tell often defied powerful social, cultural, and political rules and norms. Those who abided by the rules thought that the sanctuarians were misguided, selfish, crazy, or criminal to act as they did.

For example, it is difficult to explain, by invoking social or economic factors, why Oskar Schindler—who profited from Jewish slave labor and fraternized with Nazi officials while allowing his workers to sabotage production—risked his life to rescue Jews. Schindler seemed to act quixotically, against his own best interests, and his motives remain mysterious. I even wondered if he might have taken sociopathic pleasure in fooling the Nazis from whom he was stealing. But such an analysis would be invidious and obtuse, considering the life-saving success of Schindler's altruistic behavior in the eyes of anyone but a Nazi. At any rate I do not believe that altruistic actions can be satisfactorily explained by standard social-science logic, which tends to assume that human behavior is rational, orderly, and consciously self-interested, in accordance with functional social norms. Life is messier and more confounding than that. As Charlie Chan once said: "Theory like mist on eyeglasses, obscures facts" (Bernstein 2010: 16). In the interests of scholarship, however, those who are theoretically inclined are welcome to use this book as a launching pad.

Still, I have tried to put sanctuarians' behavior in its social, political, and economic context, precisely because it may be inexplicable without such background. For example, it would be difficult to understand why Catholic churches in late medieval Britain insisted on giving permanent sanctuary to thieves and other criminals without our knowing something about the church's struggle with the state for political dominance. That kind of contextual information is woven throughout the stories I tell.

Because of the wide-ranging nature of this subject, I had to place limits on what I covered. For example, I have not discussed topics such as the social construction of the Other or the history of refugees in the 20th century in great detail; they have been the subjects of many other books.[2] Instead I decided to focus, especially in the later chapters, on individual asylum seekers and their experience with the state apparatus. Accordingly I have reported many facts about modern asylum policies and practices, about which most people know little. Citizens should be aware of how their government treats people seeking refuge and what their taxes are paying for. I also wanted to educate the public about the many grassroots, community, and non-profit organizations that seek to help asylum seekers and refugees. In the chapters about present-day asylum and sanctuary I write as an engaged activist as well as an anthropologist, because I want to encourage those who work on asylum and immigration issues to continue their important work. As a defender of asylum and an admirer of sanctuary I do not pretend to be neutral; but I am very concerned about being accurate and coherent and backing up my claims. Above all this book should be useful to many kinds of readers, from scholars to resettlement workers.

The story of asylum goes back to prehistoric times, because sanctuary for those accused of crimes or fleeing persecution is one of our most ancient customs. Human beings may have given refuge to strangers for 100,000 years or more. So many societies around the world practice or have practiced it that it can be considered a human universal, a characteristic of our species as a whole.

Over the past five centuries travelers, historians, moralists, and anthropologists have found examples of asylum and sanctuary in hundreds of traditional societies, from the Arunta of central Australia to the Ovambo of southwestern Africa and the Berbers of Morocco. In these cultures sacred sites or important figures, such as religious and political leaders, have provided refuge to people accused of serious crimes, runaway slaves, debtors, and those fleeing war or persecution, from time immemorial.

Among the first recorded asylum seekers in Western tradition was Cain in the Old Testament. After Cain killed Abel, God told him there would be no place where he could stay safely. Every man's hand would be raised against him, because he had killed his brother. Cain argued with God, saying the penalty was too harsh, and God relented. The mark he put on Cain's forehead was not to punish but to protect him. Thus Cain gained asylum from God, the ultimate sanctuary.

In the Old Testament the Hebrews established cities of refuge, where those accused of serious crimes, especially murder, could escape vengeance. A fugitive could remain in one of the cities of refuge until his accuser, usually the chief rabbi, died. Then the charge would lapse.

The Western traditions of asylum and sanctuary are also rooted in classical civilization. The Greek word *asylos* means "inviolate" and refers to a place or a person. The closely linked word "sanctuary" comes from the Latin word for a sacred place. The ancient Egyptians, Greeks, and Romans provided sanctuary mainly to runaway slaves, who had no rights under the law. In addition certain places in ancient Greece—groves, rock formations, and temples—were traditional sanctuaries where those accused of crimes could remain unmolested.

After Constantine made Christianity the state religion of the Roman Empire in the 4th century c.e., the already ancient custom of sanctuary continued. In medieval Europe an accused malefactor could seek asylum from a bishop or abbot by throwing himself at the holy man's feet. The Catholic Church also codified sanctuary through an elaborate system of rules and rituals in designated places. Sanctuary is recorded in 6th-century Britain in the laws of King Ethelred of Kent. The secular ruler (who was considered to hold his power by the grace of God) gave the power of granting sanctuary to religious institutions and authorities: cathedrals, abbeys, churches, monasteries, convents, bishops, and abbots.

Most sanctuaries gave temporary refuge—usually 40 days—but a few major churches in Britain provided permanent sanctuary. Widespread abuses of the privilege led in the late Middle Ages to secular laws abridging the practice. Henry VIII introduced cities of refuge after he destroyed the Catholic religious houses that had given sanctuary for a thousand years. Finally in 1624 the British Parliament abolished church sanctuary.

This did not mean the end of sanctuary and asylum in Britain or anywhere else. Sanctuary survived in the debtors' prisons, and mental asylums were intended to shelter those who could not take care of themselves. By the end of the 17th century asylum had gone through a great transformation and revival, becoming a secular institution, protecting state sovereignty under international law. Meanwhile thousands of refugees were crossing borders to escape religious or political persecution. They arrived in America from Britain and Europe, in Britain from Europe and America, in Europe from other European countries.

The first people to be called refugees in English were thousands of Protestant Huguenots who fled from Catholic France to Britain and America from 1685 until the late 18th century. But they were by no means the first to seek refuge in those countries. As early as 1494 Jews arrived in Britain, Islamic countries, and several New World territories after their expulsion from Spain. They and their successors found a mixed welcome.

Members of persecuted minorities arriving in sheltering countries brought special skills, labor power, or wealth, but they also aroused resentment, envy, and hostility. Each group that arrived in large numbers was subject to the same stereotypes: Jews, Huguenots, Irish, Germans, Italians, East Indians, West Indians, Mexicans, and many others were said to be dirty, oversexed, smelly, greedy, rude, mentally retarded, sickly, and criminal. After the first fit of self-congratulation, hosts often reacted negatively to those they had received with kindness. They passed laws and acted in ways calculated to make refugees feel unwelcome, stop more from arriving, or expel those already in residence.

Yet host societies benefited from the newcomers. By the second or third generation some refugees had been incorporated into the receiving society. The age-old argument continued about whether giving refuge to the stranger was a good idea. Meanwhile, persecution went on, and the strangers kept coming. For the most part there were no laws codifying asylum in the late 19th century, but large numbers of Europeans arrived in the New World, fleeing persecution or starvation in their home countries. In reaction, in the early 20th century some countries passed laws to limit the entry of refugees.

After World War I, which created millions of refugees, countries including the United States and the United Kingdom tried to prevent their entry through restrictive laws and regulations. The League of Nations created a special department to assist refugees, but it became increasingly difficult for them to escape persecution and war. The golden door of Emma Lazarus's poem, inscribed on the Statue of Liberty, slammed shut.

In the years before the outbreak of World War II, refugees from religious or political persecution in Germany encountered overwhelming difficulty in finding shelter elsewhere. In 1939 the *St. Louis* left Germany for New York with 930 Jewish and seven non-Jewish refugees on board (Miller and Ogilvie 2006: 174–75). Prevented from docking anywhere in North America, the ship returned to Germany; 254 of its passengers later died in concentration or extermination camps. Even the *Kindertransport*, which facilitated the escape of almost 10,000 Jewish children from Germany, Austria, and Czechoslovakia in 1939, was hedged with restrictions and red tape. These widely publicized incidents and others showed that refuge was not established in international law as a human right and was only grudgingly conceded.

After World War II some 40 million displaced people wandered Europe. In response the Universal Declaration of Human Rights (1948), the UN Convention Relating to the Status of Refugees (1951), the UN Protocol Relating to the Status of Refugees (1966), and other international agreements were supposed to establish a high standard for the treatment of asylum seekers by the signatories, including Britain and the United States. As of 2009, 147 nations had signed and ratified the refugee convention and its protocols, which guarantee the right to seek (although not to gain) asylum and govern the treatment of asylum seekers. But their implementation of these international agreements varies greatly. A few countries have not signed and do not pretend to abide by the convention. These nations are not the only ones that export asylum seekers to other countries or forcibly return them to the places where they were persecuted.

The Cold War may have been the heyday of political asylum, as Western countries welcomed those fleeing persecution by communist states. Asylum became an instrument of foreign policy. From

Rudolph Nureyev to the Dalai Lama, celebrities and artists, writers, intellectuals, and dissidents went West for freedom. Some asylum seekers also fled tyrannical Third World or right-wing regimes, and others fled the West for the East or the South. But after the Cold War ended and persecution continued in many countries, from Yugoslavia to Kenya, nations that had received asylum seekers and refugees for almost 50 years felt overwhelmed by them. From the early 1990s on governments passed increasingly restrictive laws and implemented punitive policies to staunch the inflow of asylum seekers from Iran, Somalia, Colombia, Democratic Republic of Congo, Afghanistan, and many other countries.

Individuals seeking asylum or sanctuary are few in comparison to the floods of refugees fleeing war, genocide, and natural disaster, as well as immigrants seeking jobs and a better life. Yet in Britain they are publicly scapegoated, labeled "bogus," regarded with suspicion or fear as possible terrorists, pushed into destitution and often deported. In the United States, perhaps because of its self-identification as a country of immigrants, asylum seekers are portrayed more sympathetically in the media but still detained in jails and prisons with convicted felons and frequently denied refuge and deported. European countries have more or less compassionate policies toward asylum seekers, depending on local and national economic and political factors. In every receiving country, asylum and immigration are hot issues, used by politicians to mobilize support, win elections, and exercise power.

Over time and under pressure, many nations' commitment to the rights of asylum seekers has eroded. The reasons for this erosion include:

- Eligibility for asylum is difficult to establish;
- Increasing numbers of asylum seekers fleeing human rights abuses have overwhelmed receiving countries, resulting in judicial backlogs that sometimes go on for years;
- Small numbers of terrorists and criminals have gained asylum in countries they later sought to attack or victimize;
- Easily manipulated xenophobia has resulted in exclusionary laws and policies that prevent asylum seekers from obtaining sanctuary;
- Countries with limited resources cannot afford to host asylum seekers;

- Economic refugees have gained political asylum under false pretenses.

In the 1980s and 1990s receiving countries with similar problems and views of immigration borrowed strategies from one another to prevent asylum seekers from gaining sanctuary. These included:

- Drastically limiting numbers of those who could seek asylum;
- Giving immigration officers at ports of entry the option to summarily deport a wide range of people;
- Detaining asylum seekers in poorly maintained facilities, jails, or prisons in remote areas for months or years;
- Subjecting asylum seekers to cruel, inhuman, or degrading treatment in custody;
- Making it difficult or impossible for detained asylum seekers to obtain legal representation;
- Denying permission for asylum seekers to work or obtain certain social benefits while waiting for their cases to be adjudicated, sometimes for years.

Today asylum is under threat in many countries that once welcomed asylum seekers. Numbers of asylum seekers arriving in the United States, United Kingdom, and other countries have decreased markedly, because governments have instituted policies that prevent their entry.[3] Those who do manage to request asylum on or after arrival in another country often fail in the attempt. Host societies have become increasingly hostile to asylum seekers. Many endure destitution, illness, and the isolation of exile, sometimes for years, only to be deported back to the place where they were persecuted. Some die as a result.

Yet thousands of groups and individuals in countries around the world are offering help to these threatened, vulnerable strangers. Throughout history people have organized or made special efforts to offer refuge to the stranger, sometimes at great risk to their own lives. The compelling question this book raises is Why?

The answers may lie in close study of several cases: sanctuary in ancient and tribal societies; the elaborate rituals of church sanctuary in medieval Britain; the Underground Railroad in 19th-century America; the Kindertransport that sent thousands of Jewish children to England in 1939; the rescue of thousands of Jewish refugees in several French villages during World War II; the 1980s Sanctuary Movement in the United States; peace communities in Colombia during a half-century-long civil war; the Sans-Papiers movement in France; and grassroots refugee-integration projects in present-day Glasgow. These are only a few among a multitude of examples.

Give Refuge to the Stranger traces the evolution of sanctuary from its ancient beginnings up to the present day. It focuses not only on the asylum seekers and the governments or authorities who give or refuse asylum but also on the social groups that mobilize to provide sanctuary, often outside the law and at great risk. Finally it speculates about the future of asylum in a world seemingly overwhelmed by strife and persecution on a massive scale. What does the persistent human proclivity to give refuge say about our species and its prospects? Will the history of asylum have a happy or a tragic ending? Fortunately it is too soon to answer this question; we are still in the midst of the story and the struggle for the right to refuge.

One of the most striking things I have noticed over the years is how little Americans know about the situation of asylum seekers and the inhumane, inefficient, and ineffective system of detention and adjudication our tax dollars pay for. When I tell friends, acquaintances, or groups that in this "land of the free and home of the brave" people guilty of no crime, survivors of systematic persecution, abuse, and torture, are incarcerated for months or even years, denied legal representation, and deported without mercy by our government, they are shocked and incredulous. The stubborn refusal of the U.S. government to improve detention conditions and of lawmakers to reform the immigration system seems enough to lead any caring person to despair.

But thousands of organizations, community groups, and people of good will are trying to do something to change this depressing state of affairs. Having already published *Fierce Legion of Friends: A History of Human Rights Campaigns and Campaigners*, about the generations of activists who have organized and mobilized to protect and advance human rights, I felt it was time to focus on the people who are working with persistence, courage, and determination to help asylum seekers, refugees, and immigrants in the United States and other countries. My research has given me many opportunities to meet and learn from them. I hope the story of their efforts is as inspiring and heartening to readers as it has been to me. And I hope it moves you to take action, however modest, to protect and advance the ancient, noble institution of sanctuary, a vital part of our human heritage.

CHAPTER ONE

Asylum Seekers' Stories

A well founded fear of being persecuted

CONVENTION RELATING TO THE STATUS OF REFUGEES, 1951

Every day thousands of individuals seek asylum in scores of countries around the world.[1] In doing so they are exercising a basic human right as defined in article 14 of the Universal Declaration of Human Rights (1948): "Everyone has the right to seek and to enjoy in other countries asylum from persecution" (Center for the Study of Human Rights 1992: 7). The vast majority do not immediately obtain refuge through the elaborate systems established by international and national laws and policies. Many wait years for a definitive decision. In the meantime they may go underground, living precariously or in destitution, denied social welfare benefits, the right to work legally, and the right to participate freely in their adopted society. Others, including torture survivors, children, pregnant women, the elderly, and the seriously ill, are detained for indefinite periods in jails, prisons, and detention centers. Only a few have the opportunity to tell their story to the public or the media. Usually these stories remain unread, except by government officials and lawyers, in moldering files. For the most part asylum seekers are voiceless, invisible, forgotten. As a result many citizens have only the vaguest notion—or none at all—of what or who they are.

According to the UN Refugee Convention of 1951, a refugee is a person who

owing to a well founded fear of being persecuted for reasons
of race, religion, nationality, membership of a particular social
group or political opinion, is outside the country of his nationality and is unable or, owing to such fear, is unwilling to avail
himself of the protection of that country; or who, not having a
nationality and being outside the country of his former habitual
residence as a result of such events, is unable or, owing to such
fear, is unwilling to return to it.[2] (Chapter 1, article 1 [2])

Governments use this rather narrow definition to exclude as well
as to include asylum seekers.[3] In many countries they are confused
or conflated with illegal immigrants or even criminals and treated
as scapegoats, accused of causing economic and social problems for
which they are not responsible. They may be subjected to xenophobic reactions and even lethal violence that deepen their isolation and
suffering.

A relatively small proportion—no more than 30% in major receiving countries such as the United States and Britain—does gain asylum
and the benefits that are supposed to go along with this legal status.
They may succeed because they arrive with copious documentation
of the persecution they suffered and have the financial resources to
hire a good lawyer or the luck to find skillful pro bono representation.
But most do not.

Following are a few of the stories of asylum seekers that have
come to light in recent years. They give an idea of what many asylum
seekers experience in their search for refuge. Most of these stories remain unfinished, their protagonists lost in a Kafkaesque maze of red
tape and systematic cruelty.

Mary's Story

The most dangerous moment of Mary's year in prison came in the
solitary-confinement cell, when a guard demanded that she kneel before him.[4] She refused: "That is an act of worship, and I worship only
God; I will not kneel before any man." Mary is not sure what he did
to her after that; the next thing she remembers is waking up in the
intensive-care unit of the local hospital, shackled to the bed.

After much pleading and bargaining, she was unshackled, and
the guards watched television in her room (against regulations). She

stayed in the hospital for a week. Eventually she was paroled from prison and allowed to work, but she must keep immigration authorities informed of her whereabouts until her case is decided—if her case is decided.

Mary is no criminal; she is an asylum seeker. In the early 1990s, after a relative who was a high-ranking government official was assassinated, she fled the African country that was her home. Most members of her family also fled and now live in various European and Asian countries. She sought refuge in the United States.

In her search for asylum Mary had bad luck with a series of incompetent, over-committed, or crooked lawyers who took her money but did nothing. Her case got lost in a backlog of hundreds of thousands of cases. After several years, having heard nothing from her lawyer or the immigration authorities, she presented herself at the district office of the Immigration and Naturalization Service (INS, now known as Immigration and Customs Enforcement, whose grimly apposite acronym is ICE). There she learned that an immigration judge had signed an order to deport her after she did not appear at a hearing she had known nothing about. She was taken into custody at the immigration office and sent first to a local jail, then to a maximum-security prison 200 miles from the town where she was living.

The next year was a trial by ordeal, marked by physical and psychological abuse that violated federal detention guidelines, not to mention international law. Transferred to a prison in another state without warning or explanation in the middle of the night, malnourished because she was lactose-intolerant, kept in a cell with a murderer, denied vegetarian food in accordance with her religious beliefs, unable to contact her lawyer because she had no money to pay for a long-distance call, Mary kept her sanity by documenting the mistreatment she and other detainees endured. After she and two others threatened to expose conditions at the prison to federal authorities, they saw some improvements. The detainees were taken out of cells housing convicted felons and placed in a warehouse with no windows.

It took months of dedicated efforts by a pro bono attorney and Amnesty International to secure Mary's release on parole. Two years after her parole she was unwilling to discuss her experience publicly for fear of retaliation by ICE or corrections officials. Asked in 2006 how it felt to be in her situation, with her case still unsettled, she said: "Dreadful; I cannot make plans. I cannot visit my family, I cannot leave the country." Asked when she began seeking asylum, Mary replied sadly, "1992." How long could the process go on? "Forever." In 2010 Mary was still awaiting resolution of her case.

Leah's Story

Leah fled the African country of her birth for reasons she is too traumatized to discuss.[5] After arriving in Britain in 2001 she sought asylum, but her petition was denied. She married a UK citizen who died while she was pregnant. Because she was a "refused asylum seeker," local social services refused to give her accommodation, so she slept in a church. Six years later, after detention, an attempted deportation, expulsion, a desperate flight back to Britain and countless trips to the Home Office, her ordeal at the hands of the British immigration authorities continued with no end in sight.

Leah told her story almost dispassionately. One morning at dawn in 2006 men in plain clothes came without warning to her flat in a London suburb and announced that she and her three children would be deported that day. They would give her 10 minutes to pack. The children, including a daughter who had been raped at age nine and a son with emotional problems, started to scream in terror. After she filled a few plastic bags with the stuff of their existence in exile, the guards cuffed her hands and feet and forced her into the back of a white van. They missed the flight. The guards dumped Leah, the children and the plastic bags at the airport. Somehow they found their way home at 1 the next morning.

A few weeks later the guards came again. One of them pushed her head between her knees, and she was forced to sit in that position all the way to the airport as her children sobbed and shrieked. This time they did not miss the flight. In a few hours she was back in Africa, in a city she knew was not safe for her or her family. Again something terrible happened, and she fled to Britain as soon as she could, leaving her children with her brother, who died a few months later. After two years her youngest child (a British citizen) came to join her, but the older ones now live with strangers in her home country.

Her little boy refused to believe her when she told him she was his mother. "My mummy's gone," he replied. It took months to convince him he was her son. Meanwhile, she reported to the Home Office on the advice of people at a community women's center.

"Do you have any proof that we deported you?" the Home Office interviewer asked. All her records, it seemed, had been lost.[6] Now Leah waits to find out what will happen to her. She is not allowed to work and gets by with the help of an evangelical church and a refugee women's group.

Jason's Story

Hiu Lui (Jason) Ng entered the United States from China on a tourist visa in 1992, when he was 17 years old.[7] According to *The New York Times* of August 13, 2008, he "stayed on after [the visa] expired and applied for political asylum. He was granted a work permit while his application was pending, and though asylum was eventually denied, immigration authorities did not seek his deportation for many years."

Jason worked his way through community college and became a computer engineer, working in the Empire State Building. In 2001 he married, and his wife petitioned for him to be granted a green card (permanent residence) as the spouse of a U.S. citizen. The couple waited more than five years for this request to be processed.

Meanwhile the immigration bureaucracy was looking for him as a refused asylum seeker. A notice ordering him to appear in court went to a nonexistent address, and as a result Jason did not show up for a hearing in 2001. At that time the judge automatically issued a deportation order for him.

Unaware of this turn of events Jason and his wife appeared for a green card interview in July 2007. ICE agents arrested him under the old deportation order and sent him to two jails and a federal detention center in New England. "Over the next year," the *Times* reported, "his family struggled to pay for new lawyers to wage a complicated and expensive legal battle."

In April 2008, still in detention, Jason began complaining to his family about severe back pain and skin irritation. At the time he was in a county jail in Vermont that had no medical personnel. He asked to be transferred to Wyatt Detention Facility in Rhode Island, because it had medical staff who he hoped would provide treatment for his extreme pain. For the first three days at Wyatt he was kept in a dark isolation cell. "Later," the *Times* reported, "he was assigned an upper bunk and required to climb up and down at least three times a day for head counts, causing terrible pain." He told his sister he had informed the nursing department he was in pain, "but they don't believe me. . . . They tell me, stop faking." The *Times* described him as "once a robust man who stood nearly 6 feet and weighed 200 pounds. . . . Mr. Ng looked like a shrunken and jaundiced 80-year-old."

Jason got help from other detainees, who helped him go to the toilet, brought him food, and called his family. "He no longer received painkillers, because he could not stand in line to collect them," the *Times* said. When his lawyer tried to visit him on July 26, 2008, he was too weak to walk to the visiting area, and he was denied use of a wheelchair. Detention center officials refused to arrange for an independent medical evaluation of his condition.

Jason's final ordeal began on July 30. According to affidavits obtained by the *Times*, "guards . . . dragged him from his bed . . . , carried him in shackles to a car, bruising his arms and legs, and drove him two hours to a federal lockup in Hartford, where an immigration officer pressured him to withdraw all pending appeals of his case and accept deportation." Then they drove him back to the detention center.

Calling this treatment "torture," one of his lawyers filed a habeas corpus petition on his behalf. A U.S. District Court judge ordered that Jason be taken immediately to a hospital for testing. "The results were grim: cancer in his liver, lungs and bones, and a fractured spine," the *Times* reported. After waiting three days for the detention center director to give permission, his family visited him in hospital, "hours away from death and still under guard." Jason died on August 6, 2008; he was 34 years old and left a wife and two children, all U.S. citizens.

The Slave's Story

The scene is a hearing room in the Asylum Tribunal in London.[8] The Home Office attorney (apparently the son of immigrants) is in conversation with a visiting researcher from the London School of Economics. "I have an MA in economic history from there," he says, admitting that he could not find a job in his area of expertise so he became a lawyer. "I'm new at this, so I won't be very impressive," he jokes.

A young woman who looks no more than 16 comes into the room, pushing a stroller containing a tiny new baby. An interpreter arrives along with the young woman's lawyer. The judge enters hastily, looking as if he did not have time to comb his hair before leaving home that morning.

The judge explains to the young woman that he is an independent immigration judge. As the interpreter translates, the judge asks her if she feels her human rights have been violated. She murmurs something to the interpreter, who says, "She asks, what are human rights?" The judge explains that she has the right to ask for protection against deportation.

The young woman is asking for "exceptional leave to remain" in the United Kingdom on humanitarian grounds. The Home Office is proposing that she be deported to Benin because she was born there. But it seems that her parents took her from Benin to Nigeria when she was an infant, and she knows no one in Benin. She speaks Yoruba, a major language in Nigeria, and very little English. Her lawyer interjects that the Yoruba interpreter is not translating the judge's remarks accurately and that he knows this because he, too, is Yoruban. He tries to explain the complexities of her origins. The story gets worse as it goes along. The young woman, whom I'll call La Beninoise, seems bewildered by the proceedings.

Her lawyer explains that she was "brought" to the United Kingdom in 1998, when she was nine years old, to be a servant in the house of her "guardians," immigrants from Nigeria.[9] La Beninoise describes the life of a child slave, taking care of younger children, cleaning, and cooking. She was not allowed to go out by herself or attend school but had to take the guardians' children to school in the mornings. Speaking no English she had only the vaguest notion of where she was. Finally, at age 13 or so, she fled the house because of beatings and overwork and sought refuge with a "friend," a woman she had met at the children's school.

Her baby is fussing, and the judge observes that it looks overdressed. He kindly asks if she could take it to a witness waiting outside. Everyone smiles at the cute baby as La Beninoise carries it out of the room.

La Beninoise returns and explains that after a short time she had to leave her friend's house and live on the street. The judge points out that some things in her written statement are missing from her testimony. He asks her to clarify how she escaped from her guardians' house. He asks, "Have you lived on the streets?" Yes, she replies. But that is not in the written statement.

The judge asks where her parents are; she does not know. She has had no contact with them since arriving in the UK. She met the father of her child when she was living on the streets. He disappeared when she became pregnant. A local church has been helping her care for her baby. Her lawyer asks where she would like to be sent. Helplessly she replies she does not know. She has no education and does not know how to find her parents. Sometimes she considers killing herself, but church teachings keep her from doing it.

The judge asks for details about her life at the guardians' house and how she escaped. One day, when the guardian was out, La Beninoise called her friend and asked her to pick up her clothes before the guardian returned. She waited until the guardian came home, because she was not supposed to leave the children alone. When the guardian went into the kitchen she quietly left the house.

The Home Office lawyer shuffles his papers. Looking down, never making eye contact with La Beninoise, he asks, "Couldn't you have escaped at an earlier date?" The absurdity of the question does not seem to occur to him. She explains that with an acquaintance she met on the street she went to a church, and the people there took her in.

The Home Office lawyer asks, "Did they tell you to report your guardian to the police?"

"Yes, but I thought they'd get in trouble. I didn't know what to do." She was 13 or 14 years old at the time.

Later, after additional pitiable testimony, the Home Office lawyer (still looking down at his papers) asks, "What can you remember about your parents?"

"I miss them; I don't remember anything about them. . . . It's been a long time." The judge comments that it is difficult to understand how she cannot remember anything about her parents. He asks if they wanted to send her away to give her a better life. She does not know. When asked if she has ever had a social worker, she says she does not understand the question.

A witness enters the hearing room; it is not clear who he is, but he is smartly dressed and wears a gold link bracelet. He explains that he has known La Beninoise for five or six years. Watching her deliver smaller children to school, he and his wife used to speak to her there. After three or four years she asked for his help. He works for a social service agency, but he did not refer her to a social worker right away. He did not want to get involved, he explains, so he responded only to what she asked him to do. Eventually he started giving her financial support and paying her rent. A social worker investigated, calling him the girl's uncle, although he is not related to her. He felt she was a victim of circumstances, unfairly treated, and needed support and help.

When she became pregnant he acted as an intermediary with social services. It is all very vague.

The Home Office lawyer sums up. He asks the court to find La Beninoise not credible. Her account of her escape does not add up, he says, and no one can substantiate her claims. Incredibly, he says there is no reason she could not go to another country and adapt there. In Benin, he says, the government is reported to be trying to re-unite trafficked people with their families. He does not mention that her family is not in Benin.

Her lawyer emphasizes that La Beninoise was only nine years old when she arrived in the UK and was not allowed to go to school. "In a way she is disabled," he says. Expecting her to recount the whole story of her escape is impossible; all she needs to do is to provide a probable explanation, since this is not a criminal case. He cites letters from her church supporting her story, but he presents no medical report, no testimony from the guardian or the friend who helped her escape. Her lack of knowledge of her parents should not be compared to a Western child's knowledge, he says. She is illiterate, and she has nowhere to go. The judge interjects that the law stipulates that she must have a family in the UK to be allowed to stay. He seems to have forgotten her tiny British baby in the hallway.

Her lawyer describes her as a "traumatized child." As the witness said, she is a victim of circumstances. Citing article 3 of the European Convention of Human Rights, he concludes that it would be disastrous to deport her to Benin.

A month later her petition for exceptional leave to remain is denied. Her likely fate is destitution in London's underground of refused asylum seekers. And her baby?

Aisha's Story

The hearing in the Asylum Tribunal has not even started, but already the asylum seeker's lawyer is complaining to his government counterpart that the Home Office has improperly introduced a new issue, "deliberate verbal deception," during the appeal process.[10] He continues muttering as he shuffles his papers, then leaves the room in a huff. One of the Home Office attorneys is coaching the other about how to react and what to say to the judge. He refers to the asylum seeker's lawyer as "a bit of a drama queen."

The appellant is a young Somali woman, a medical resident at a London hospital. She expresses concern that "deliberate verbal deception" might be a criminal offense, but the judge reassures her that her failure to request asylum as soon as she entered Britain is not a crime. She speaks so softly that it is difficult to hear her, but she does manage to point out that the case record is wrong; her brother was killed in 2006 in Somalia's civil war, not in 2001. In 2006 she finished medical school in Pakistan. Before that time she and her family had been living in the United Arab Emirates. A confusing exchange takes place among the lawyers about her visa to live in the UAE. (Asylum decisions can hinge on such small points.)

In late 2005 Aisha started planning to return home to Somalia. Her friends were going back there, and she thought she should, too. Her brother went home in early 2006, telling her he would help her relocate. But meanwhile, with her UAE visa expired, she accepted a temporary appointment as a medical resident in the UK. While she was in the UK her brother was killed.

"You claimed asylum because you thought the situation was dangerous, am I right?" the judge asks. The Home Office lawyer asks about her upbringing; was it "westernized"? She replies that although she was identified as a member of a particular clan, she was not interested in clan politics. She neither wore the hijab (headscarf) nor associated herself with her family's clan. Her lawyer asks if she would be forced to live under strict Muslim controls if she were to return to Somalia. Her life would be in danger, she replies.

In summation the Home Office lawyer says it is "incredible" that she knows nothing about her clan origins just because her father was unwilling to discuss his clan affiliation. Even if she grew up in a sheltered environment, it is difficult to believe that she had no curiosity to explore her ethnicity on reaching adulthood. Her ignorance of her clan affiliation, he says, "seriously undermines the credibility of her claim." She has not been subjected to ill-treatment, and so she has no well-founded fear of persecution in Somalia.

The Home Office lawyer goes on to say that an independent country expert's report supporting Aisha's claims is "circumstantial and speculative"; the expert, hired by Aisha's lawyer, is not qualified and was merely expressing an opinion. He says that the Islamic Courts, a fundamentalist social movement that took over Somalia, brought law and order to the country when Aisha sought asylum in 2006, and Somalia was "enjoying relative peace" at that time.

Aisha replies that she does not want to live in the strict Islamic manner the Islamic Courts are trying to impose. She has no plans to wear the hijab, and the authorities in Somalia do not accept women living their own lives. The Home Office lawyer insists her fears do not amount to a fear of persecution. Later he claims that the situation in Somalia "has begun to stabilize." Aisha shakes her head no. Besides, he continues, civil war is not a sufficient ground for asylum under the Refugee Convention. Furthermore, she has relatives in the UAE, Canada, and Malaysia; she could go to any of those places and live safely there.

Aisha's lawyer responds with barely concealed indignation. She is a member of a minority clan and grew up in circumstances where she was not familiar with clan structure. According to an appeals court decision the expert witness *is* qualified to give his opinion, he insists, and the Home Secretary made incorrect statements about her clan in his asylum refusal letter. He reminds the court that only a low standard of proof is necessary in asylum cases. Aisha does not have to prove that she was ill-treated, only that she fears persecution. Her brother's killing is the basis of her fear. If she returned to Somalia she would be forced to live in a "strict Islamic situation," even if the Islamic Courts were no longer in control of the country. If she refuses to wear the hijab there, she faces harassment and even death.

Her lawyer quotes the Home Office guidelines for Somalia, according to which Aisha is eligible for asylum, because her minority clan has no militia to protect her. He points out that Aisha would be one of no more than a dozen women physicians in the country and would "stand out like a sore thumb." She would be a target for kidnapping, extortion, or rape. Being forced to wear a hijab to avoid violence constitutes subjection to degrading treatment under article 3 of the Refugee Convention. Therefore she deserves humanitarian protection under Home Office rules.

Aisha's lawyer concludes by pointing out that she has been self-supporting as a resident physician. She would promote health and the economic well-being of British citizens and residents through her medical work. She is "exceptional," the only doctor among the Somalis he has encountered.

A month later Aisha is granted asylum.

Jeff's Story

David Ngaruri Kenney (Jeff) resisted the dictatorship of Daniel arap Moi in Kenya in early 1992 by organizing a tea farmers' demonstration and boycott.[11] He was about 20 years old at the time. According to his lawyer, Philip G. Schrag, "In response, the security police nearly executed him, tortured him, and put him in solitary confinement for months. When he was finally released, he was subjected to police surveillance and controls. He had no future in Kenya, and he was told that if he engaged in political acts, he would be rearrested."

The torture Jeff experienced included being confined for about a week in an unlighted tank or box that jailors would fill with water "at apparently random intervals." He could not sleep for long periods "because I was afraid that the water would rise and drown me while I was asleep." This ordeal and other abuses at the hands of Kenyan security forces traumatized him for many years afterward.

With the help of some sympathetic Peace Corps volunteers, Jeff managed to flee Kenya and go to the United States legally to attend college in 1995. When his brother got into trouble with the Kenyan authorities a couple of years later, Jeff returned there briefly and bailed him out. Then he went back to the United States and finished college.

In 2000, unable to return to Kenya because Moi was still in power, Jeff applied for asylum in the United States. He encountered many obstacles, starting with the complex application form, which included a request for documentation supporting his claim. "When I left Kenya, I had not taken with me any documents about my arrest and imprisonment. The security forces provided no records showing that they had jailed and tortured me. Even if they had done so, I would have left them behind, because they would have reminded me of the pain, fear, and suffering I had endured," he wrote in his book.

He made many mistakes, such as going to an asylum interview without consulting a lawyer beforehand or taking one with him. "I told my story as best I could, but I was relating events that had occurred eight years earlier and dredging up memories that I had worked hard to suppress. I got some of the details wrong." The asylum officer did not believe him and placed him in deportation proceedings.

The immigration authorities also made many mistakes, such as failing to send his case file to the judge. Delays stretched on for months, during which time he was not permitted to work. While Jeff was waiting for a hearing to be scheduled, he applied to law school at Georgetown University. The dean he spoke to there urged him to consult a lawyer about his case and directed him to the university's immigration law clinic, where he found free legal representation.

Student lawyers worked hard on his case. Meanwhile, in going over the details of his torture and imprisonment, Jeff suffered severe flashbacks. He would sit for hours, banging his head on the wall to avoid falling asleep and having nightmares; he contemplated suicide. His lawyers referred him to a psychologist, he began taking antidepressants, and his symptoms lessened. In addition he managed to obtain documentation from Kenya proving his leadership of the tea farmers' protest movement.

Jeff's brief return to Kenya in 1997 to rescue his brother from prison was problematic, however. Despite the submission of 561 pages of evidence including Kenyan newspaper clippings, his 47-page affidavit and the psychologist's findings, Jeff was denied asylum. Nobody questioned his credibility, but according to the judge, his brief trip to Kenya showed he was not "unwilling to return" as the Refugee Convention dictated.

Changes in immigration procedures after the 9/11 attacks doomed Jeff's appeal. Then-Attorney General Ashcroft had instructed immigration judges to eliminate the huge backlog of cases within six months by forgoing written opinions. The result was an enormous number of appeals hastily rejected without explanation. Jeff, who had married his American sweetheart in late 2003 while awaiting an appeal judgment that seemed likely to deny him asylum, opted to leave the United States voluntarily in early 2004 to avoid deportation and 10 years' banishment. He tried unsuccessfully to resettle as a businessman in Madagascar and Tanzania. While there he perceived that he was being followed, apparently by Kenyan security agents.

Jeff had several misadventures in Africa, including being kidnapped by bandits. With the help of his wife and Philip Schrag, he finally obtained an immigrant visa as the husband of a U.S. citizen, but he had to cope with a verbally abusive U.S. consular official in Dar es Salaam, demands for unnecessary paperwork by obtuse U.S. officials in Nairobi, serious errors in government documents and a visa left unsigned. He arrived back in Washington, D.C., in January 2005. Jeff could not obtain asylum from the U.S. government, but he did find refuge in the United States, in his wife's welcoming arms.

These cases are not unique or even unusual. Mary and Jason both presented themselves voluntarily to immigration authorities and were immediately detained because of outstanding deportation orders. Neither had received notice of an asylum hearing held years before. At such hearings the judge automatically issues deportation orders to anyone who does not appear, no matter what the reason, and then the cumbersome, arbitrary system moves clumsily and haltingly into action. Immigration authorities took years to find Mary and Jason, by which time they had established themselves as law-abiding, taxpaying U.S. residents. Jason started a family whose other members were U.S. citizens. All the people described in this chapter suffered family break-up, either as a result of going into exile or through detention in or expulsion from the country of refuge.

Both Mary and Jason were thrown into jails and prisons and detained there under inadequate and inhumane conditions for many months. In those facilities the staff callously, even viciously, violated the basic human rights of the detainees in their care. Their apparent negligence might have caused Jason's agonizing and premature death.[12]

Philip Alston, United Nations Human Rights Council special rapporteur on extrajudicial, summary, or arbitrary executions, reported on visits he made to U.S. immigration detention facilities in June 2008:

> There have been at least 74 deaths in immigration detention facilities since 2003. I received credible reports from a variety of sources of denials of necessary care, long delays in the provision of treatment, and the provision of inadequate care and incorrect medication. . . . The standards and procedures for medical care in all of these facilities are set by ICE. They are designed primarily to provide emergency care and generally exclude other care unless it is judged necessary for the detainee to remain healthy enough for deportation. Specialty care and testing believed necessary by the detainee's on-site doctor must be pre-approved by the Division of Immigration Health Services (DIHS) in Washington, D.C. Reliable reports indicate that, in practice, an often very restrictive interpretation is applied. In their defense, DIHS and ICE explained to me that truly emergency care is formally provided at the discretion of medical personnel at each detention center without prior authorization from DIHS. But it is still necessary to obtain DIHS authorization in order for the care provider to get reimbursed for such emergency care. Denials of

such requests have a chilling effect on decisions taken subsequently about whether to go ahead without authorization.

In addition, the ICE standards are merely internal guidelines rather than legal regulations. This has insulated ICE policy-making from the external oversight provided by the normal regulatory process and limits the legal remedies available to detainees when the medical care provided is deficient. ICE reassured me that there are internal grievance procedures, but detainees and their lawyers regularly report no or delayed responses to complaints, and complaint hotline telephones that simply don't work. The DHS should promulgate legally enforceable administrative regulations, and these should be consistent with international standards on the provision of medical care in detention facilities.

. . . ICE has no legal reporting requirements when a death occurs in ICE custody. This has resulted in a clear failure of transparency by ICE in relation to deaths in custody. Both civil society groups and Congressional staff members told me that for years they were unable to obtain any information at all on the numbers of deaths in ICE custody. ICE's recent public reporting of the number of deaths, and their voluntary undertaking to report future deaths is encouraging, but insufficient. ICE should be required to promptly and publicly report all deaths in custody, and these deaths should be fully investigated. (Alston 2008)

Leah and La Beninoise were subjected to institutional cruelty in the British immigration system. Leah's account of her botched deportation and later expulsion is not unusual. Dawn deportation raids on the houses and apartments of refused asylum seekers attracted so much negative publicity in Scotland, where thousands of asylum seekers have been relocated in recent years, that the Home Office suspended such raids there in 2007; despite public protests, however, dawn raids resumed in 2008 (Mackay and Money 2008). Leah is also a member of a London solidarity group of African women asylum seekers who have been sexually assaulted, either in their home country or in Britain.[13] In general, it is extremely difficult for Africans, especially women, to gain asylum in Britain, even from countries with a high level of internal conflict and government repression. The British government was reportedly shipping planeloads of refused asylum seekers back to Iraq, Uganda, Congo, Zimbabwe, and other dangerous countries in 2009.

La Beninoise, who evidently had been trafficked into Britain, did not benefit from the United Nations Protocol to Prevent, Suppress and Punish Trafficking in Persons, Especially Women and Children (2000/2003), one of whose purposes is to "protect and assist the victims of trafficking in persons with full respect for their human rights" (I, article 2[b]). Articles 6 and 7 of the protocol call for governments of receiving countries to provide assistance to and protection of trafficking victims and to give consideration to humanitarian and compassionate factors when determining their immigration status.

Although the United Kingdom signed this protocol in 2006, the Home Office apparently made no attempt to investigate her case. Nor did the judge take into account her status as a trafficking victim when he denied her petition for exceptional leave to remain. The British government's only concern seemed to be to get rid of her and her baby by ordering their expulsion to a country she did not know, where she had no relatives or friends, from a country that had failed to protect her human rights, arguably owed her educational and other social benefits, and was the birthplace of her child.

La Beninoise was ill served by her lawyer, who seemed well intentioned but did not know how to argue effectively on her behalf. He was not a specialist in immigration law and seemed to have taken on the case at the request of the church members who were trying to help her. Aisha's barrister, a skilled veteran of many legal battles, commented that he could have won La Beninoise's case. Unlike her lawyer, on behalf of Aisha he made strong and convincing arguments based on the Home Office's own guidelines and country reports, expert opinion, and legal precedents. He shifted the focus from his client to the Home Office's technical mistakes. He convinced the judge that Aisha was an asset to the United Kingdom, whereas La Beninoise's lawyer unsuccessfully tried to elicit pity for his unfortunate client, who needed more help than the British state was willing to give. Like her, Mary also suffered dire consequences of bad lawyering: years of delay, prolonged detention, and apparently endless uncertainty.

Jeff's confounding experience with the U.S. immigration bureaucracy illustrates how governments can foil even the most determined and best documented attempts to gain asylum. After September 11, 2001, it became even harder to obtain asylum in the United States and other developed countries. Unable to cope with a huge backlog, immigration judges rushed to dismiss thousands of cases, giving little or no explanation for their decisions.[14] Like Aisha, Jeff was lucky to have highly skilled and experienced lawyers who spared no effort on his behalf. Both were also fortunate to avoid detention, which would have made it extremely difficult for them to keep in touch with their lawyers. As a torture survivor Jeff could have suffered retraumatization in detention, with little hope of competent medical attention and the constant possibility of the outrageous abuse to which Jason succumbed.

At one time or another all these asylum seekers were victims of what scholars and advocates have called "a culture of disbelief," which permeates immigration bureaucracies. Members tend to assume that asylum claimants are all liars who present fraudulent documents and deliberately misrepresent their reasons for seeking refuge. Thus Home Office lawyers sought to deny refuge to La Beninoise and Aisha by questioning their credibility. The asylum officer who interviewed Jeff disbelieved his account of his political activity, arrest, and torture because of internal inconsistencies that might have resulted from posttraumatic stress. In Aisha's and La Beninoise's cases Home Office experts generated accounts of country conditions that distorted, minimized, or denied the grim reality in Somalia and other countries undergoing extreme civil disorder.

These and many other stories lead to the overwhelming impression that present-day asylum systems are designed *not* to work—or at least to deny asylum in most cases, to deserving and undeserving applicants alike.[15] Despite a well-developed body of international and national laws that are supposed to protect their human rights, asylum seekers are often treated more harshly than criminals. At every opportunity legislatures and governments pass laws and implement policies that make it increasingly difficult for victims and survivors of harassment, discrimination, torture, genocide, and other crimes to find a safe haven where they can remake their lives and contribute to their new societies.

In the face of such systematic abuse, what can be done to help asylum seekers and ensure that they can exercise their right to seek and enjoy asylum? Despite unfavorable public opinion and official obstruction, myriad groups and individuals try to help asylum seekers by lobbying, advocating, protesting, and providing sanctuary inside or outside the bounds of the law. They follow an ancient tradition, at least 5,000 years old and perhaps much older than that. As contradictory as it may seem, along with rejecting and expelling outsiders, giving refuge to strangers may be one of the fundamental acts of humanness.

CHAPTER TWO

From the Beginning

I was a stranger, and ye took me in.

MATTHEW 25: 35

Homo sapiens is a migrating species. Scientists have traced our wanderings across continents and oceans through a history that stretches back more than 2 million years. During this long process we have adapted to our varied surroundings by developing diverse practices and beliefs, as well as forms of behavior that distinguish us from our primate relatives. And in the relatively brief 125,000 years that we have had language, we have evolved further, from discrete, isolated communities into a worldwide community. According to anthropologist Adam Kuper:

> Five hundred years ago, the history of the human population began to come together again into a single process, for the first time since the origin of modern humans. After a history of dispersal and differentiation that lasted perhaps a quarter of a million years, there is once more something approaching a single world economy, culture and political system. (1994: 95)

A highly sociable species characterized by sharing, exchange, cooperation, and hospitality, we are also quarrelsome and violent, excluding and rejecting those we define as different from us. "Social living is characterized by conflict; that is, by competition over scarce resources such as food, status, and mates, as well as by cooperation and reciprocal altruism," Allman claims (1994: 230). Yet anthropologists have found some cultures in which food, status, and mates are not particularly scarce; the only generalization one can make with assurance about human beings is that our circumstances and actions vary considerably—within certain broad limits determined by biology, environment, and culture.

As Allman acknowledges, we have in common with other species a tendency to act altruistically. The great primatologist Frans de Waal observes: "Aiding others at a cost or risk to oneself is widespread in the animal world." Like other primates, humans extend help not only to their biological kin but also to unrelated individuals or groups. "Helpful acts that are costly in the short run may produce long-term benefits if recipients return the favor," de Waal notes (1996: 12). Such reciprocal altruism follows rules laid out by Robert Trivers in 1972:

1. The exchanged acts, while beneficial to the recipient, are costly to the performer.
2. There is a time lag between giving and receiving.
3. Giving is contingent on receiving. (de Waal 1996: 24)

De Waal links reciprocal altruism among primates to the evolution of morality, "a tendency to develop social norms and enforce them, the capacity for empathy and sympathy, mutual aid and a sense of fairness, the mechanisms of conflict resolution, and so on." Morality among humans extends beyond single communities, as disparate groups "join to socialize, trade, court, perform." Anthropologists have documented how the social relationships that develop at such gatherings endure over long periods and great distances. "A significant way in which human societies differ from those of chimpanzees is that kin bonds have become elaborated and maintained even beyond the boundaries of the group, in part by exchange of females in marriage," de Waal points out (2001: 34).

Giving asylum or sanctuary can be seen as one of the basic manifestations of altruistic behavior and human morality. In the face of conflict humans wander or even flee, sometimes thousands of miles from home, seeking safety among strangers who may have little apparent reason to welcome us. We seek sanctuary from pursuers and offer asylum to strangers in this richly contradictory context. Thus sanctuary and asylum may be considered ancient, perhaps primordial, institutions, part of the foundation of humanness. Why should that be so? Aside from saving the lives of those fleeing persecution, what larger purposes does sanctuary serve?

Other primates' social lives may be suggestive. *Homo sapiens* is not the only species whose members offer or seek sanctuary. Among our closest primate relatives, the chimpanzees and bonobos, females often move from one group to another, fleeing sexual overtures or attacks by local males they do not want to mate with, perhaps because they are related to them. According to primatologists, female primates are more averse to incest than males and therefore more likely to leave home to avoid it. About chimpanzees Lynne Isbell writes: "Because inbreeding is more costly to females than to males, selection should favor females that minimize incestuous matings. Males disperse because limited mating opportunities in their natal groups or home ranges create greater mating opportunities in other groups or home ranges, all else being equal" (2004: 96).

Chimpanzees manage to find shelter in groups where they have no relatives, even though their social life is characterized by chronic conflicts, including raids and killings, between communities. Perhaps sanctuary or asylum could be considered an integral part of inter-group hostility within a species, since it can be defined as the reception and protection of a fleeing member of a strange or "enemy" group.

However one chooses to interpret primate migration, it is a delicate business to extrapolate from other primates' behavior to our own. Humans are different from chimpanzees and other primates in important ways. Most strikingly, unlike other primates we form enduring nuclear and extended families; we keep in touch with distant relatives; unrelated humans—especially females—become friends and maintain those friendships for long periods; we maintain elaborate kinship groups, based on social as well as biological ties; we socialize and trade with hundreds or even thousands of other humans, creating huge communities that span continents; we make war but we also make peace; we codify and change social rules; and we give refuge to unrelated individuals and groups on a scale unknown to other primates. As a result our sociability is far more complex than that of our primate relatives. And to a far greater extent than other primates we are an unfinished species: we have tried to take our evolution into our own hands, through our wholesale alterations of the natural environment, with unforeseen and as yet unknown results. Our evolution is still going on.

Kuper warns us "not to expect to learn very much about our present nature from a study of remote ancestors scratching a living some 40,000 years ago" (1994: 101). Nonetheless, it is instructive to look at the long history of human groups to find the commonalities that define us as members of one species.

Nineteenth-century theorists disagreed about the mechanisms of human evolution on the basis of their observations of other species, ancient Greek and Roman sources, and reports of recently contacted human groups. In *Primitive Marriage* (1865) John McLennan speculated that early human males had avoided incest by seizing women from outside their local group. Darwin played down ideas about generalized promiscuity among early humans by pointing out that mating is never random; but Freud apparently believed that such promiscuity had existed. Early 20th-century anthropologists including Westermarck and Malinowski theorized that incest was the first human taboo.

Westermarck went further, proposing that association with close relatives during childhood inhibits later sexual attraction in humans and other primates; this has come to be known as the Westermarck effect. Evolutionary biologists' research over the past 100 years has proven him right. They have also found that in some primate species, such as chimps and bonobos, males tend to be philopatric (remaining in their birth communities), whereas females migrate to other communities to mate. Thus primates, including humans, practice exogamy (mating outside their family or community) to avoid incest, which has damaging effects on reproductive fitness over time.

In the process humans create and maintain trade and other relationships outside their home community. Relations with other communities may be friendly, antagonistic, or both: "Strangers can be viewed in many contexts as important sources of information or potential partners in exchange, rather than dangerous interlopers or murderous assailants—yet which of these they will turn out to be cannot be known in advance" (Chapais and Berman 2004: 401). For this system of communication and exchange to work, communities must take in strangers at least some of the time.

Furthermore, "social inclusion is absolutely central to human morality, commonly cast in terms of how we should or should not behave in order to be valued as members of society. . . . Universally, human communities are moral communities; a morally neutral existence is as impossible for us as a completely solitary existence," de Waal maintains (1996: 10). However, he insists, "human sympathy is not unlimited. It is offered most readily to one's own family and clan, less ready to other members of the community, and most reluctantly, if at all, to outsiders" (1996: 88). Accepting strangers makes them part of the moral community. That is the basis of sanctuary. But the ever-present tension between incorporating and rejecting strangers limits humans' willingness to bestow it.

Thus in many societies sanctuary is only temporary or is hedged with restrictions. Inspiring stories of Christian Holocaust rescuers sheltering Jewish children at the risk of their own lives must be juxtaposed against today's punitive and exclusionary asylum policies, which break up families or return refugees to their death in the country that persecuted them. Decisions about whom to accept and whom to reject may seem arbitrary, but they are not; they are based on our willingness to incorporate members of certain groups but not others into our moral community. The criteria we use to make such decisions change over time, depending on a complex combination of economic, social, and political factors and circumstances. And sometimes sanctuary is given *despite* these factors, as individuals and groups defy custom and law, risking their lives and livelihoods to give refuge to strangers.

Often these decisions come out of deeply held beliefs that form the foundation of our moral community. Almost every major religious tradition includes concepts and rules governing sanctuary. Religious texts codify customs that probably existed long before the texts were written. For example, rules establishing "cities of refuge" for manslayers are laid out in the Old Testament, in the Book of Numbers and Deuteronomy, compiled more than 2,500 years ago. Siebold explained:

> Exodus XII: 14 ruled that whosoever transgressed against his neighbor, killing him by cunning, should be removed from the altar and slain. Deuteronomy marked a new epoch in the administration of criminal justice: blood vengeance was divested of its private character and replaced by public punishment; the purchase of freedom from punishment by the murderer was no longer permitted; and a clear distinction was made between premeditated and unpremeditated crimes. All shrines were abolished except for the temple at Jerusalem, where the entire cult was centralized, and the institution of sanctuary was completely transformed. (1937: 534)

The ancient Hebrews created six cities of refuge, linked to former religious sanctuaries. They were intended only for unpremeditated killers, "so that protection of the innocent, like punishment of the guilty, became a public matter, a secular legal institution" (Siebold 1937: 534).

Bau points out that the city of refuge "mitigated the harshness of the blood feud" by giving refuge to unintentional killers, who were in a different category from murderers. Once they had arrived in the city of refuge, manslayers had to undergo a trial to prove that they had killed accidentally. Then they could stay in the city until the reigning high priest died. After that they could return home safely.

Traditions of sanctuary in the Mediterranean world are even older. Among the ancient Egyptians, Siebold notes, "in the earliest times every shrine, including places dedicated to the gods, royal altars, pictures and statues of the ruler, or sites used for the taking of oaths, was a protected region sought out by all the persecuted, by mistreated slaves, oppressed debtors and political offenders" (1937: 534).

The very word "asylum" comes from the ancient Greek, *asylos*, inviolable. Three thousand years ago Diana's sanctuary at Ephesos was famous throughout Greece as a place of asylum, and people also sought refuge in groves, temples, and other places associated with the gods. Boundary markers, including rocks and trees, "marked out the core sacred space, which being sacred was inviolable. Since it was a place where nothing might be damaged and no might be harmed with impunity, it became a place of asylum. Fugitives had to do no more than sit at the foot of a statue or an altar, or even attach themselves by a rope to a statue, and no one, in theory, could touch them" (Pedley 2005: 57). Sometimes the area around a sanctuary was also held sacred. Mithradates of Pontos declared "all the space within bow shot range of the corner of the roof of the temple [of Ephesos] . . . sacred ground" (Pedley 2005: 58).

Outlaws and refugees, the guilty and the innocent alike, fled to sanctuaries, and "dreadful punishments—for example, a plague—might fall on anyone who broke these rules (or on that person's community). All that the refugees, whether defeated soldiers, slaves, exiled politicians, or social outcasts, had to do was to cross the boundary into the sacred space and they were safe. They could not be removed by force" (Pedley 2005: 97).

The Greek city states were constantly at war with one another, producing a stream of refugees and exiles seeking sanctuary with their enemies. Sanctuaries on the frontiers of city states were well known. Promontories, considered sacred to the god Poseidon, were often places of asylum, because they were accessible by both land and sea. According to Siebold, "Temples enjoyed the character of sanctuaries and under all circumstances could protect the oppressed and the persecuted, slaves, debtors, malefactors and criminals. Even deliberate murderers and those under sentence of death had a claim to protection and could dwell in the sanctuary grounds surrounding a temple, secure under the sheltering wing of the divinity, until death overtook them" (Siebold 1937: 534).

Sanctuaries are often referred to in ancient Greek literature. In the great tragedy *The Eumenides*, Westermarck noted, "Aeschylus puts the following words into the mouth of Apollo, when he declares his intention to assist his suppliant, Orestes: 'Terrible both among men and gods is the wrath of a refugee, when one abandons him with intent'" (1909: 164). The dramatist Euripides wrote: "Beasts have their rocky retreats to fly to—Slaves have their altars" (Mazzinghi 1887: 4).

Under Roman rule during the 3rd and 2nd centuries c.e., Greek sanctuaries were still giving shelter to fugitives, often escaped slaves. "One [Roman] emperor, hearing that rights of asylum and sanctuaries were being abused, referred the matter to the Senate. Decisions were normally favorable to the sanctuaries and justified on the basis of ancient practice. In matters regarding their own sanctuaries, for the most part the Greeks were thought to know best," Pedley wrote (2005: 98).

Although the ancient Romans were not known to be merciful, they also considered certain places as sanctuaries. According to Westermarck, an old Roman tradition held that "Romulus [the mythical cofounder of Rome] established a sanctuary, dedicated to some unknown god or spirit, on the slope of the Capitoline Hill, proclaiming that all who resorted to it, whether bond or free, should be safe" (1909: 162). He also noted that a temple built in honor of Julius Caesar in 42 b.c.e., two years after his assassination, gave sanctuary to fugitives. Statues of Roman emperors were considered places of sanctuary as well. According to Siebold, "Beginning with the imperial period, when the protective power was extended to persons and objects connected with the cult of the emperor, so that statues, portraits and temples of the Caesars and flags and eagles of the military legions were invested with the properties of asylum" (1937: 535).

In the Roman *campagna* the 19th-century historian of asylum, Thomas Mazzinghi, noticed "small pieces of ground staked in, and

forming squares, strongly fenced on all sides with huge logs of wood
. . . permitting entry . . . through uprights to a body of human dimensions" (1887: 3). Such ancient shelters had become refuges for people
when herds of cattle were passing by; but in ancient times, Mazzinghi
believed, they might have served sacred purposes.

Cultures and societies remote from Western civilization also
have long traditions of sanctuary and asylum. Ethnographers, historians, explorers, invaders, and travelers since the 15th century have
observed and reported the acting out of such traditions, which may
date from ancient times. Margaret Mead observed in her study of the
island of Manus, in Papua New Guinea: "In a primitive community,
sanctuary and hospitality are so intermixed that it is difficult to distinguish between them . . ." (1956: 315).

In cultures where honor is a central virtue, it usually "has a large
number of aspects, of which the most important are the obligation
of vengeance, safeguard and sanctuary, the integrity of women, and
hospitality" (Masters 1953: 180). Ideals of honor predate major religious traditions in the Middle East and Mediterranean. For example,
in the 1960s the Bedouins of western Egypt preserved an ancient
practice called

> the *nazaala*, i.e., "the act of taking refuge." If a killing is com-
> mitted, the killer immediately seeks protection by going to
> the residence of a neutral third party. . . . During the period of
> sanctuary, it is hoped that two things will happen: that the killed
> man's group will be placated and agree to compensation rather
> than retaliation as a means of conflict regulation; and that over
> this period of one year the killer's family will pay the [compensa-
> tion]. (Obermeyer 1969: 201)

Seeking or giving sanctuary or asylum to forestall blood vengeance is
a frequent theme in the anthropological literature.

Sanctuary also serves other purposes in "honor" cultures. Boehm
wrote that in Montenegro, a Balkan tribal society, "malefactors" might
be exiled temporarily or permanently. "This did not deny the malefactor the right to live, since both in Montenegro and in the surrounding Turkish territory, people who were refugees from trouble of
one sort or another continually were showing up and asking permission to settle. The moral code was such that whenever it was possible
to award the desired sanctuary, this was done" (1984: 75).

In many African societies sanctuary was based on animist religious beliefs and thus was a sacred institution. Among the Igbo, a
major ethnic group in Nigeria, "The shrine of the goddess became a
sanctuary for such social offenders as thieves, adulterers, debtors and
those sent there as gifts to the goddess. . . . As the stream was considered sacred, all creatures in it were considered sacred and taboo by
the community" (Amadiume 1987: 53).

Nilotic groups, such as the Nuer in Sudan, combined several
beliefs about sanctuary and its purposes: "The slayer seeks sanctuary with the leopard-skin chief [a religious figure], who will ritually
cleanse him and make a sacrifice to protect him from the vengeance of the spirit of the slaughtered man and his kinsmen" (Butt
1952: 141).

Among many examples of sanctuary throughout the world,
Westermarck cited one from India: "Among the Kafirs of the Hindu-
Kush there are several 'cities of refuge,' the largest being the village of
Mergron, which is almost entirely people by . . . descendants of per-
sons who have slain some fellow-tribesman" (1909: 161).

Half a world away, Native American groups that had tense relationships with one another still offered and received sanctuary. After
their rebellion against the Spanish in the 1680s, for example, the Tewa
fled west and sought refuge with the Hopi. Courlander noted:

> Through the centuries there have been continuing and frequent
> contacts between the Hopis and the Eastern Pueblos. . . . Various
> Eastern Pueblos came west from time to time to settle in Hopi
> country. The Hopi mesas were a sanctuary for Lagunas, Acomas
> and others seeking escape from Spanish authority virtually
> throughout the seventeenth century. At one time or another
> there were Eastern Pueblo settlements close to every one of the
> extant Hopi villages. (1987: 12)

A *History of American Indians,* published in 1775, describes "several peaceable towns" among the tribes of the Southeast: "They seem
to have been formerly 'towns of refuge,' for it is not in the memory
of their oldest people that human blood was ever shed in them, although they often force persons from them, and put them to death
elsewhere" (Westermarck 1909: 161).

Hawaiians seem to have been more forgiving. According to
Westermarck:

There were two . . . cities of refuge, which afforded an inviolable sanctuary even to the vilest criminal who entered their precincts, and during war offered safe retreat to all the noncombatants of the neighboring districts who flocked into them, as well as to the vanquished. . . . After a short period, probably not more than two or three days, the refuge was permitted to return unmolested to his home, the divine protection being supposed still to abide with him. (Westermarck 1909: 161)

In what later became New York State, in the 18th century the Seneca "maintained a sanctuary for dispossessed Indians of diverse origins and kinds, from all quarters. Many of these alien Indians had remained among their hosts to be easily assimilated in the Iroquoian way" (Deardoff 1951: 82).

Over the past 500 years, as societies changed under the pressure of Western colonialism and imperialism, they transformed ancient traditions to respond to modern conditions. For example, Catholic Church historian John Noonan pointed to the re-use of ancient concepts of sanctuary in 19th-century America:

In the 19th century, churches were to be used as safe places for slaves who had fled their masters in slave states. . . . Here sanctuary was not incorporated into the law to limit the law but operated in bold defiance of the law. Nonetheless the ancient idea of the special character of a holy place was at work. Somewhere on earth, it was believed by religious people, the hunted should be beyond their pursuers. (Bau 1985: 2–3)

During the Iranian Revolution of the early 20th century:

the Shah's failure to respond to protests by the religious establishment, the merchants and other classes led the merchants and clerical leaders in January 1906 to protest by taking sanctuary in mosques in Tehran and outside the capital. . . . 10,000 people, led by the merchants, took sanctuary in June in the compound of the British legation in Tehran. In August the Shah was forced to issue a decree promising a constitution. . . . (Bakhash 1989: 23)

Catholic ideas of sanctuary were applied in Spain in the 1960s, when "the Basque lower clergy has also been in the forefront of protest. . . . They have participated in strikes, demonstrations and have allegedly given sanctuary to members of ETA pursued by the Spanish police" (da Silva 1972: 147).

Members of the Sanctuary Movement in the United States often cited Canon 1179 of the Catholic Church's 1917 Code of Canon Law to justify giving refuge to Salvadorans, Hondurans, and Guatemalans during the Central American wars of the 1980s: "A church enjoys the right of asylum, so that guilty persons who take refuge in it must not be taken from it, except in the case of necessity, without the consent of the ordinary, or at least of the rector of the church" (Bau 1985: 91). Despite its omission from the Code of Canon Law of 1983, this provision continued to have moral force for some Catholics. Bau commented: "Sanctuary is shocking to the secular mind. How can there be any place within the confines of a nation that the law does not operate? How can religion claim a privilege to say it is beyond the law? How can the law stultify itself by acknowledging that in certain places the law ceases to hold sway? Religious history teaches otherwise" (1985: 2). Thus contemporary sanctuary seeks legitimacy in ancient traditions.

Certain generalizations may be made about sanctuary and asylum:[1] Human cultures are characterized by diversity and variety, and the apparently contradictory tendencies both to exclude and to integrate strangers seem widespread in our species. As a result, it is incorrect to assume that human nature leads inevitably to rejection of the Other. We are as likely to accept strangers as to drive them away, depending on complex factors that cannot be reduced to the immediate self-interest of a particular group. Sanctuary and asylum may be informally or spontaneously given, but they are rule-bound institutions based on shared values and well-established cultural codes. Nevertheless, individuals and groups may defy powerful social, political, and economic forces to give sanctuary.

Giving refuge to strangers is an act of reciprocal altruism, an adaptation we share with our primate relatives and other species. It may have its roots in the avoidance of incest and the practice of exogamy in various species. Sanctuary is often associated with sacred or otherwise special places where extraordinary exceptions may be made to normal rules, punishments, and restrictions. Asylum may be given to complete strangers from distant societies or to known individuals from neighboring communities or nearby kin groups. Whoever gains sanctuary is protected from violence, usually temporarily but sometimes permanently. The religious nature of sanctuary seems to be a constant across otherwise dissimilar cultures, from Hawaii to Macedonia.

Medieval church sanctuary provides a prime example of religious practice overlapping with and sometimes superseding secular law. Because of its complexity and widespread influence on Western culture over more than a thousand years, it deserves a chapter of its own.

CHAPTER THREE

A Thousand Years of Sanctuary

*God in heaven forbid / We should infringe the holy
privilege /Of blessed sanctuary! Not for all this land/
Would I be guilty of so deep a sin.*

SHAKESPEARE, *Richard III*. Act 3, Scene 1

In the 4th century C.E. the Roman Empire made a transition from one state religion to another by transforming pagan practices and institutions into Christian ones. Sanctuary was already an ancient custom among many peoples of the empire, from Germans to Hebrews. Historians differ in their accounts of exactly when the Emperor Constantine embraced the institution of sanctuary. In the 19th century Cox dated it from the time of Constantine's Edict of Toleration in 303 C.E. In the 20th century Robert Tomsho wrote that Constantine guaranteed sanctuary in Christian churches throughout the empire in 324.

In any case the Theodosian Law Code of 392 formally codified church sanctuary, limiting it according to the type of crime and the character of the accused. Debtors, embezzlers of state funds, Jews, heretics, and apostates were to be excluded from its benefits. Around 450 C.E. Theodosius the Younger extended sanctuary from the church interior to the churchyard walls or precincts, including the bishop's house, cloisters, and cemeteries. About 50 years later Justinian's Law Code excluded public debtors, tax officials, murderers, rapists, and adulterers from sanctuary. But such people often did obtain refuge on church premises over the next 1,100 years.

Catholic Church councils laid down rules for church sanctuary throughout the Christian world. As early as 344 the Council of Sardia officially recognized sanctuary in churches, but it did not proclaim any *right* to asylum in churches. Fourth-century church fathers such as Augustine, John Chrysostom, and Ambrose personally protected fugitives and preached on the inviolability of churches. The Council of Orange, 511 c.e., declared,

> No one was permitted of his own authority to remove by force from churches those who had fled to them, but they had to apply to the bishops, who took cognizance of the complaints of the slaves, and the wrongful acts of their masters, and interposed to obtain pardon for the former, guaranteed by an oath of the master to observe it or pay two slaves to the church. (Mazzinghi 1887: 90)

In the late 7th century the Council of Toledo declared excommunication as the penalty for violating sanctuary. It should be kept in mind, however, that transportation and communication were so poor and the rule of law so precarious that legal codes and conciliar proclamations often had little effect unless officials, clerics, and secular rulers saw the advantages of upholding and enforcing them on the local level. On the one hand, rulers understood that "protection of sanctuary was a matter of upholding royal authority"—the peace of the church was also the king's peace (Sartain 2002: 34). On the other hand, the Catholic Church struggled to exert exclusive control over sacred spaces and objects, such as relics housed in churches. To maintain the sanctity of church premises (and the power of the church as an institution) it was necessary to protect everything and everyone, even fugitives, within them.

Above and beyond secular law codes the church exercised its authority by regulating sanctuary. Pope Leo I (440–61 c.e.) decreed that church officials were to examine all sanctuary seekers. As sanctified personages bishops could then grant sanctuary. They could act as intercessors and advocates on behalf of fugitives, becoming intermediaries between accused wrongdoers and those seeking private vengeance or the legal system. They also assumed the authority to subject sanctuary seekers to "penitential discipline" and "spiritual punishment" (Siebold 1937: 535). The Council of Reims, 630 c.e., decreed that "a person delivered by the church from pain of death had

to promise before he left to make penance for his crime and to ful-
fill whatever canonical punishment might be imposed" (Sartain 2002:
42). The church undertook to exercise mercy and dispense justice in
a world that had little time for either.

As far as the church was concerned its power to grant sanctuary
came from God and thus superseded that of the state. As a result secular officials were not allowed to pursue sanctuary seekers into the
church. Such pursuit would amount to sacrilege. Siebold points out:
"The legal effect of flight to a church sanctuary was that . . . the right
of public authorities to take possession of the refugee was suspended"
(Siebold 1937: 535). Conflicts between church and state over the extent and exercise of each institution's authority led to a gradual erosion of church power, a process that took many centuries.

During early medieval times in European countries and Britain
the secular legal system was thoroughly corrupt and ineffective, if it
existed at all. The king was the lawgiver, and if he was absent from the
kingdom or in conflict with the nobility, lawlessness reigned. Gangs
composed of nobles or their vassals controlled parts of kingdoms.
Bellamy remarks: "Because men of lower rank as a matter of course
carried knives and the gentry swords, any quarrel was likely to end in
the shedding of blood, especially since society viewed martial deeds
and a willingness to engage in them as a valuable quality in any man"
(1973: 25). Armed men could bribe, intimidate, or even kill judges,
juries, and witnesses and get away with it. Violent feuds were common among the nobility and gentry, and private individuals avenged
killings with impunity. Crime was not the monopoly of the lower
orders. Nobles and gentry were as likely to commit crimes as the poor,
although most crimes were thefts caused by poverty. Penalties were
severe. In England the penalty for stealing goods worth more than
1 shilling was death. It was in this context that people (usually men)
accused of serious crimes fled to church sanctuary.

To the clergy, "crime was a natural consequence of man's original
fall from grace," and the church stood for mercy to sinners (Bellamy
1973: 32). Thus violence within the church's sacred precincts was forbidden. Sanctuary seekers had to sign an oath upon entry that they
would not commit violent acts in the church. Innocent people also
sought sanctuary. During the limited time they were allowed to stay
in the church (three to 40 days, depending on the period and the
place), negotiations could be conducted with the secular authorities
to forestall private vengeance killing.

The German tribes that came into contact with the declining Roman Empire also had a tradition of sanctuary, but their customs differed. According to Cunningham, their temples "were places of supreme peace and purity; any desecration of this peace was punishable by death. Hence . . . religious shrines were never places of asylum for criminals who had been tainted by vice or misfortune. . ." (1995: 221). Under the Merovingian kings, who ruled in the former Roman province of Gaul from the mid-5th to the 8th century, Roman and German concepts of sanctuary combined so that criminals could find refuge from private vengeance and severe punishments but remained subject to the public legal system. The sanctuary seeker who was delivered to the secular court was guaranteed no capital punishment or brutal treatment. The German kings also borrowed exile and banishment, accompanied by confiscation of personal property, from Roman law.

Charlemagne, who ruled the Holy Roman Empire from 768 to 828 C.E., allowed sanctuary but intervened to prevent feuding and assert the royal right of pardon and punishment. His Saxon Capitulary of 785 declared: "If anyone seeks refuge in a church, no one should attempt to expel him by force, but he should be permitted to have his peace until he presents himself to judgment; and his life should be spared in honor of God and Holy Church." However, the king reserved the power to send the fugitive "wheresoever he pleases" (Jones 1994: 27). He was one of many kings who tried to bend the ecclesiastical system to their own political purposes, proclaiming themselves monarchs by divine right and challenging the authority of the pope and his bishops to greater or lesser extent.

In the 7th century C.E., while European kings and clerics proclaimed and regulated church sanctuary based on ancient precedents, in Arabia the Prophet Muhammad was creating what would become the world religion of Islam. Encountering resistance and violent persecution, An-Na'im wrote, the Prophet "sought a more receptive environment for his message, which he eventually found in Medina, a mainly agricultural community in western Arabia. In 622 C.E., Muhammad and his first followers, who became known as *al-muhajirin* (the migrants), left Mecca and settled in Medina" (1990: 12). In other words, they found sanctuary in Medina. This flight to refuge is known as *hijra*, and that year marks the beginning of the Muslim calendar.

Hijra had ancient roots in Arab traditions of hospitality. According to Westermarck (1909: 162), "At certain Arabian shrines the [pre-Islamic]

god gave shelter to all fugitives without distinction." Among the desert Arabs, Bau noted, "any tent could serve as a sanctuary" for a short
period (1985: 127–28). In many tribal cultures that adopted Islam,
sanctuary was (and is) connected to the practice and prevention
of vengeance. In Afghanistan, for example, the traditional Code of
Pashtunwali includes not only vengeance and feuding but hospitality
and sanctuary. *Nazaala*, a traditional practice among the Bedouin of
western Egypt, mentioned in Chapter Two, is an example of the link
between sanctuary and conflict resolution (Obermeyer 1969: 201).

Muslim religious practices have preserved and continued these
venerable traditions. In late 19th-century Morocco, Westermarck
noted, "the tombs of saints and mosques offer shelter to refugees, especially in those parts of the country where the Sultan's government
has no power" (1909: 161). Muslims have taken the idea of sanctuary
with them as they spread their religion around the world, from Arabia
to Indonesia to Detroit, Michigan. A recent study of Iraqi refugees in
the Detroit metropolitan area found that many of them considered
themselves *muhajirin* on a migration from "the Domain of Disbelief
to the Domain of Faith" as they struggled to maintain their Islamic
beliefs in a secular society. A Sunni man, aged 35, told an interviewer,
"The Prophet said that he who escapes with his faith from one land
to another, even if it is only the distance of an inch, will be worthy of
Paradise" (Shoeb, Weinstein, and Halpern 2007: 449).

In the medieval western world sanctuary was consolidated
through royal edicts, laws, and clerical customs. The first Christian
king in England, Ethelbert of Kent (c. 560–616), set up a penalty for
violation of the peace of the church, or *fryth*, in a law code of 597. "A
protection created by the power of the church and vested in any sacred place (the Germanic root of the word . . . refers to the sanctuaries
of sacred woods)," fryth was one of the foundations of sanctuary (Bau
1985: 135).

As in Germany and Arabia, in Anglo-Saxon England sanctuary was
related to blood feuds and vengeance. The offender was subject to
punishment by the group or individual that had been injured, and his
offense was considered a crime against the entire community, clan
or tribe. The victim or relatives had the right to carry out vengeance.
In some societies compensation was supposed to substitute for violent punishment. The church served as an intermediary between the
fugitive and the offended group, helping to determine what punishment or compensation would be levied. Later the crown or the state

intervened, turning compensation into a fine and vengeance into capital punishment or imprisonment. Thus a public legal system gradually emerged over many centuries from rougher, private forms of justice. But over a thousand years, by stepping between the accused perpetrator and the injured parties, church sanctuary played an important role in the progression from private vengeance to public law. During this time England "transformed itself from a society governed by a folk law of private vengeance and compensation to a society that had begun to submit itself to the transcendent authority of a modern state," Jones wrote (1994: 19).

In 680 King Ine of Wessex provided for sanctuary as an alternative to punishment or death in his law code, and in 887 King Alfred gave his protection to all churches and some monasteries, "which were permitted to give temporary refuge to fugitives in the expectation that they would shortly leave sanctuary and be reconciled with their enemies" (Jones 1994: 21). Alfred offered "immunity from peremptory retribution" if the sanctuary seeker confessed and surrendered to local authorities (Jones 1994: 21). Under his law code sanctuary seekers could gain refuge for seven to 30 days. Anyone harming the fugitive during that time had to pay compensation to the fugitive's kin for breaching fryth.

Another of Alfred's laws extended the number of days the fugitive could stay in sanctuary but did not allow the church to provide food, thus guaranteeing the fugitive's eventual departure. Even so, church officials were supposed to ensure that sanctuary seekers did not suffer capital punishment or torture after leaving sanctuary, in line with the church's duty to ensure mercy for sinners.

Toward the end of the first millennium c.e. kings granted sanctuary privileges to almost two dozen abbeys, monasteries, minsters, and other religious houses throughout England. These included Beverley Abbey, Durham Cathedral, Wells Cathedral, York Minster, and Westminster Abbey. Royal laws imposed fines to protect the inviolability of sanctuaries, depending on the distance from the altar where violations took place. A violation of the altar itself was irredeemable. This rule had momentous consequences in the 12th century, when King Henry II's vassals assassinated Thomas Becket, the archbishop of Canterbury, inside the cathedral near the altar. According to Cox, one chronicler says Becket had resisted Henry's repeated denials of sanctuary, "and it was for resisting this royal action, among other causes, that Thomas à Beckett incurred the hatred of the king and

his eventual assassination" (Cox 1911: 35). In addition to being archbishop of Canterbury, he was also the provost of Beverley, one of the
most important sanctuary abbeys in England.

Becket's murder on December 29, 1170, had tremendous repercussions, including the development of a cult in his honor that
brought numerous visitors and considerable revenues to Canterbury
Cathedral. (Chaucer portrays the pilgrims in the *Canterbury Tales* as
they wend their way to the cathedral to worship at Becket's shrine.)
Henry had made progress in consolidating the justice system and the
state's power over the feudal lords. But his involvement in Becket's
murder made it impossible for him to exercise effective control over
the church. He had to do public penance in the streets of Canterbury
and spend the night in the cathedral crypt to atone for his violation of
sanctuary. Becket's murder had the unintended effect of strengthen-
ing church sanctuary under church control.

As sanctuary law developed it began to reflect conflict and competition between church and state. In 1014 King Ethelred's law con-
ferred sanctity on churches themselves rather than the clerics who
officiated there. The church collected fines for violations of sanctuary under this royal law. As time went on, Bau points out, "the
churches and the clergy would claim that the sanctuary privilege was
rooted in the sanctity of the place, irrevocable by the monarch. On
the other hand, the king would claim that the privilege was merely a
personal privilege granted to the clergy, revocable at the king's will"
(1985: 141).

In the second half of the 11th century William the Conqueror's
laws affirmed church sanctuary and established stiff fines for its violation. Such fines were to be paid not only to the church but also to the
king. Riggs wrote that during this period, "the institution of asylum
appears to have been one of the most effective instruments the times
provided for bringing men to submit to the law" (1963: 60). The law
was supposed to approximate or be modeled on divine justice. As it
developed, it protected the guilty and the innocent through due process. Secular procedures such as habeas corpus (which seems to have
appeared in England in the 12th century) and the concept of "innocent until proven guilty" may have evolved from royal laws protecting
sanctuary seekers. In the 12th and 13th centuries English and French
kings created a criminal justice system in which royal courts claimed
a monopoly over criminal prosecution, making formerly private justice public.

The crown had strong reasons to support sanctuary, however. If private parties summarily executed a criminal, the crown would lose the revenue (fines, seized property) it could hope to gain if it successfully prosecuted him. Sanctuary gave the crown time to prepare a prosecution and made it more likely the criminal would be brought to justice. The monarch also used sanctuary to protect a particularly stigmatized group, the Jews, on whom he often depended for funds to fight both civil and foreign wars. According to Winder, in the 12th and 13th centuries, threatened by great public hostility and pogroms, "many Jews survived only because their [loan] contracts stipulated that they had the right to take refuge in royal castles" (Winder 2004: 47).

Sanctuary could be and was abused by criminals who used the church as a safe house. Some abbeys could even provide permanent sanctuary from private vengeance or the king's justice. As a result kings placed various restrictions on sanctuary. Siebold notes, "From the 12th century a felon could be harbored in a church for only 40 days, in which period, if he desired safety, he had to confess his crime and abjure the realm" (1937: 536).

Abjuration of the realm was a form of voluntary exile. It apparently arrived in England from Normandy and was first mentioned in a royal document around 1130. Bracton's *On the Laws and Customs of England*, compiled in the mid-13th century, described the procedure in detail. After gaining sanctuary, the fugitive would publicly confess the crime before a royal official called a coroner, who would come to the church for that purpose. Coroners kept legal records of sanctuary cases, some of which still exist today. These and other documents indicate that around a thousand people a year may have gained church sanctuary in England over several centuries. The fugitive could either surrender to the secular authorities for trial or abjure the realm. In the latter case he would swear before the coroner: "Hear this, justices or ye coroners, that I shall go forth from the realm of England, and shall not return thither again, except with the license of the lord the king or of his heirs, so God me help" (Cox 1911: 14).

Bracton's law treatise, *De Corona*, describes what happened next:

> If having acknowledged his misdeed he has elected to abjure the realm, he ought to choose some port by which he may pass to another land beyond the realm of England. . . . And there ought to be computed for him his reasonable traveling expenses as far

as that port, and he ought to be interdicted from going out of the king's highway, and from delaying anywhere for two nights, and from entertaining himself anywhere, and from turning aside from the high road except under great necessity or for the sake of lodging for the night, but let him always continue along the straight road to the port, so that he shall always be there on the appointed day, and that he shall cross the sea as soon as he shall find a ship, unless he shall be impeded by the weather; but if he does otherwise, he shall be in peril. (Cox 1911: 13–14)

Other sources say the abjurer was to wear white sackcloth, carry a cross in his hand, and go bareheaded and barefoot. The usual port of departure was Dover, but some northern abjurers would walk to Berwick and thence to Scotland. Sometimes the coroner gave the abjurer little time to reach the port, and he might have to walk as many as 33 miles per day. Once at the port he was supposed to wade into the water up to the knees (some sources say up to the neck) and hail a boat. Jones insists: "It is . . . very unlikely that most abjurors actually departed the kingdom. . . . Given the limited ability of medieval legal administration to enforce even its most solemn judgments, the best that could be hoped for was that the identities of abjurors would be publicized as widely as possible" (1994: 25). From exile abjurers could petition the king to return to England, and a few records indicate that some were allowed to return by paying a large indemnity. Abjurers could be pardoned only once, however.

With its elaborate rules, privileges, and restrictions, sanctuary was one of the most powerful and important medieval institutions. Three types of sanctuary existed: first, a general privilege inhering in every parish church and churchyard; second, sanctuary chartered by the king, where permanent refuge was possible; third, secular sanctuary controlled by the local lord in churches under his jurisdiction, beyond the king's authority. In all cases sanctuary "was a useful means towards a settlement or resolution of conflict, not simply an irrational way of avoiding due punishment and retribution," according to Musson (2005: 5). It also served broader purposes, defining the boundaries of the law and the sacred meaning of justice. "Sanctuary confirmed a complex cluster of ideas about the purpose of dispute resolution and the redemptive significance of punishment that permeated early medieval culture" (Musson 2005: 39). Doing wrong injured not only the victim of crime but the soul of the wrongdoer. Redemption lay in the perpetrator making an offering to God in search of forgiveness. Retribution for wrongdoing was supposed to be "an offertory act of conciliation and repair," mediated or supervised by the church without violence (Musson 2005: 42). Punishment would lead to justice only if it included mercy and charity. The wrongdoer could return to the community of believers by making a sacrifice, an act of penance, which "reflected an acknowledgment that by strict justice, all were lost. One could only achieve reunion through grace, be it the Deity's, lord's or victim's" (Musson 2005: 46).

The Catholic basis of sanctuary survived until the Reformation in Europe and Britain, but the rules governing it changed as the state tried to exert more control over the justice system. With adoption of the Magna Carta in 1215, trial by jury became part of the secular law. Sanctuary seekers who wanted to avoid trial in the royal courts had to abjure the realm. Thus sanctuary continued to be a recourse for fugitives, but increasingly kings sought to limit its use. They tried to prevent traitors, debtors, and other categories of criminals from gaining refuge in churches and even went to the pope to gain support for their policies. For example, Henry VII obtained a bull (decree) from Pope Innocent VIII in 1486 regulating sanctuary in England. The bull proclaimed that sanctuary men could not return to sanctuary if they committed crimes after leaving it; sanctuary men's goods were not protected from creditors; and "if any man took sanctuary for a case of treason, the king might appoint keepers to look after him in sanctuary" (Mazzinghi 1887: 112).

Both religious and secular sanctuaries marked the limits of royal authority. The courtyards of feudal lords were out of bounds to state authorities and private seekers of vengeance. Entire cities, such as Durham, were classified as "liberties," where royal authorities could not pursue fugitives. During periods of civil war armed vassals and soldiers could flee to a liberty and stay there permanently. Thus the liberties' inhabitants were effectively beyond the reach of the law. Numerous disputes between the king, the city, and the church ensued over liberties and sanctuary during the late Middle Ages. By the 15th century kings tried to undermine the institution at every opportunity. The legal authorities also disliked it. In 1399 English judges issued a manifesto against the erection of new sanctuaries, declaring that the king could not give away his own prerogative of pardoning felons. Alleged abuses of sanctuary gave the monarch an excuse to limit or abolish it. But medieval laws limiting sanctuary were often ineffective:

"Medieval legislation was always in the nature of a manifesto of policy, or the enunciation of a wholesome principle, to which practice should but frequently did not conform," Thornley wrote (1924: 187).

Despite the royal restrictions churches continued to take in fugitives during the 14th, 15th, and 16th centuries. They had strict rules. For example, at Durham Cathedral two men were stationed in chambers inside the north door to receive fugitives at all hours. The sanctuary seeker would ring the bell and then declare why he was there in front of witnesses. Once inside he had to don a black gown with a yellow cross on the left shoulder and stay in certain areas of the cathedral for a maximum of 37 days. From 1464 to 1524 Durham's records indicate that 332 fugitives involved in 243 crimes were inside the church. Almost 200 of the crimes were homicides. At Beverley between 1478 and 1539, 469 sanctuary seekers included 173 murderers and 200 debtors (Kesselring 1999: 348).

In 1456–57 the regulations of St. Martin le Grand in London declared that the sanctuary seeker could bring no weapons into the church. Gates and doors were closed from 9 P.M. to 6 A.M. between All Hallows and Candlemas. During the rest of the year they were closed from 9 P.M. to 4 A.M. "Any sanctuary man roving forth by night or day to do any evil deed" was to be compelled to stay inside the church (Cox 1911: 90). Counterfeiters, strumpets, and bawds were not allowed entry, and betting was prohibited. Barbers were not to work on Sundays or feast days, although many tradespeople did live and carry on business within protected church precincts.

Sometimes sanctuary seekers waited many years, even decades, before fleeing to the church. Kesselring reported one man who abjured the realm in 1519 for a murder he had committed 40 years earlier. Some sought sanctuary far from the scene of the crime. Others confessed to a felony committed nearby on the same day they had fled to the church. Christopher Brown sought sanctuary in July 1477 after

> he insulted one Thomas Carter who was riding and holding in front of him his little boy of three years of age; whereupon the said Thomas hastily dismounting on account of the insult, suffered his son to fall on the ground, and the horse, by an unfortunate accident, set its feet upon the child who died within two days from the wounds. Christopher, recognizing that he was the indirect cause of the child's death, hastened to Durham. (Cox 1911: 110)

By the late Middle Ages sanctuary was a tarnished institution in Britain. The Elizabethan poet Michael Drayton expressed a common sentiment when he wrote,

Some few themselves in sanctuaries hide
In mercy of that privileged place,
Yet are their bodies so unsanctified,
As scarce their souls can ever hope for grace,
Whereas they still in want and fear abide,
A poor dead life this draweth out a space,
Hate stands without and horror sits within,
Prolonging shame, but pardoning not their sin!
(Mazzinghi 1887: 112)

Kesselring notes that "the most prevalent criticisms of sanctuary focused not on the institution itself, but on the abuses to which it was susceptible" (1999: 354). Thieves and debtors who used sanctuary as a base or to escape punishment were particularly despised. People knew and disapproved of the fact that fugitives could lead comfortable lives in permanent sanctuary in one of the liberties. Some became lay brothers with trades and skills a monastery could use to maintain itself. During periods of civil conflict, liberties welcomed sanctuary seekers who were able fighters. According to Thornley, "In 1487, upon the false news that Henry VII had been defeated by the rebels, the Westminster sanctuary men mustered in a body to rob the houses of those whom they knew to be with the king in the field" (Kesselring 1999: 186).

Westminster Abbey's precincts, which extended quite some distance beyond the church itself, were part of a sanctuary chartered by the king. In a famous incident in 1378 Sir Robert Hawley, an escapee from the Tower of London, was killed in the choir of the Abbey Church "during High Mass, while the Gospel was being read" (MacMichael 1970: 12). Cox noted: "This murder in such a place, apart even from the peculiar sanctuary privilege, aroused the deepest feeling of dismay. For four months the abbey remained closed to all religious rites, and even the sittings of Parliament were suspended lest they should be contaminated by assembling near the scene of the outrage" (1911: 52). As a result Parliament gave Westminster permanent sanctuary status, even for debtors.

Rosser describes the Abbey's residents as "a large assembly of marginal types, destitute or criminal, or both, who were glad of this protection from the law. At the same time, the sanctuary population also included a substantial minority of wealthy merchants. . . . To a trader desiring both complete immunity and convenient proximity to the city, nowhere offered greater safety than the sanctuary of Westminster Abbey" (Rosser 1989: 156). Merchants accused of theft and fraud sometimes lived within the Abbey gates for many years. Political dissidents also found a home in the Abbey. The most famous was the poet laureate John Skelton, who wrote broadsides in verse against Cardinal Wolsey during the reign of Henry VIII. He died in sanctuary in 1529.

The sanctuary seeker in Westminster Abbey

> had to state the cause of his flight and to give the names and conditions of those he had wronged, to swear to behave properly, to observe the privileges and the customs of the sanctuary, to honour contracts entered into within the sanctuary and to satisfy his creditors as soon as possible, if he was a fugitive for debt. He might only sell food or drink with the area, or admit fugitives to his house, if he had a license to do so from the Archdeacon. He was neither to carry weapons, nor to go out of sanctuary by day or night until he had satisfied his adversaries, nor was he to defame other fugitives, nor to do violence or let it be done by any other inmate. (MacMichael 1970: 10–11)

The Abbey's special status as a sanctuary "arose from the fact that the land around the Abbey was an independent liberty. The king's writ did not run there, and royal officers had no authority" (MacMichael 1970: 11). The 15th century, during the Wars of the Roses, was the heyday of sanctuary at Westminster Abbey. Among the prominent sanctuary seekers there were Eleanor, Duchess of Gloucester, in 1441; Henry Holland, Duke of Exeter, in 1454; and Queen Elizabeth Woodville in 1470 and 1483.

As the Tudor kings consolidated state power by force and through the law, the church lost its dominance; sanctuary declined as a result. Determined to prevent traitors from gaining sanctuary, Kings Henry VII and Henry VIII severely limited its operation. A series of parliamentary acts between 1529 and 1540 decisively damaged the institution. Abjuration of the realm was abolished in 1530, and anyone claiming sanctuary had to remain there permanently under pain of death. This law may have been passed because people with expert knowledge, such as mariners, were abjuring the realm and taking state secrets and technical expertise abroad. A law of 1534 declared that traitors could not gain refuge, and in 1540 serious felons were excluded from sanctuary. All sanctuaries except for churches and churchyards were abolished after Henry VIII dissolved the monasteries and ended the chartered privileges of the country's major abbeys. The Reformation effectively destroyed not only the primacy of the Catholic Church but also sanctuary as a refuge from and alternative to the claims of secular law.

In a famous speech Henry VIII declared, "I argue that St. Edward, King Edgar and the other kings and holy popes who made the sanctuaries never intended that sanctuary should serve for willful murder and larceny outside the sanctuary, done in the hope of re-entering and such like cases. . ." (Kesselring 1999: 355). Instead of church sanctuaries he established eight cities of refuge based on the Old Testament model. Apparently the inhabitants of the eight cities objected, and few if any fugitives were sent there.

Queen Mary Tudor allowed sanctuary at Westminster Abbey but did not try to restore it in all places. Near the end of her reign, in 1558, the abbot of Westminster successfully defended the abbey's privileges in Parliament, noting that "all princes, throughout the history of Christendom, had preserved 'places of succour and safeguard for such as have transgressed laws and deserve corporal pains.'" He argued that "the maintenance of places of refuge continued to be a legitimate way to ensure the temperance of the law" (Kesselring 1999: 355).

Mary's successor Queen Elizabeth weakened sanctuary by restricting it to debtors. During her reign voluntary abjuration of the realm was transformed into "transportation," a secular judicial penalty. In 1624, during the reign of James I, Parliament finally ended sanctuary. It continued to exist until the early 18th century in a few churches, but it was finished as a recognized legal institution in Britain. Even so, in Scotland debtors could—and did—gain sanctuary at the royal palace of Holyroodhouse until 1880. Debtors' prisons, which allowed them and their families to live unmolested in relative comfort until they could find the money to repay their outstanding debts, could also be seen as a continuation of sanctuary.

Even as the religious institution of sanctuary was declining, however, the underlying principles of sanctuary survived in the new secular invention of asylum, an important part of international law that developed during the 17th century as a right of nation states.

Meanwhile, the Catholic Church tried to preserve sanctuary in predominantly Catholic countries such as France, where King Francis I had abolished it in 1539. The Council of Trent (1545–63) declared sanctuary a divinely instituted right of the church. A papal bull of 1591 pronounced church buildings inviolable, and fugitives were not to be removed without the rector's permission. Violation of this rule would result in excommunication. As late as 1727 Pope Benedict XIII threatened secular officials with excommunication if they violated sanctuary but barred street robbers, assassins, political offenders, and counterfeiters from refuge in churches. According to Jones, "Severely restricted in its application, sanctuary was tolerated in some parts of southern and eastern Europe into the nineteenth century" (1994: 35). The 1919 Code of Canon Law upheld sanctuary but dropped excommunication as a penalty for its violation.

Ironically, in his 1937 article on asylum in the *Encyclopaedia of the Social Sciences*, Siebold remarked: "In an orderly state with a systematized legal procedure sanctuary is superfluous" (1937: 537). At that moment thousands of refugees from the Spanish Civil War were receiving sanctuary in France, Mexico, and other countries, and late in the following year charitable organizations began sending almost 10,000 Jewish children from Germany, Austria, and Czechoslovakia to sanctuary in Britain. During World War II Catholic clergy, including the future Pope John XXIII, revivified sanctuary by hiding Jewish and other refugees from the Nazis in churches, monasteries, convents, and other religious houses. The 1983 Code of Canon Law did not include sanctuary at all. But at about that time Catholic, Protestant, and Jewish clergy and laypeople in the United States were risking prosecution by giving sanctuary to refugees from the Central American wars.

The elaborate belief structure of sanctuary, mandating forgiveness and mercy, existed in a brutal world of blood feud, summary killing, torture, and trial by ordeal. Since then the world has changed in some ways but not in others. However sanctuary worked in practice during the Middle Ages, its success as an institution can be measured chiefly by its enduring influence on Western societies and beyond, up to the present day.

CHAPTER FOUR

From Sanctuary to Asylum

*A permanent residence ought not to be denied to
foreigners who, expelled from their homes, are seeking
a refuge, provided that they submit themselves to the
established government and observe any regulations
which are necessary to avoid strifes.*

HUGO GROTIUS, 1625 (Stevens 2004: 12)

On August 3, 1492, Isabella and Ferdinand expelled the Jews from
Spain. A few left with Columbus that day for the New World. Some
others fled to England, where they lived very quietly indeed, since
the Jews had been expelled from that country two centuries before,
in 1290. James I expelled their descendants in 1609, but from the
mid-1620s on, small numbers of Jews again sought to enter England.
In 1656, during the Protectorate of Oliver Cromwell, 20 Jews arrived
in London, declaring themselves refugees from the Spanish Inquisi-
tion. In essence, Winder observed, they were asylum seekers, and "by
identifying themselves as anti-Catholic, they successfully ingratiated
themselves with the authorities" (2004: 76). They were allowed to stay
and practice their religion. More followed, establishing a small community in the East End of London. By the end of the century they
numbered about a thousand.

The Jews were not the only, and certainly not the largest, group
to seek refuge from religious persecution in England. Protestants
from other nations, such as the Huguenots who left France after the

St. Bartholomew's Day Massacre of 1572, fled to Protestant England during the Reformation. Many other foreigners arrived in the country for economic and political reasons. In the 14th century Flemish weavers fled unrest on the Continent and settled in England, where protectionist trade policies helped them prosper. These economic immigrants were much disliked, however. For example, riots in London drove Italian merchants out of the city in 1456–57, and unemployed people aimed their rage at foreigners during the May Day riots of 1517. Parliament repeatedly passed laws against "aliens" and restricted their economic activities. The British crown also had extradition treaties with other states; it used these agreements to get rid of "traitors" (people we would now consider political refugees) as well as criminals. Yet despite a generally negative attitude toward outsiders, the British became known for their willingness to take in strangers, especially when they believed that doing so served their interests.

English law divided aliens into two categories, friends and enemies. The Jews were defined as eternal enemies until the courts overruled that designation in 1697. As far back as the 16th century, the government had feared that foreigners were arriving under false pretenses, claiming to be religious refugees but actually coming to take jobs away from native-born subjects. Throughout that century rabble-rousing pamphlets aimed hostility at foreigners, who were commonly called "fugitives," as if they were criminals. Queen Elizabeth set an example for monarchs by allowing certain kinds of people, such as Protestant Walloons from Flanders, into Britain while mercilessly expelling others, such as German Anabaptists who did not believe in the Trinity. Her government also kept strict records of the numbers of foreigners in the kingdom. Nevertheless European Protestants referred to Britain as "asylum Christi."

Even so, the British Puritans could not find the religious toleration they craved in their native land and sought refuge first in Holland, then in the New World, which they considered a sanctuary from persecution. The Massachusetts Bay Colony and other early European settlements in America did not have sanctuary laws, but some did give refuge to religious and political dissidents who fled other colonies.

The first recorded sanctuary case in the American colonies took place in the 1660s, when Edward Whalley and William Goffe, officers in Cromwell's army and members of the court that had condemned King Charles I to death 15 years earlier, arrived in the New Haven

Colony (Bau 1985). They were fleeing indictments handed down under Charles II, who sent officers to the colony to arrest the two and return them to England for trial. A pastor in New Haven preached a sermon to the officers in support of sanctuary, and the Puritans hid the fugitives in a cave. The two stayed in the colony for 10 years before dying of natural causes. Nobody invoked sanctuary, but it was given.

The first people to be called "refugees" in English were the Huguenots, who fled to England for a second time after the revocation of the Edict of Nantes in 1685. As many as 250,000 Huguenots left France in the following years for England, Germany, Switzerland, Holland, Denmark, Sweden, Russia, and America. The origin of asylum as a legal concept in international law predates this event, however.

The Peace of Westphalia, which ended the Thirty Years' War in 1648, established a community of nation-states that had certain rights, including sovereignty, in Europe. The idea of state sovereignty based on physical territory was an invention of this peace treaty. It followed that the native inhabitants of a state had a natural right to live there, as opposed to outsiders or strangers who had to obtain special permission to enter or reside in the territory. The Peace of Westphalia brought new order, based on international laws and agreements, to the relations between and among European nations. Part of sovereignty, Gibney and Hansen explained, was "the right to grant asylum to whomsoever [the state] wished and to have that right respected by other states" (2005: I: 23). An important aspect of asylum was the limitation it established on the right of a state to ask for extradition of enemies who had fled to another state. It should be kept in mind that modern asylum came into formal existence as a universal right of *states* to grant, not of *individuals* to receive. In contrast to sanctuary, a religious institution in Europe, asylum was a secular and political institution, a part of the modern international system of sovereign states.

The acceptance of the Huguenots as refugees was an important early test of the new system. They were granted permanent asylum in their new countries, and their descendants live and prosper there to this day. Each generation seemed to have a group of refugees who sought refuge outside their native land. For example, some 40,000 émigrés arrived in England during the French Revolution. Although the British government supported the French monarchists, it feared that revolutionary spies might be sent to England to overthrow the British king. As a result Parliament passed the first law regulating asylum in Britain, the Aliens Act of 1793. Refugees would have to register upon arrival in the country, and this requirement has been included in successive immigration laws for more than 200 years.

Often governments would admit refugees only to expel them later on. Charles Talleyrand, prime minister and foreign minister of France, was granted asylum in England in 1792, during the Reign of Terror, but expelled two years later; he spent two more years in exile in the United States before returning to France. In 1803 King George III issued a proclamation ordering 1,700 French refugees to leave the country. When they were refused entry in France, they returned to England and were allowed to stay. In these instances the enemy of England's enemy was England's friend—for a while.

During this very repressive period, when public meetings and even private correspondence on political matters could lead to treason charges, paranoia became official policy in Britain. In 1798 the Act for Establishing Regulations Respecting Aliens distinguished "between persons who either really seek refuge and asylum from oppression and tyranny . . . and persons who, pretending to claim the benefit of such refuge and asylum . . . have or shall come to . . . this kingdom with hostile purposes" (Stevens 2004: 21). This very suspicious attitude toward strangers can be found in almost all asylum legislation and policy up to the present, where it survives in the bureaucratic "culture of disbelief"—the assumption that asylum seekers are liars.

The Alien Acts passed during the Napoleonic Wars allowed the government to deport enemy aliens, and 218 were removed between 1801 and 1815. Even so, the government was ready to make exceptions to its draconian rules on a case-by-case basis. In 1802 the British secretary of state allowed the Bourbon princes to find refuge in Britain, saying, "His Majesty . . . feels it to be inconsistent with his honor, and his sense of justice, to withdraw from them the rights of hospitality, as long as they conduct themselves peaceably and quietly" (Stevens 2004: 22). This is an example of the state using asylum or the denial of asylum for political purposes, as an instrument of state power in foreign affairs.

In the United States the Alien Act of 1798 gave the president the authority to deport anyone he found dangerous to national security. This law and the accompanying Sedition Act were highly unpopular.

In general U.S. borders were open, and regulation of immigrants was the responsibility of local authorities until the late 19th century.

The British Parliament continued to pass Alien Acts from time to time during the 19th century, but between 1836 and 1905 the government did not deport a single refugee, including hundreds of revolutionaries who had been expelled previously from various European countries. The most illustrious political exiles included Giuseppe Mazzini and Karl Marx, who lived in Britain for decades. Thus Britain consolidated its reputation as a free country. A conspiracy bill, "aimed at refugees plotting attacks on European rulers," did not pass Parliament and brought down the government in 1858, so great was the public opposition (Stevens 2004: 24).

Fifty thousand refugees were registered with the British police in 1851; 100,000 in 1871. Public attitudes toward them were contradictory. On the one hand, in 1849 the *Times* called England "the favoured receptacle of all the scum and refuse which the continental revolutions have thrown up" (Stevens 2004: 22). On the other hand, the same newspaper proclaimed in 1853: "Every civilized people on the face of the earth must be fully aware that this country is the asylum of nations, and that it will defend the asylum to the last ounce of its treasure and the last drop of its blood. There is no point on which we are prouder or more resolute. . . . We are a nation of refugees" (Stevens 2004: 27). In line with this sentiment an 1870 law specifically protected political exiles from extradition.

Thousands of European political dissidents began to move to England and France in the early 1830s, after revolution swept from France and Belgium to Holland, Switzerland, Germany, Italy, and Poland. Around 12,000 Poles went to Western Europe and England in 1830–31. Thousands more fled from Portugal, Spain, Italy, and Germany. The French government reacted by placing restrictions on refugees. They were dispersed to different parts of France, where they would not threaten national security, and they had to carry identity cards after 1837. Sometimes they were forced to join the Foreign Legion and fight in colonial campaigns. They could be imprisoned. Or they might be expelled or extradited if they left the place to which they had been sent or if their home country wanted to prosecute them. Bade wrote: "Refugees were only guaranteed asylum in France if they lived inconspicuously and abstained from all political activity" (2003: 136).

The revolutions of 1848 led to another wave of refugees arriving in France and Belgium. For political and economic reasons both governments tried to discourage them from staying, although Belgium had achieved independence with the help of refugee soldiers and officers in 1830. Even before 1848 Karl Marx was kicked out of France and went to Belgium. Then he was kicked out of Belgium and eventually went to England in 1849. Other revolutionaries left Europe for the United States. But many European exiles wanted to stay as close to their home country as possible, so they could continue to influence political developments there. Bade observed: "The significance of political refugees depended not on their numbers but on their role as a voice of the opposition abroad. The abundance of their writings and the activities of their groups and clubs convey the image of lively populations of political exiles" (2003: 138). Their influence was disproportionately large compared to their small numbers.

Pressured by the French government the Belgians made it more difficult for political refugees to stay in the country. In 1849, for example, they prevented scores of Italians and Hungarians from crossing their border because another country (France) had previously taken them in. About 150 years later European Union member states promulgated a similar regulation to keep asylum seekers out.

Similarly, Switzerland pushed asylum seekers on to England and the United States in 1848–49. "Only those who were persecuted in their native country for political crimes and could not return because of threat to life and limb would be acknowledged as refugees" (Bade 2003: 140). The Swiss government considered asylum a "humanitarian concession" that could be "refused or revoked at any time." As Switzerland became a haven for revolutionaries, the government reacted by restricting refugees' activities, banning them from participating in any organizations as long as they stayed in the country. Then Switzerland expelled Mazzini and other revolutionaries and the focus shifted to England, which became "the most consistent and thus significant asylum-granting country in the 19th century" (Bade 2003: 143). After 1851 France, Belgium, and Switzerland deported political refugees to Britain rather than back to their home country. Sometimes the British government encouraged political refugees to emigrate to the United States, and in 1858 it "secretly financed the emigration of 960 men, 305 women and 233 children" (Bade 2003: 146).

During the 19th century Britain did not pass the kind of restrictive laws that made European countries increasingly inhospitable to refugees. Indeed, they could become British citizens after three years' residence, unless they were notorious troublemakers like Marx, whose petition for naturalization was denied in 1874. Nevertheless he lived unmolested in Britain until his death in 1883, and he rests in peace near several of his followers in Highgate Cemetery in London.

The life of political exiles in Britain was not easy unless they were wealthy. A few managed to become university professors or publish journals. Others struggled as tutors or governesses. Marx was a freelance journalist, writing mostly for U.S. newspapers, but he never earned enough money to support himself and his family; he depended on the beneficence of his wealthy friend and fellow exile Friedrich Engels for many years.

On arriving in England many exiles felt free, since no government spies shadowed them and they could associate with one another without constraint. After the Post Office opened Mazzini's correspondence in 1844, the House of Commons attacked the government for introducing "the spy system of foreign states . . . repugnant to every principle of the British Constitution and subversive of the public confidence" (Ashton 1986: 41). Certain activities classed as crimes in Europe, such as political conspiracy, propaganda, and incitement to revolution, were not criminal offenses in Britain; furthermore, Britain boasted the right to assemble, freedom of the press, and an elected Parliament, which many European countries lacked. British asylum policies provided a humanitarian model in contrast to the repressive laws of the Continent.

Over time the exiles suffered from penury, isolation, and disillusionment, however. In his journal, *The Star of Freedom*, G. J. Harney of the Association of Fraternal Democrats wrote in 1852: "The exile . . . is free to land upon our shores, and free to perish of hunger beneath our inclement skies" (Ashton 1986: 34). Although the government did little or nothing to harm political refugees, it also did nothing to help them. Organizations such as the Association of Fraternal Democrats provided limited financial assistance to refugees, but some disappeared into the morass of poverty, went mad, or subsisted by begging. In 1854 the London police estimated that of almost 2,000 exiles in the city, two-thirds were "in straitened circumstances" (Ashton 1986: 226).

A few political exiles became famous in Britain. For example, Gottfried Kinkel, a university professor, was sentenced to life in prison for his involvement in the 1848 revolution in Prussia. He managed to escape to Britain with his family. Well connected with British intellectuals who became his patrons, he was asked to deliver lectures all over the country. The press covered his activities favorably because he was seen as the victim of "excessive punishment at the hands of an oppressive state" (Ashton 1986: 155). As Britain admitted Italian political refugees in 1874, the Italian ambassador wryly observed, "England is very chary of making restrictions on the freedom of entry of foreigners to these shores. Deposed emperors and kings, princes in trouble, persecuted ecclesiastics, patriots out of work—all find an asylum in little England" (Winder 2004: 186).

In 1880 the British Institute of International Law passed the Oxford Resolutions, one of which stated: "Extradition shall not take place for political acts" (Grahl-Madsen 1980: 4). However, in an 1856 extradition law Belgium declared that "murder, assassination or poisoning of the head of state of a foreign country or of members of his family shall not be considered a political crime or as an act connected with such a crime" (Grahl-Madsen 1980: 25). Governments generally agreed that political asylum could be given only to certain kinds of political dissidents—usually nonviolent ones—and political crimes were of a different nature from common crimes. Like medieval kings and popes, they wanted to restrict sanctuary to those they classified as deserving. But the essence of traditional sanctuary is openhandedness: anyone who sets foot on sacred ground must be admitted, no questions asked. It is too difficult to tell on the spot who might be innocent, who guilty. As a result, sanctuary has an ambiguous quality that makes it seem both compassionate and dangerous.

The United States became known as a country that welcomed immigrants and refugees, but it restricted entry in some ways. The Immigration Act of 1875 barred the entry of prostitutes and convicts. The Chinese Exclusion Act of 1882 was not repealed until 1943. Another 1882 law imposed a head tax on immigrants and prohibited entry of "idiots, lunatics, convicts and persons likely to become public charges" (Bau 1985: 40).

Immigration became a hot political issue in many countries at the end of the 19th century because of growing unemployment, poverty, industrial unrest, urban overcrowding, and the sweatshop system. At the same time millions of people were leaving their home countries for economic, political, and religious reasons. About 2.5 million Jews fled persecution in Eastern Europe and Russia from the 1880s to 1914. Only about 120,000 of them arrived in Britain during that period, and the 1901 census reported a total of 339,000 foreigners in a national population of 32 million. Nonetheless they were seen as "hordes." In 1891 Sir Howard Vincent, an MP from Sheffield, said they were arriving "in battalions and taking the bread out of the mouths . . . of English wives and children" (Stevens 2004: 34). There was a forceful anti-Semitic reaction: the British Brothers' League, a precursor of the far-right National Front, was established in East London, where many Jewish refugees lived, to fight Jewish immigration in 1901. Their agitation inspired the Alien Act of 1905, the first law since 1836 restricting immigration into Britain. As a result many Eastern European emigrants pushed on to America.

The 1905 Alien Act did contain a provision protecting asylum seekers:

> In the case of an immigrant who proves that he is seeking admission to this country solely to avoid prosecution or punishment on religious or political grounds or for an offence of a political character, or persecution involving danger of imprisonment or danger to life or limb, on account of religious belief, leave to land shall not be refused on the ground merely of want of means, or the probability of his becoming a charge on the rates. (Stevens 2004: 39)

This law could be said to be the first legislation to "enshrine the concept of asylum in British law," even though the words "asylum" and "refugee" were not mentioned anywhere in the law (Price 2007). Nonetheless the home secretary insisted at the time that there was "no such thing as a 'right' of asylum" (Price 2007). According to Stevens, he mentioned the Huguenots as desirable immigrants, because they had brought money and skills to Britain, expressing a "willingness to protect refugees so long as they brought with them tangible benefits and did not become a burden on the state, with a concern also to distinguish between genuine and bogus applicants" (2004: 38). These attitudes have been constant features of government refugee and immigration policies in Britain and other countries up to the present.

The main purpose of the 1905 Alien Act was to keep "undesirables" out of Britain. Only immigrants traveling in steerage (third class) were examined to determine their physical condition and means of support. Winder points out:

> Immigrant ships—those with more than 20 foreign passengers— could be refused entry. Customs officers were invited to turn

back those unable to support themselves. While aimed above all at Jewish migrants from the Baltic, the Act could be invoked against any would-be immigrants. For the century that followed, immigration would cease to be a right and would be buffeted by the shifting whims of party politics. (2004: 259)

Before passage of the 1905 act, asylum was said to be "writ in characters of fire on the tablets of our Constitution"; after its passage, asylum "became a privilege granted by the state and not an automatic right" (Kushner and Knox 1999: 397). Numbers of political refugees admitted to Britain decreased markedly. Yet, in the words of an official 90 years later, the British government continued to claim: "This country has a proud and consistent record in its treatment of refugees. Our humanitarian record is second to none" (Kushner and Knox 1999: 399). This is true only because other countries' treatment of refugees has been no better.

The significance of the 1905 Alien Act was its establishment of administrative and legal procedures to decide refugee cases and its linkage of asylum with immigration. Its limitations on foreigners' entry into Britain had grievous consequences for refugees.

The tumult of war in the early 20th century decisively ended Britain's long period of hospitality and sanctuary. The Aliens Registration Act of August 1914 included internment of "enemy aliens," a term that had not been heard in the country in almost a century. The right to appeal adverse immigration decisions was removed, as was the exception in the 1905 law benefiting political and religious refugees. In 1915 the British government made compulsory the presentation of a passport upon entry into the country; it had been optional since 1858. Also in 1915 the Germans erected a high-voltage electrical fence between occupied Belgium and Holland; about 3,000 people died trying to cross over it.

During World War I thousands of foreigners were interned in Britain, and 24,000 were still in camps in November 1918. In Germany 110,000 foreign civilians were interned in 18 camps at the end of the war. In all the warring countries about 400,000 enemy aliens were interned during the war. The French government revoked the citizenship of all naturalized citizens who had been born in an "enemy state." After the war a series of restrictive laws made entry into the UK a privilege. An overtly racist, "Special Restriction (Coloured Alien Seaman) Order," apparently aimed at East Indians, required all foreigners to register with the police (Winder 2004: 286).

Meanwhile the United States was closing its "golden door" to immigrants and refugees. One late-19th century law authorized the deportation of indentured workers. Bau comments: "This expansion of the deportation power reflected the slow but certain shift of U.S. immigration policy from one of open welcome to an increasingly complicated system of selection and exclusion" (1985: 41). The Immigration Act of 1917 imposed a literacy requirement, codified previous grounds for exclusion, extended exclusion to Asians, and allowed deportation up to five years after entry. After 40 years of relatively easy entry by more than 23 million immigrants from all parts of Europe, the 1921 Quota Law "limited the annual immigration of persons of a given nationality to 3% of the number of such persons already in the United States in the year 1910" (Bau 1985: 41).

The law was frankly racist in its intention to keep Southern and Eastern European immigrants out and allow Northern and Western Europeans in. From 1917 on the government used immigration laws to deport foreign-born political activists, antiwar campaigners, and trade unionists. The U.S. National Origins Act of 1924 removed time limits for deportation of anyone who entered the country without a proper visa and restricted entry to 164,000 immigrants per year. In 1927 the annual quota was lowered still further to 150,000. As a result Argentina and Brazil received more immigrants between 1925 and 1930 than the United States did.

Thus did intolerance of the dangerous Other become official policy, and it still casts a long shadow over asylum.

CHAPTER FIVE

Asylum outside the Law

I will shelter, I will help, and I will defend the fugitive
with all my humble means and power. I will act with
any body of decent and serious men . . . in any mode
not involving the use of deadly weapons, to nullify and
defeat the operation of [the fugitive slave] law.

REV. THEODORE PARKER, 1850 (Siebert 1968 [1898]: 90)

Among the many fugitives who sought sanctuary in England was Frederick Douglass, perhaps the greatest human rights advocate of the 19th century. In 1845, soon after the publication of his autobiography, he fled from the United States to avoid recapture by his owner in Maryland and became a wildly successful lecturer in England and Ireland. While he was there British supporters purchased his freedom, enabling him to return to the United States in 1846.

For Douglass and a few other prominent runaway slaves, England was the most remote station of the Underground Railroad (UGRR), the last stop in a long and complex network that stretched from Florida to Canada and beyond. It operated successfully for more than 30 years—perhaps as long as 60 years, between the turn of the 19th century and the beginning of the Civil War. Hundreds of escape routes ran through 17 states, from North Carolina to the Canadian border, and as many as 10,000 people, black and white, may have been involved in conducting 40,000 to 100,000 slaves to freedom.[1] Because the UGRR served as a model for many later sanctuary efforts that took place outside the law, it is worthwhile to examine its structure, participants, and operations.

The 18th-century roots of the UGRR lie in the decline of slavery in northern states. In Pennsylvania a law passed in 1780 mandated gradual emancipation, banned slave trading, and automatically freed slaves brought into the state after six months' residence. Although blacks were "excluded from most schools, denied the right to vote, barred from many public places, and relegated mostly to menial occupations," they were legally free in Pennsylvania (Bordewich 2005: 47). In addition, the national Ordinance of 1787 created five new "free" states on the western frontier—Ohio, Indiana, Illinois, Michigan, and Wisconsin—to which slaves could flee. However, the United States Constitution said in Article 4, paragraph 2: "No person held to service or labor in one state under the laws thereof, escaping into another, shall, in consequence of any law or regulation therein, be discharged from such service or labor, but shall be delivered up on claim of the party to whom such service or labor may be due." The Congress passed a fugitive slave law in 1793 to implement this provision. Slaves had no right to contest the law, because they were considered to be property, not human beings.

Nevertheless, small communities of free people of color and escaped slaves established themselves in northern and western cities. Between 1765 and 1800, for example, the number of free blacks in Philadelphia grew from 100 to almost 6,500, about 9% of the city's population. Bordewich notes: "For fugitive slaves, and eventually for the development of the UGRR, the growth of northern cities was crucial. There, fugitives could hope to disappear among friends, and former slaves learned the autonomy and self-reliance that were necessary to build lives in freedom" (2005: 45).

Escape was extremely difficult and dangerous. Most slaves had little idea of how or where to escape. Vigilantes patrolled communities, steamboat captains searched for stowaways, and black travelers were subject to arrest if they could not present proof of their status on demand. If they failed they could be beaten, tortured, mutilated, sold south, or killed. Most fled alone and emancipated themselves without help from anyone. Even if they did succeed, life in the north and west was precarious. Slave catchers, who operated with little or no interference even in northern cities, could invade black residences and terrorize and seize inhabitants with impunity. Blacks could not afford to trust any white person. Frederick Douglass himself received no help from whites, only from blacks, when he escaped to New York City from Maryland in 1838.

Yet a decentralized, grassroots network of black and white preachers, teamsters, peddlers, slaves, sailors, ship stewards, lawyers, business owners, family members, friends, and parishioners did aid and protect fugitive slaves. Bordewich believes the "underground road" began around Philadelphia, perhaps coordinated by Quakers, at the turn of the 19th century. (Only after the introduction of the railroad to the United States in the early 1830s did its name change.) According to Switala:

> The Underground Railroad did not operate like a well-oiled machine. . . . There was never a network that began in the South and ran uninterruptedly all the way to Canada. . . . the Railroad [was] somewhat organized into small operations. These could have as large as a county, and the network within this geographic area was well run. Those regions were then loosely connected to other regions, and a fugitive using these connections could eventually reach the 'promised land' of Canada. (2004: 21)

The UGRR consisted of western, central, and eastern routes. The western route went up the Mississippi River Valley through Kansas and Missouri to Iowa and Illinois, then through Michigan to Canada, usually via Detroit. The central route went from the "heart of the South" via Kentucky, West Virginia, western Maryland, Ohio, Indiana, and Pennsylvania to Canada. The eastern route went from the southeastern states via Maryland, Delaware, Virginia, Pennsylvania, New Jersey, New York, and New England to Canada. The Ohio River Valley was an especially important corridor. After crossing the river, "fugitives who managed to make contact with the underground could, with some confidence, hope to be passed in safety from town to town and from farm to farm all the way to the Great Lakes" (Bordewich 2005: 196). Sometimes the journey to freedom could take hours or days— Douglass reached New York City from Maryland in less than 24 hours by train and boat—months if slaves traveled by foot all the way to Canada.

Of necessity the UGRR's operations were secret; after passage of the 1793 Fugitive Slave Act, helping slaves to escape was a federal crime. Most of those who helped knew the names of collaborators who lived nearby but might not have known anything about the network beyond 20 or 30 miles away. One of the participants, Isaac Beck of southern Ohio, said: "The method of operating was not uniform but adapted to the requirements of each case. There was no regular organization, no constitution, no officers, no laws or agreement or rule except the 'Golden Rule,' and every man did what seemed right in his own eyes" (Bordewich 2005: 5). Most participants said or wrote nothing about their activities, and as a result few names of those involved are recorded. Family stories and folklore kept alive the memories of what Bordewich calls "the country's first racially integrated civil rights movement" (2005: 4).

The first history of the UGRR was by William Still, an African American freeman who worked for the Pennsylvania Anti-Slavery Society in Philadelphia from 1847 to 1861 and the Philadelphia Vigilance Committee from 1852 until the Civil War. Still "coordinated the activities that made Philadelphia one of the nation's strongholds of abolition. He was also one of the Underground Railroad's most significant historians, maintaining meticulous records of the 649 fugitives who were sheltered in the city prior to the Civil War . . ." (Blight 2004: 178). Still carefully hid the records, which included information about UGRR participants, routes, and safe-house locations, until after the war ended. In 1872 he published *The Underground Railroad* himself and sold it by mail for many years.

In 1898 historian Wilbur Siebert published *The Underground Railroad from Slavery to Freedom*, based on thousands of questionnaires sent to UGRR participants and other documentary materials. He collected the names of 3,211 "practical emancipationists" and said there were many more. (Bordewich notes that Siebert's list included only white men.) He recorded the work of many "conductors," including Daniel Gibbons, a Quaker farmer in Lancaster County, Pennsylvania, who helped fugitives for 56 years. Gibbons kept records of about 1,000 slaves whom he assisted between 1824 and 1853.

Quakers were among the best-known UGRR conductors, not only in Pennsylvania but in North Carolina, Illinois, Indiana, and Ohio. A network of Quakers was helping runaway slaves in Philadelphia as early as 1786. Later, via their regional Yearly Meetings in Philadelphia and other cities, they collected and sent funds to coreligionists farther south who used the money to smuggle runaway slaves to free states. According to Bordewich, for the Quakers "the trek out of North Carolina . . . was not merely a geographical journey, but a spiritual one from the darkness of moral depravity into the light of redemption" (2005: 79).

Among the most effective and best known UGRR organizers was Levi Coffin, a Quaker who lived and operated first in North Carolina and later in Indiana and Ohio. He and his cousin created "the earliest known scheme to transport fugitives across hundreds of miles of unfriendly territory to safety in the free states" in 1819. Of his work Coffin said: "The dictates of humanity came in opposition to the law of the land, and we ignored the law" (Bordewich 2005: 63–64).

In 1826, when things got too hot for Coffin in North Carolina, he moved his family to southern Indiana. Later he moved to southern Ohio. Many other Quakers and some free blacks also settled in these border areas. As a prominent businessman and director of the Richmond branch of the Indiana state bank, Coffin was able to operate openly. Willing to take risks, use trickery, and work under difficult conditions, he "represented a new, pivotal kind of figure in the clandestine network, sometimes called a 'general manager,' who exerted a combination of managerial efficiency and moral suasion to rationalize the operation of what had formerly been a fairly haphazard system" (Bordewich 2005: 219). He declared: "I expressed my antislavery sentiments with boldness on every occasion. . . . I told the sympathizers with slave-hunters that I intended to shelter as many runaway slaves as came to my house, and aid them on their way, and advised them to be careful how they interfered in my work" (Bordewich 2005: 220).

In his 1845 autobiography Douglass criticized such boldness:

I have never approved of the public manner in which some
of our western friends have conducted what they call the
Underground Railroad. . . . I honor those good men and women
for their noble daring, and applaud them for willingly subjecting
themselves to bloody persecution, by openly avowing their participation in the escape of slaves . . . while, upon the other hand,
I see and feel assured that those open declarations are a positive
evil to the slaves remaining, who are seeking to escape. They do
nothing toward enlightening the slave, whilst they do much toward enlightening the master. . . . (Bordewich 2005: 238–39)

A decade earlier divisions among Quakers had led to their general withdrawal from leadership of the abolitionist movement. Some Quakers objected to the movement's militant rhetoric and actions.

Coffin and seven other Quakers were expelled from the Indiana Yearly Meeting for divisiveness in 1842. He replied: "We were proscribed for simply adhering to what we believed to be our Christian duty. We asked only liberty of conscience—freedom to act according to one's conscientious convictions" (Bordewich 2005: 229). He continued to help runaway slaves until the outbreak of the Civil War, later estimating he had directly or indirectly assisted around 100 runaway slaves a year, some 3,300 fugitives in all. As a result he was widely known as the "president of the Underground Railroad." But the UGRR was much more extensive than the sphere of his operations in the Ohio River Valley.

Other well-known UGRR organizers included Thomas Garrett and Isaac Hopper, both Quaker businessmen. Garrett lived in the Wilmington, Delaware, area for many years. Around 1815, at age 24 or 25, he found out that one of his father's black servants had been kidnapped. He traced the track left by a wagon to Philadelphia, where he found the abducted woman and set her free. After that he dedicated himself to rescuing slaves. Married to the daughter of a director of the National Bank of Wilmington, he obtained funds for his work from the wealthy DuPont family. In the early 1850s "he was the linchpin, if not the formal director, of a diverse network that . . . included Quakers and Catholics, farmers, whites within the law enforcement establishment, black fishermen and watermen and, as he called her, 'that noble woman,' Harriet Tubman" (Bordewich 2005: 354). She was said to have rescued some 300 slaves from the South and later served as a scout and spy for the Union army during the Civil War.[2] By 1860, Garrett estimated, he had assisted about 2,750 slaves.

Hopper recounted that he had first helped a runaway slave in 1787, when he was 16 years old. Bordewich tells the story:

> Soon after Hopper's arrival in Philadelphia, he encountered his first fugitive, an enslaved sailor who had jumped ship and was desperate to escape recapture. Wanting to help in some way, Hopper asked among his neighbors until he heard about a Quaker in rural Bucks County who was reputed to be "a good friend to colored people." He then found someone to provide the fugitive with a letter of introduction and directions to the man's house where, Hopper was later assured, the sailor was kindly received and provided with a job. (2005: 47)

Hopper and others "pioneered the technique of passing fugitives from hand to hand among members of their extended family, personal friends, Abolition Society activists and others whom Hopper decided should be asked to live up to their principles, until they reached a permanent haven, usually somewhere in the countryside outside Philadelphia" (Bordewich 2005: 59). This pattern of action became standard procedure for the UGRR.

Hopper once told a magistrate: "I would do for a fugitive slave whatever I should like to have done for myself, under similar circumstances. If he asked my protection, I would extend it to him to the utmost of my power. If he was hungry, I would feed him. If he was naked, I would clothe him. If he needed advice, I would give him such as I thought would be most beneficial to him" (Bordewich 2005: 56). He received death threats, his family members were attacked, and his house was burned down. But "antislavery work was for him a profoundly religious act," and nothing could stop him from continuing it (Bordewich 2005: 52).

Philadelphia, where William Still, Isaac Hopper, and other UGRR participants worked and lived, was also the center of the Society of Friends or Quakers, many of whose members opposed slavery. The city also had a sizable community of free blacks and escaped slaves; some were prosperous business owners who financially supported the UGRR. The mother church of the African Methodist Episcopal Church was located there, and AME churches in the vicinity became UGRR "stations." Nevertheless, there were race riots, anti-abolitionist disturbances, and anti-black pogroms in Philadelphia, and slave catchers operated there for many years. In response Pennsylvania became a sanctuary state in 1820, when its legislature passed a law making kidnapping blacks a felony, in defiance of the Fugitive Slave Act of 1793.

During the 1830s the UGRR steadily expanded as the abolitionist movement grew. Some antislavery campaigners were also UGRR conductors or organizers, but the antislavery societies did not endorse the activities of members who carried out illegal actions. Many committed abolitionists were unwilling to break the law; others came to a decision to go underground over time, as the "slave power" gained influence and its representatives wielded increasing clout in Congress. Blacks formed their own "vigilance committees" that cooperated with white allies or acted independently. For example, the New York Vigilance Committee started operating in 1835 with David Ruggles, a courageous 25-year-old black journalist, as its secretary. It became "the hinge upon which the UGRR's operations turned in New York, with links that extended southward to Philadelphia and north to central New York state, New England and Canada" (Bordewich 2005: 172). It gave direct assistance to fugitives such as Frederick Douglass. During its first year the committee helped 335 men and women. Composed of about 100 members and a steering committee of five or six men, it raised funds in the local black community. Prominent New York abolitionists might also have given it financial support.

A determined new generation of activists, black and white, was starting to make its mark in the 1830s and 1840s. In 1834 white students at an evangelical seminary in Cincinnati debated slavery and came out against it. Some went into the city's black neighborhoods to work with their residents on an equal basis. Shocked, the seminary's trustees ordered the students to stop discussing slavery. Many of the students moved to Oberlin College, a known center of abolitionist fervor, "where they formed the nucleus of one of the most ardent UGRR communities west of the Appalachians" (Bordewich 2005: 131).

The Rev. John Rankin was an agent of the Ohio Antislavery Society who became one of the state's foremost UGRR operatives in the 1830s and 1840s. He was one of 100 to 200 abolitionists in Ripley, Ohio, a town overlooking the Ohio River and the border with Kentucky. Rankin was a "moral entrepreneur" who worked with Presbyterian churches and black communities, where "blacks worked as underground conductors and agents, and black hamlets scattered through the region served as key holding areas, or way stations, where fugitives could rest and recuperate before being moved farther north" (Bordewich 2005: 199).

Harriet Beecher Stowe, who lived nearby in Cincinnati and hid fugitive slaves in her home, based the character of Eliza in *Uncle Tom's Cabin* on a woman who escaped across the partly frozen Ohio River in 1838 with her baby in her arms. Collapsed on the river bank, she was discovered by a slave catcher who had watched her make her way across. He directed her to Rankin's house at the top of the hill. Rankin sent her to the next UGRR station without learning her name. A few years later Levi Coffin sent her north.

Bordewich notes: "The underground network, in Ripley and elsewhere, was built on a cellular structure consisting mainly of discrete, farm-based units that were linked to one another only at their outer edges, and whose members typically did not know the names of fellow members who lived more than two or three towns away" (2005: 206).

Rankin's UGRR work was very risky, endangering his entire family. In 1841 his house and barn were attacked in the middle of the night, but the family fought off the attackers, including one they shot and killed. Rankin then published an announcement in the local newspaper that he would shoot anyone who came onto his property after dark. This warning did not apply to runaway slaves, who arrived at all hours. His four sons, who all became Presbyterian ministers, took care of the new arrivals. "At least one of the Rankin boys was expected to be on call at any given moment to saddle up and hasten his charges to the next friendly home." The UGRR stations were 15 to 20 miles apart, "the maximum distance for mounted riders or a wagon to travel at night and return before dawn" (Bordewich 2005: 207).

Rankin's example shows how the UGRR and the abolitionist movement "existed . . . in a symbiotic relationship with the societies serving as a fertile recruiting ground for clandestine activists, and the Underground Railroad in turn supplying abolitionist lecture halls and fundraisers with a steady stream of flesh-and-blood fugitives who . . . were living proof of slavery's inhumanity" (Bordewich 2005: 162). Echoes of this kind of relationship may be seen in the U.S. Sanctuary Movement of the 1980s, described in Chapter Seven.

Women's contributions to the UGRR received little recognition, but Bordewich points out:

> Women had always done much of the Underground Railroad's unsung work of feeding, sheltering and nursing fugitives. When they arrived travel-worn and hungry at the Hayden home in Boston or the Douglass home in Rochester, it was Harriet Hayden and Anna Douglass who made their beds and cooked their meals. Many women did much more than that. In one Michigan community, women were responsible for giving the alarm if slave catchers appeared, and in Cleveland four of the nine members of that city's very active, all-black Vigilance Committee were women. White women as well as black women sometimes served as conductors. (2005: 369)

Women's antislavery societies and committees specialized in helping escaping female slaves.

Although the new free states provided refuge to fugitives, they also passed laws discouraging them from settling there. Northern states also passed discriminatory ordinances, the "black laws," that made life difficult for free people of color. Nowhere in the United States was a truly welcoming place for blacks. But in Canada slavery was in steep decline by 1800, and after the War of 1812 Canada welcomed blacks to help defend its underpopulated southern borders from invading Americans.[3] As an incentive blacks were given the right to vote there. By the 1820s black runaways were building settlements in Canada opposite Buffalo, New York, and Detroit, Michigan. These modest towns—Amherstburg, St. Catherines, Buxton, and others—became the northern terminuses of the UGRR.

Also in the 1820s the United States and Britain were at odds over the flight of slaves to Canada. U.S. Secretary of State Henry Clay, a professed opponent of slavery who owned dozens of slaves, tried to negotiate extradition agreements guaranteeing the return of escaped slaves. But the British government "steadfastly refused . . . on the ground that the British government could not 'depart from the principle recognized by the British courts that every man is free who reaches British ground'" (Siebert 1968 [1898]: 193).

Canada may have been legally hospitable to escaped slaves, but the situation there was very difficult. The climate was poor, diseases—including tuberculosis—were rife, and the settlements had few resources. Quakers, Indians, and philanthropists tried to help. Josiah Henson, who had escaped to Canada in 1830 from slavery in Maryland, founded a settlement called Dawn that struggled to provide subsistence for about 500 inhabitants. By 1860 between 20,000 and 60,000 black refugees had settled in Canada, moving from rural areas to towns where they could find employment more easily.

With the passage of the Fugitive Slave Law (FSL) of 1850 Canada became the only really secure destination for runaway slaves. The law was passed because it had become so difficult during the 1840s to apprehend runaways in the free states. Part of the Compromise of 1850, the new law was draconian:

Anyone who hindered a slave catcher, attempted the rescue of a recaptured fugitive, "directly or indirectly" assisted a fugitive to escape, or harbored a fugitive, was liable to a fine of up to $1,000 and six months' imprisonment, plus damages of $1,000 to the owner of each slave that was lost. Commissioners were to be appointed by the federal circuit courts specifically to act on fugitive slave cases, and provided with financial incentives . . . to facilitate the recovery of runaways: the commissioner would receive a fee of $10 each time he remanded a fugitive to the claimant, but only $5 if he found for the alleged slave. Commissioners could be fined $1,000 for refusing to issue a writ when required, and they were personally liable for the value of any slave who escaped from their custody. (Bordewich 2005: 318)

Slave catchers could arrest slaves without a warrant, and slaves had no way to contest their seizure. The federal government undertook to pay the costs of returning the escaped slave to his or her owner, on a federal vessel if necessary.

Resistance to the Fugitive Slave Law throughout the free states was immediate and tremendous. The city council of Syracuse, New York, "voted that if the Central Railroad, which ran through the middle of the town, ever carried a recaptured fugitive back toward slavery, its rails should be physically taken up from the streets" (Bordewich 2005: 412). Vigilance committees took direct action to prevent escaped slaves from being arrested, hearings from taking place, and apprehended slaves from being returned to their masters. Armed bands of rescuers invaded courtrooms, seized slaves from custody, and sent them to Canada.

One of the first such rescues took place in 1851 in Christiana, Pennsylvania, a district where Congressman Thaddeus Stevens and many others hid slaves in their homes. William Parker, a fugitive slave, ran a secret black militia in Lancaster County, where Christiana is located. When slave catchers attacked the town, Parker and his men killed a slaveowner and wounded his son in a confrontation. Parker and the slave escaped to Rochester, New York, where Frederick Douglass helped them get on a boat to Canada at great risk to himself. Canada's governor-general personally granted Parker asylum.

The federal government sent 45 troops to Christiana, whereupon 35 blacks and three white Quakers surrendered. They were indicted for treason by a grand jury, but the presiding judge at their trial found that "the efforts of a band of fugitive slaves in opposition to the capture of any of their number . . . was altogether a private object, and could not be called 'levying war' against the nation" (Siebert 1968: 281). The defendants were acquitted. During the first year after passage of the FSL, at least 60 rescues of more than 100 fugitives took place. As such rescues proliferated in the free states during the 1850s, it became almost impossible to find a Northern jury that would convict anyone of defying the law.

In 1852 Stowe published *Uncle Tom's Cabin*, which portrayed the UGRR as "a Homeric endeavor that was part Christian drama of self-sacrifice, part frontier saga ripped from the pages of James Fennimore Cooper" (Bordewich 2005: 370). An international bestseller, the book sold 300,000 copies in its first year of publication and effectively inflamed public sentiment against slavery. Its powerful message can be found in a passage describing the private debate over the Fugitive Slave Law between a U.S. senator and his wife. Here a woman strongly expresses a religious argument for giving sanctuary and breaking the law, opposing the pragmatic position of her husband.

"Now John, I want to know if you think such a law as that is right and Christian?"

"You won't shoot me, now, Mary, if I say I do!"

"I never could have thought it of you, John; you didn't vote for it?"

"Even so, my fair politician."

"You ought to be ashamed, John! Poor, homeless, houseless creatures! It's a shameful, wicked, abominable law, and I'll break it, for one, the first time I get a chance; and I hope I *shall* have a chance, I do! Things have got to a pretty pass, if a woman can't give a warm supper and a bed to poor, starving creatures, just because they are slaves, and have been abused and oppressed all their lives, poor things!"

"But, Mary, just listen to me. Your feelings are all quite right, dear, and interesting, and I love you for them; but then, dear, we mustn't suffer our feelings to run away with our judgment; you must consider it's not a matter of private feeling,—there are great public interests involved,—there is such a state of public agitation rising, that we must put aside our private feeling."

"Now, John, I don't know anything about politics, but I can read my Bible; and there I see that I must feed the hungry, clothe the naked, and comfort the desolate; and that Bible I mean to follow."

"But in cases where your doing so would involve a great public evil—"

"Obeying God never brings on public evils. I know it can't. It's always safest, all round, to *do as He* bids us. . . . Turning a woman out of doors in a snow-storm, for instance; or, maybe you'd take her up and put her in jail, wouldn't you? You would make a great hand at that!"

"Of course, it would be a very painful duty," began Mr. Bird, in a moderate tone.

"Duty, John! Don't use that word! You know it isn't a duty—it can't be a duty! If folks want to keep their slaves from running away, let 'em treat 'em well—that's my doctrine. If I had slaves (as I hope I never shall have), I'd risk their wanting to run away from me. . . . I tell you folks don't run away when they are happy; and when they do run, poor creatures! They suffer enough with cold and hunger and fear, without everybody's turning against then; and, law or no law, I never will, so help me God!"

"Mary, Mary! My dear, let me reason with you."

"I hate reasoning, John—especially reasoning on such subjects. There's a way you political folks have of coming round and round a plain right thing; and you don't believe in it yourselves, when it comes to practice. . . ." (Stowe 1952 [1852]: 78–79)

At that moment a runaway slave carrying a baby arrives fainting at their door, and of course they take her in.

Also in 1852 Isaac Hopper died at age 80 after more than 50 years of helping fugitives. By that time, spurred by the FSL and having overcome widespread disapproval, "radical abolitionism had . . . become a mighty movement" (Bordewich 2005: 341). Opposition to slavery that had been covert became overt. Abolitionists thundered that the law violated the biblical injunction in Deuteronomy 23: 15–16 "not to deliver unto his master the servant that hath escaped." The abolitionist movement became violent and revolutionary as some of its members took drastic action that went beyond civil disobedience. The Rev. Jermain Loguen, a fugitive slave living in Syracuse, New York, publicly declared: "What is life to me if I am to be a slave in Tennessee? I have received my freedom from heaven, and with it came the command to defend my title to it. . . . my ground is taken. I have declared it everywhere. I don't respect this law [FSL]—I don't fear it—I won't obey it! It outlaws me, and I outlaw it. I will not live a slave, and if force is employed to re-enslave me, I shall make preparations to meet the crisis as becomes a man" (Bordewich 2005: 325). At about that time the mayor proclaimed Syracuse a sanctuary city.

During the 1850s, as the nation moved toward civil war, the UGRR stepped up its activities, helping tens of thousands of runaway slaves to reach Canada. Loguen, who handed out business cards describing himself as an "Underground Railroad Agent," helped about 1,500 fugitives escape to Canada via Syracuse. As a result, "the widespread opposition to the law led to prosecutions of underground workers in various places, and these prosecutions greatly helped to keep the slavery question before the attention of the country, despite the wishes and endeavors of the politicians who strove to silence the issue" (Siebert 1968 [1898]: 317).

For example, from the 1830s on Calvin Fairbank, who worked with Levi Coffin, helped 47 slaves escape. He served a total of 17 years in prison for his UGRR work. In 1852 he was kidnapped from Indiana to Kentucky, convicted of stealing a slave from the latter state and sentenced to 15 years, of which he served 12 years in harsh conditions that broke his health. Other UGRR workers were prosecuted and fined heavily. In some cases their friends raised funds to save them from destitution. As a result of their sacrifice, the work of thousands of other activists and the courage of the self-emancipating slaves, during and after the Civil War the United States outlawed involuntary servitude and mandated the equal protection of the law for former slaves.

Estimates of the number of runaway slaves helped by the UGRR between 1800 and 1860 vary from 40,000 to 100,000, a small percentage of more than 4 million persons in bondage at the beginning of the Civil War. But the UGRR's significance goes far beyond the number of slaves it rescued. Bordewich calls it "the greatest movement of civil disobedience since the American Revolution, engaging thousands of citizens in the active subversion of federal law and the prevailing mores of their communities" (Bordewich 2005: 438). As such it was the forerunner of the labor, civil rights, antiwar, sanctuary, and women's movements of the late 19th and 20th centuries.

The UGRR was also "the seedbed of religious activism in American politics" (Bordewich 2005: 438). Its rhetoric and principles were biblical. Bau points out: "The churches providing sanctuary did not seek to claim a legal privilege but only sought to respond to religious commands regarding hospitality" (1985: 160). He quotes the Rev. Leverett Griggs of Bristol, Connecticut, who preached after the Dred Scott decision of 1857: "Fugitives from American slavery should receive the sympathy and aid of all lovers of freedom. If they come to our door, we should be ready to feed, clothe and give them shelter, and help them on their way. If we make the Bible our rule of life, if we are willing to do unto others as we would they should do unto us, we can have no difficulty on this subject" (Bau 1985: 160). But in this statement Griggs went beyond "religious commands regarding hospitality" by expressing political as well as religious convictions. He addressed himself to "lovers of freedom," and what he proposed was illegal.

Likewise, in its Declaration of Sentiments, the first national conference of abolitionists in 1833 used evangelical language, saying opponents of slavery had "the highest obligation" to "remove slavery by moral and political action" (Bordewich 2005: 146). The declaration expressed support for nonviolent action and did not call on abolitionists to break the law. The UGRR applied such principles but carried out acts of civil disobedience against secular law in the name of a higher law.

Abolitionism and the UGRR flourished in the places where the evangelical revival of the early and mid-19th century was strongest. As evangelical Methodists, Presbyterians, Scotch Covenanters, Congregationalists, and Quakers moved west, they took along both their antislavery convictions and the determination to resist slavery. Preachers not only inveighed against slavery in their sermons, they also helped slaves to escape. Churches put traditional religious beliefs about providing sanctuary to escaped slaves into practice. Laypeople extended the meaning and reach of sanctuary to their own homes. Armed with religious conviction this widespread social movement developed in spontaneous but coherent resistance to constituted authority. It acted both secretly and publicly, informally but effectively. After 60 difficult years of iron-willed struggle it attained its objective. No wonder, then, that it became the template of almost every American political movement that has succeeded it.

CHAPTER SIX

The Delight of Rescue

And above all, I beg of you—don't make me and my
wife into heroes. What we did we could not have done
otherwise! That's all!

French Protestant pastor who sheltered Jews during World
War II (Joutard, Poujol, and Cabanel 1987: 22)

Sanctuary was and is a religious institution, and it often flourishes outside the law; modern asylum came into existence and continues as a secular institution hedged by legal constraints. The conductors of the Underground Railroad (and many of the slaves who freed themselves) saw their actions as divinely inspired and protected. They provided and sought sanctuary and freedom. But the officials who granted asylum to political refugees acted in accordance with policies and regulations. Since the 17th century governments have given or denied refuge as an assertion of their rights and sovereignty. Asylum seekers tried to fit into the categories the governments created. The typical 19th-century asylum seeker was "a European leader of a nationalist movement forced to flee after losing a round in his prolonged battle against the ruling order," Stastny pointed out (1987: 294).

Twentieth-century refugees, however, were "attacked for what they are: a pariah group marked by a separate religion, 'race,' etc. Refugees now come wholesale rather than retail" (Stastny 1987: 294). Unlike earlier asylum seekers, they often had no political involvement and were forced to flee for their lives merely because of their identity. Genocide accounted for millions of deaths at a time and triggered a general exodus from danger by anyone and everyone who could manage to escape.

In the face of massive population movements caused by economic, political, and social upheavals, in the late 19th and early 20th centuries governments sought to prevent, limit, and control the large-scale entry of strangers. Restrictive laws closed the open door of immigration, especially after World War I, which left tens of millions of refugees wandering about Europe in desperate conditions. The British government, which had accepted thousands of Belgians during the war, tried to force them to return home in 1919. The new Aliens Restriction (Amendment) Act of 1919 merely extended provisions of the 1914 Aliens Act. Renewed annually until 1971, it had no provisions benefiting refugees or asylum seekers and allowed no appeal of negative decisions. One MP explained the reason for the restrictions: "We have been the dumping ground for the refugees of the world for too long" (Stevens 2004: 54). The Conservative politician Lord Hailsham later commented that Britain had "one of the least liberal and one of the most arbitrary systems of immigration law in the world" (Stevens 2004: 55).

The new League of Nations established the so-called Nansen Office after World War I to help refugees overcome the obstacles that governments placed in their way. Its most notable achievement was introducing the principle of *non-refoulement* to international law. Non-refoulement is a prohibition on sending asylum seekers back to a country where they might be persecuted. The League of Nations also named a High Commissioner for Refugees who had to raise funds to run his office and repay money the League lent him to start operations. Governments gave him little help.

In 1930 the British home secretary stiffly told a Jewish delegation that the right of asylum belonged to "the sovereign state to admit a refugee if it thinks fit to do so" (Kushner 2006: 146). Three years later, after Hitler came to power, hundreds of thousands German Jews began applying for asylum in Britain and other countries. The British government insisted that British Jews guarantee the maintenance of Jewish refugees so they would not become charges of the state. Only a relative few were admitted under these conditions from 1933 to 1938. By 1933, Kushner pointed out, "most western countries, with only a few exceptions such as France, had implemented a policy of almost total control on alien entry. Britain formally had no refugee policy or entry during the 1930s. . . . it proved unwilling to provide permanent rather than temporary refuge to Jews escaping the Third Reich" (2006: 41).

The home secretary had absolute discretion to deport aliens. In the mid-1930s a committee was set up to advise him, but it fell into abeyance in 1939. Because of the dire economic situation, the Aliens Act was enforced more rigidly as the 1930s went on. In a 1938 memo the Home Office candidly said that the point of a visa system for Germans and Austrians was "to prevent potential refugees from getting here at all" (Stevens 2004: 58). Kushner estimates that of 500,000 Jews who applied for entry to the UK in the 1930s, only 80,000 were admitted, most on temporary visas. In deciding who could enter, officials overtly discriminated by age, sex, and class.

As Europe drifted toward world war refugees from various conflicts came desperately knocking. Millions fled Spain during and after the civil war (1935–38). Some 500,000 fled to France; in 1939 two camps held 180,000 on the French Mediterranean coast. By the end of that year more than 300,000 Spanish refugees left France for Latin America, especially Mexico. Despite the reluctance of the UK government and negative press coverage, 4,000 Basque children were admitted to Britain on three-month visas in 1937. The Lord Mayor of London and the National Joint Committee for Spanish Relief raised funds privately to maintain them. "British people . . . soon tired of their 'guests' and . . . gradually came to regard them as an unwanted problem" (Stevens 2004: 62). Even so, a Basque Children's Committee functioned in Britain until 1951, and some of the children who arrived in the country in 1937 remained there all their lives.

In 1938, under pressure from his wife, President Roosevelt convened the Evian Conference of 20 nations to discuss "the refugee problem in Europe." It came to no firm conclusion, but far-off Australia offered to accept 15,000 Jewish refugees from Germany and the Sudetenland. Half of them arrived, but the other half did not make it. Meanwhile thousands of leftwing politicians and activists were fleeing Germany and Italy for other European countries. Like their 19th-century predecessors, many "tried to remain in Europe as long as possible in order to be able to continue their political work from abroad" (Bade 2003: 203). Some were interned and deported to Germany or the death camps; others, like the literary critic Walter Benjamin, committed suicide.

Meanwhile the United States was also closing its doors. The story of the *St. Louis* is emblematic of the late 1930s. In 1939 almost 1,000

Jews fled Germany for America on the ship. Cuba refused to accept them, as did the U.S. government when the ship asked for permission to dock at Miami. As the boat went from one east coast port to another, Eleanor Roosevelt tried to intervene on the refugees' behalf, to no avail. The ship was forced to return to Germany. About one-third of the passengers died in the Holocaust. In a less-known incident in August 1940, more than 300 European refugees arrived in New York on the *Miss Liberty*, a chartered ship. Almost 200, including 66 U.S. citizens, disembarked, but 121 others were denied asylum. Next the ship went to Mexico, where 86 were denied entry. The boat then anchored in Virginia to pick up coal. There, "a lawyer . . . managed to keep the ship in dock until Mrs. Roosevelt stealthily instructed a State Department official, against the wishes of the secretary of state, Cordell Hull, to arrange for everyone on board to get visas" (Buckley 2007). Sadly the *St. Louis* episode reflected the mentality of the U.S. government far better than the happy ending of *Miss Liberty*.

The exact number of emigrants who left Germany before the war is unknown. Bade estimates that 280,000 to 330,000 of the refugees were Jews. Emigrants from central European countries under German control numbered 450,000 to 600,000. More than 80 countries gave them refuge. Relatively few of those who tried to flee Germany and Austria—only about 100,000, of whom 80% were Jews—found refuge in the United States. Half of them arrived in the United States in 1938 or later. One reason why they did not flee sooner was that it was expensive, time-consuming, and very difficult to do so. The German government put up so many bureaucratic obstacles that most people who wanted to leave could not get out before the war started. The Nazis also extorted money and property from those who were trying to get out, so that only the well-off could afford to leave. As soon as hostilities commenced it became impossible to escape from Europe. The British government, for one, stopped issuing entry visas in September 1939.

Concerned individuals and organizations did not let the British and American governments' reluctance to admit refugees deter them from trying to rescue German Jews. British activists founded the Inter-Aid Committee for Children from Germany in 1936. It arranged for 471 children to be admitted to the UK, providing "a model of Jewish-Christian cooperation in refugee matters" (Kushner and Knox 1999: 154). The Refugee Children's Movement (RCM) grew out of the earlier body in 1938. Former Prime Minister Stanley Baldwin made a radio appeal for funds and raised £500,000 for the RCM. This was the seed money for the Kindertransport, which ferried almost 10,000 children from Austria, Germany, and Czechoslovakia to Britain from late 1938 to September 1, 1939.

The RCM's leaders believed it would be impossible to obtain the British government's permission to rescue Jewish adults from central Europe because of widespread anti-Semitic sentiment in Britain. Therefore they concentrated on helping children. Likewise, the government justified its refusal to grant asylum to foreign Jews by pointing to public anti-Semitism, thus creating a self-fulfilling prophecy. Similar attitudes can be seen today in the UK regarding people of color, as the government justifies its draconian restrictions on asylum by pointing to racist sentiments among the public.

The British public did seem to support rescuing refugee children, however. Especially after the shocking events of the *Kristallnacht* pogrom in November 1938, British people became more welcoming to refugees. The originator of the Kindertransport was a son of German Jewish immigrants to Britain, Nicholas Winton, a clerk at the British Stock Exchange. Raised as a Christian, he later said he had been motivated by humanitarian not religious feelings. "In 1938 he went on a fact-finding mission to Prague and was horrified by the plight of its Jews. On his return to London he lobbied the Home Office and charitable agencies (both Jewish and Christian) . . . to evacuate as many endangered children as possible to England" (Kushner 2006: 147). For his efforts he received an MBE in 1983 and a knighthood in 2003, when he was 93 years old. Others who helped set up the Kindertransport included Frank Foley, a civil servant, and Anglican Bishop George Bell of Chichester.

More than 160 local committees in 12 regions of England, Scotland, and Wales formed to arrange the children's placement in homes and hostels. The RCM chose children from a pool of 60,000 whose parents applied to private, British-run groups in Berlin, Vienna, Prague, and other central European cities. The British government did not want to get directly involved in making the arrangements for transport and resettlement. "Children could be brought to Britain if a sufficient cash deposit was made and 'provided that the financial situation of the would-be guarantor was sufficiently stable and that the proposed home was found to be suitable'" (Kushner and Knox 1999: 155). The required deposit amounted to £50, the equivalent of about £1,500 (U.S. $2,250) today and far beyond the capacity of most British people.

The children received temporary transit visas, not permanent leave to remain in the UK. Apparently the government expected that once the war ended the foreign children would leave. Kushner comments bitterly, "Guilt (and an attempt to compensate for it) has been the motivating force for most of the generous moments of British refugee policy in the 20th century" (2006: 147). In this instance and many others ordinary people, not the policymakers, were the ones showing the generosity.

At the same time the Kindertransport was being organized the British government closed Palestine to European Jews. And a bill to accept 20,000 German children was defeated in the U.S. Congress in early 1939.

In Britain the RCM took responsibility for the children's mainten- ance, education, religious instruction, and training for "useful work which will fit them to become self-supporting and responsible cit- izens, whether in this country or abroad." The children were sup- posed to be dispersed around the country so that they would not be conspicuous in any one place. They were told not to speak German and "not draw attention to themselves by complaining" (Curio 2004: 54). Those considered mentally or physically abnormal were not per- mitted on the trains and boats to Britain. "Priority was given to those whose emigration was specially urgent because their fathers were in concentration camps or at least no longer able to support them, or because they were homeless, or orphaned, or old enough to be in danger themselves" (Gershon 1966: 21). Sometimes the committees made mistakes; a refugee told Gershon in 1966: "I came to England at the age of 15, seven days before the war. On arrival it was discovered that my sister should have come instead. I was nearly sent back, but it was too close to the war. My sister perished at Auschwitz" (Gershon 1966: 45).

The first train left Prague on December 1, 1938. Eight more train- loads departed from Prague in 1939. At the height of the transport 300 children were arriving in the UK each week; their ages ranged from 2 to 17. Many were sent to reception centers where conditions varied from bad to intolerable. Sometimes prospective foster parents would arrive at a center and pick a child out of the crowd of new arrivals. Cute lit- tle blond-haired, blue-eyed girls stood a better chance of being chosen than gangling teenage boys, who were the most difficult to place.

Some of the children had to use their own initiative to gain refuge. One boy found out where Baron Rothschild lived and hiked to his palatial country home. He asked Rothschild to help get his father out of Germany. Rothschild asked, "Can your father work on a chicken farm?" The boy replied, "He'll do anything," and it was arranged (Harris 2000). A few parents, such as newspaper correspondent Hella Pick's mother, did manage to accompany their children on condition that they work as domestic servants. But most of the *Kinder* went unaccompanied to Britain, never saw their parents again, and found out what had happened to them only after the war.

One of the Kindertransport organizers wrote an account of his work for Gershon's 1966 collection of refugees' stories. Trevor Chadwick recounted that he was teaching at his family's preparatory school in 1938 when he heard about the children in Prague. He went there to pick up two children and returned later to pick up more, bringing out 20. When he went back to Prague for a third time, "I felt depressed. . . . Only 20!" By March 15, 1939, when the Germans marched triumphantly into Prague under the Munich agreement, he was ready to take 100 children out by air but could not find a plane to accommodate them. So he arranged for special trains to take them to Britain. In Prague he had two helpers, and the three spent all night writing begging letters to guarantors back in England. Chadwick wrote, "I can't say how many children were on my books, but it must have been in the thousands. Nor can I say how many I eventually got away, but it was only hundreds, alas" (Gershon 1966: 22–23).

Chadwick tactfully remarked that the Home Office must have taken so long to send him visas for the children because

> they just didn't realize. If only the Home Secretary could have spent a few days with me, seeing brutality, listening to, not arguing with, young Nazis, as I often did, he would doubtlessly have pushed the whole thing along fast. If he had realized that the regulations were for so many children the first nudge along the wretched road to Auschwitz, he would, of course, have immediately imported the lot. (Gershon 1966: 24)

When the visas did not arrive he made some up himself. A message from the Home Office "contained a threat to send [the children] back, but I figured the mob of legally accepted guarantors would stop that one" (Gershon 1966: 25).

The children arrived at British ports traumatized, bewildered, usually speaking and understanding no English. A refugee who was seven years old on arrival told Gershon: "We were in a room facing a man and a woman and were told that they were Mr. and Mrs. Smith. . . . They put us in their car and we set off to drive some miles to their home. We sat in the back, my sister and I, clutching hands, tired with all that had gone before, and confused with all the babble of English that we had heard, of which we could understand not a word" (Gershon 1966: 47).

Most of the prominent figures and backers of the RCM were upper-class men, but women played a prominent role in the management of the organization and other refugee agencies. Eight of the 12 organizing secretaries of RCM's regional committees were women, as well as all eight department heads of the Quakers' refugee relief organization.

Eleanor Rathbone, an independent MP, was very active in refugee work from 1933 on. She spoke out in Parliament against the government's restrictive refugee policies, criticizing "obstructiveness, . . . financial meanness and lethal delays" (Oldfield 2004: 58). During the 1930s she spoke in favor of asylum for Basque children, communist and socialist Czechs, and Austrian and German Jews. After Kristallnacht she founded the Parliamentary Committee for Refugees. In an article in the *New Statesman* in 1939 she castigated the government for overloading voluntary organizations with rescue work it should have been doing or supporting. She protested the internment of Kindertransport refugees as enemy aliens in 1940. Known as the "MP for refugees," she had "incalculable" influence on public sentiment before and during the war (Oldfield 2004: 59).

Other important women included Bertha Bracey, secretary of the British Friends' Committee on Refugees. She supervised 80 caseworkers and volunteers, mostly women, who worked on 14,000 cases of German, Austrian, and Czech refugees in 1938. She was part of the committee that successfully lobbied the Home Office for establishment of the Kindertransport. In 1945 she persuaded the British government to transport 300 child survivors of the Theresienstadt concentration camp to Britain in 10 bombers.

Anna Essinger, an educator who moved her progressive school from Germany to England in 1933, gave shelter to Kindertransport children in 1939 and prevailed on the RCM to make its placement strategy more humane. Greta Burkill, a German married to a British academic, was "a one-woman rescuer of Jewish youngsters" who "battled with university college bursars, local education committees, the Education Ministry and the International Student Service to grant funding for deserving [university] candidates" (Oldfield 2004: 63). As chair of the Cambridgeshire Refugee Children's Committee she had responsibility for 800 to 2,000 children.

Other women involved in helping Jewish refugee children included Edith Morley JP, Ruth Simmons and her mother, Hama Simmons, and Elaine Blond and her friend Lola Hahn-Warburg, both of whom worked on refugee issues until their deaths in the late 1980s. Dorothy Hardisty, RCM's general secretary until 1948, was an eloquent advocate for the children. She said they had "endured over a long period of time and in increasing severity such physical and mental suffering as had stolen their childhood from them" (Oldfield 2004: 67).

The RCM came into conflict with British Orthodox Jews who wanted the children to be raised in Orthodox homes. Solomon Schonfeld's mission was to save this remnant of the Jewish people and preserve their religious identity at all costs. An uncompromising and difficult man, he personally arranged for about 1,000 children to enter Britain. He was furious when Parliament gave legal guardianship of the Kinder to the chairman of the RCM in 1944.

Many of the Kinder lived with Christian families, and their experiences varied considerably. Some told Gershon they had felt happy, accepted, and loved. Others were haunted by fears for their relatives in Europe or placed with unsympathetic or even abusive families. Barriers to their progress included "the determination of some refugee committees to keep their charges under control, the rigid class and ethnic stratification of British society and the financial and psychological burdens which many refugees carried with them" (Kushner and Knox 1999: 156). One said: "I was 10 years old when I arrived and found it difficult to accept that life in England was 'normal,' that one could walk in the street, go into a shop or get onto a bus without fear of attack or insult" (Gershon 1966: 48).

Some of the Kinder had to overcome negative stereotypes and hidebound attitudes to achieve success in Britain. John Grenville, born in Berlin in 1928, was sent to a private school where he did well. But the Cambridge RCM committee insisted that he leave school at 16. He became a gardener at Peterhouse College, Cambridge University. When he told the college he was leaving to attend London School of Economics, "Peterhouse's bursar asked if he was sure 'because . . . we have you in mind for our head porter'" (Kushner and Knox 1999: 157). They wanted him to fill a working-class role for the rest of his life. Grenville later became the professor of history at Birmingham University.

The older Kinder were classified as "enemy aliens" after the fall of Holland, Belgium, and France in 1940. Prime Minister Winston Churchill famously said: "Collar the lot!" when a press campaign whipped up public hysteria against foreigners. The internment of refugees violated international law and had no basis in British law, but political pressure prevailed for a time. More than 20,000 people, including children, were interned on the Isle of Man and in hastily arranged internment camps for more than a year. Some of the Jewish refugees were detained with Nazi sympathizers.

About 2,500 detainees were sent to Canada on a ship that was torpedoed by a U-boat but did not sink. A Kindertransport survivor told Gershon that the prisoners were treated like animals on the boat for two long months before they finally arrived in Australia to be interned. He later returned to Britain to join the army. Eventually public support for internment dropped significantly, and most of the detainees were let go. Several thousand left Britain for the United States and other countries or joined the British armed forces and served with distinction. A Kindertransport refugee said she had joined the army at age 18 "to thank England for saving my life" (Harris 2000). In the service she finally "felt like everybody else."

Although the British government allowed the children to enter the country in 1939 with the proviso that they would leave at age 18, thousands stayed after the war ended and became naturalized citizens. A Kindertransport survivor told Gershon, "I was naturalized under a special scheme introduced after the war for young people like me who had gone into foster homes and whose parents were dead, as we could not be legally adopted until we were British subjects" (1966: 127). It seems significant that despite the government's negative attitude toward refugees, it did make it possible for the Kinder to stay permanently in the country.

The first popular account of the Kindertransport was published in 1944. *A Great Adventure: The Story of the Refugee Children's Movement* portrayed it in a wholly positive light, as part of an ancient British tradition of hospitality. But Kushner insists the British public's attitude was ambivalent, "followed after 1945 by several decades of silence, indifference and obscurity before the recent (largely) celebratory approach has emerged" (Kushner 2006: 10). Most of the Kindertransport survivors kept silent about their experiences during the war, in some cases for as long as 50 years. They went on to lead fairly normal lives for the most part, although some sustained severe emotional damage.

Some of the children felt intense "survivor's guilt" that they expressed in the Gershon book. One of the contributors defined a refugee as "someone who is not wanted in one place and given shelter in another out of pity. He is therefore forced to choose between death and charity" (Gershon 1966: 150). When Gershon's book was published in 1966, there was no organization of Kindertransport children and little public discussion of the Holocaust in general. It was almost taboo to dwell on the tragic past, and so the refugees suffered in silence. But the consequences of the trauma they experienced have affected at least two generations.

The 50th anniversary of the Kindertransport, celebrated in 1989 with great fanfare, led to the founding of the Kindertransport Association. Its members were mostly British, but almost 1,000 members lived in Canada, the United States, and Israel. A flood of Holocaust books, articles, films, and commemorations followed. A collection of 243 essays by Kindertransport survivors, *I Came Alone*, appeared in 1990. The first history of children in World War II was published in 1991. During the 1990s most attention was paid to children who had hidden or been hidden, so the Kindertransport received less attention than harrowing stories from the Continent.

In 1999 a plaque commemorating the Kindertransport was unveiled at the House of Commons, and in 2003 a memorial sculpture was installed at Liverpool Street Station in London, where many of the Kinder had disembarked. "By this stage," Kushner points out, "the campaign against asylum seekers had reached a fever pitch" in Britain; but the Kinder were respectable after 60 years (Kushner 2006: 165).

Kushner offers no comfort to anybody who would like to see the Kindertransport as a triumph of humanitarianism: "Self-contained and self-congratulatory, the story [of the Kindertransport] becomes cut off from the messiness of modern refugee movements, including the existence of enormous numbers of unaccompanied refugee children today who can be counted not in the thousands but in the millions." He also believes that the Kindertransport story has been used to legitimate discriminatory refugee policies that have existed in Britain since the early 20th century. In his view "the fatalism towards the (non)-rescue of the parents and other adults during the 1930s is replicated in the paralyzed response to the millions suffering in the world today who we convince ourselves we cannot help" (Kushner 1999: 167).

In the face of the murder of 6 million people, of whom 1.5 million were children, the Kindertransport may be seen as a well-intentioned but inadequate rescue effort whose symbolism grossly outweighed its effectiveness. Nevertheless it saved almost 10,000 children who would have been killed otherwise. It would be impossible to weigh the value and meaning of those 10,000 lives against the tragedy of the millions who were lost. As the Talmud says, "Whoever saves a single soul, it is as if he had saved the whole world" (Fogelman 1994: 18).

The rescuers amounted to a tiny proportion of the 700 million Europeans, Asians, and Africans who witnessed World War II, but they provided powerful proof of the reality of reciprocal altruism as a universal human practice. Perhaps that is why many of them, like the pastor quoted in this chapter's epigraph, felt they had done nothing special in sheltering Jews and other persecuted people. Eva Fogelman, a psychologist, did extensive research on the rescuers and found that most "were not loners or people who felt alienated from society. But the secret of rescue effectively isolated them from everyone else. Neighbors viewed people who harbored Jews as selfish and dangerous, because they risked their lives and the lives of those around them" (1994: 68). Fogelman theorizes that a "rescuer self" emerged, helping rescuers "re-center" themselves around their transformed social role. She sees rescue as "an expression of the values and beliefs of the innermost core of a person. It is a core nurtured in childhood. . . . This rescuer self was, and over the years has continued to be, an integral part of their identity" (Fogelman 1994: xviii). The rescuer had to be alert, quick-witted, a skilled liar, and a good actor. Rescuers questioned their own motivations and consulted their conscience about the lying, deception, and illegal acts they had to commit. Religious belief also helped the rescuers. "In moments of extreme danger, turning to God often alleviated their fear. Spiritual transcendence of the terrifying present made it possible to withstand regular brushes with death," Fogelman says (1994: 87).

Holocaust survivors who had not encountered or received help from rescuers found it hard to believe in their goodness. At a conference in Tel Aviv,

> they grilled the survivors about the rescuer's motivation. Were the survivors sure that their rescuer did not expect a payoff when the war was over? Did she acquire their possessions when they were in hiding? They were openly disbelieving that anyone would

respond from a deeply felt sense of morality or personal integrity. Jews whose families were dispossessed of their homes, rounded up and then murdered without so much as a murmur of protest simply did not believe in selfless acts. (Fogelman 1994: 19)

Many rescuers did not operate alone but in networks that extended dozens, hundreds, or even thousands of miles. "'In order to save one Jew,' writes Elisabeth Maxwell, referring to the French experience, 'it required 10 or more people in every case.'" Gilbert documented one case in which more than 50 people helped a Jew escape from Antwerp to Switzerland via France, not including those who "closed their eyes and did not talk" (2003: xx).

Coordinating rescue was complex, expensive, dangerous work, and it involved people of every class, occupation, age, sex, educational level, and nationality. A few prominent rescuers, such as Oskar Schindler, Varian Fry, Aristides de Sousa Mendes, and Raoul Wallenberg, were able to help large numbers of people. Schindler saved 1,200 Jews with the help of a small group who probably did not know of one another's activities. Fry and eight helpers saved 1,500 to 4,000 Jews. Mendes, the Portuguese consul general in Bordeaux, single-handedly signed visas for 30,000 refugees during a five-week period in 1940. Wallenberg saved at least 30,000 Hungarian Jews with a network of 400 people. But most rescuers could save only a few people. They usually were witnesses to Nazi atrocities or knew someone who had been a victim, so they could not deny or ignore what was happening. Although they faced many difficulties and dangers in sheltering Jews, they believed they could help. Numbering in the thousands, they hid Jews in "attics, cellars, sewers, ditches, pigsties, haystacks, brothels, closets, pantries, space behind double walls, monasteries, convents, orphanages, schools and hospital quarantine rooms" across Europe. "Network rescuers' actions infused their lives with meaning and purpose. Rather than just talking about their values and beliefs, network members had an opportunity to act on them," Fogelman wrote (Fogelman 1994: 210).

Networks of rescuers sometimes "organized around a leader whose charismatic personality and forceful presence attracted those seeking ways to express their anti-Nazi rage" (Fogelman 1994: 211). But leaders could be denounced or killed, and they were difficult to replace. Like participants in the Underground Railroad, most network members knew only a few other members and might have been unaware of the extent of the network beyond their vicinity. It was sensible and self-preservative for them not to know too much or any more than they had to. A few wide-ranging networks became known after or even during the war. For example, the "Dutch-Paris" network included 300 people who forged identity papers, found temporary shelters for fugitives, obtained money, and escorted people across borders. Networks operating between France and Switzerland and involving Catholic clergy sheltered Jewish children in abbeys and churches. They saved some 7,000 Jewish children.

About 20,000 Danes formed six independent rescue networks composed of students, physicians, taxi drivers, clergy, and many others as part of the general resistance to German occupation. The networks carried out the famous rescue of most of Denmark's Jews over a two-month period in 1943. A German official had warned that deportations of all of the country's Jews would start in three days' time. Ordinary citizens warned their Jewish friends and neighbors. Fishing boats and other craft transported the Jews to Sweden, a two-to-three-hour trip, under intense German surveillance.

Similar networks formed in other occupied countries, such as Holland. They comprised Protestant and Catholic church groups, liberal political groups, anarchist university students, and others. Individual Dutch people also operated as rescuers under extremely perilous conditions. Johtje and Aart Vos hid 36 people—up to 14 Jews at a time—in their house. The local police chief would warn them when the Nazis were coming, and they would take their Jewish guests through a tunnel to the nearby woods. The obituary of Mrs. Vos, who died at age 97 in 2007, recounted: "Mr. and Mrs. Vos resisted the notion that they had done something out of the ordinary. . . . Mrs. Vos said, 'I want to say right away that the words "hero" and "righteous gentile" are terribly misplaced. I don't feel righteous. . . . We didn't sit at the table when the misery started and say, OK, now we are going to risk our lives to save some people'" (*The New York Times* 2007).

Miep Gies was a better known Dutch rescuer because of her association with the family of Anne Frank. She estimated that

> she was one of 20,000 Dutch men and women who helped shelter Jews. Some acted alone; others were part of an organized network effort whose work and safety depended on secrecy and anonymity. These nameless forgers, businessmen and homeowners provided false identity papers, food coupons, money and shelter. Caution

dictated that people should know as little as possible about one another. Families who opened their homes to people the resistance sent avoided introductions. Over a three- or four-year period, Jews might stay in as many as 40 different places. Some of these unknown rescuers were caught and killed. (Fogelman 1994: 15)

Many networks grew spontaneously without formal structure or rules. In Utrecht, for example, students started helping fugitives during their summer vacation. Hetty Dutihl Voute told Fogelman: "[Of those] who were left, we knew who we could trust and rely on. That same core group stayed together until the end." In Amsterdam Tina Buchter, her mother, and grandmother hid more than 100 Jews, five at a time, on the top floor of their house. They were part of a network that helped fugitives escape to Switzerland, walking at night for three months. Before expected raids someone at Gestapo headquarters would phone to warn them, and they would hide their visitors. They set up a special bell that rang on the third floor, and "when the Germans rang the front doorbell, Tina and her mother rang the second bell—and the Jews on the third floor left the house through the back doors and back windows to the roof. If there was no time to leave, the Jews would crouch in a tiny secret attic compartment that had been built by a carpenter who was a member of the Dutch underground" (Gilbert 2003: 332).

Dutch rescuers hid Jews in homes, on farms, and at children's holiday camps. The Dutch were the second largest group of rescuers, after the Poles, honored by Yad Vashem, the Holocaust memorial in Jerusalem. Nonetheless, most of Holland's Jews—107,000 out of 140,000—were deported and killed during the war (Gilbert 2003: 332). Many, like the Frank family, were denounced by Dutch collaborators. But the high toll of treachery makes the examples of the rescuers seem all the more noble and daring.

In Italy Jews were hidden at farms and in houses, monasteries, convents, and abbeys. The abbot of the Assisi Franciscan monastery, Bishop Giuseppe Placido Nicolini, sheltered 300 Jews. Catholic religious establishments in several other countries independently decided to shelter Jews. In Poland "at least 189 convents hid more than 1,500 Jewish children" (Fogelman 1994: 173).

On the Greek island of Rhodes in 1944, when the Jews were interned, "the imam of the mosque went to see the rabbi, and offered to bury the synagogue's Scrolls of the Law in the mosque garden. This was done, and the rabbi retrieved them safely after the war" (Gilbert 2003: 379).

Among the most unusual rescuers were Muslim peasants who hid Jews after the Nazis invaded Albania in 1939. They acted in accordance with *besa*, a strict honor code. The word means "to keep one's word and includes a moral imperative to offer one's home to protect and shelter any guest in need." The Raoul Wallenberg Foundation wrote: "At the start of the war, the Jewish population of Albania numbered about 200. As persecution increased, Jews from other European countries sought refuge in Albania. By war's end there were some 2,000 Jews living there, making it the only nation in Europe where the Jewish population increased during those years" (Dunn 2008).

At a commemorative ceremony in Connecticut in 2008, Arian Myrto "explained how his father rescued a Jewish brother and sister. . . . The guests shared a room with family members, he said; they were dressed in traditional Albanian costumes and passed off as extended family." Another family sheltered four Jewish families. A son recounted that his father had told the Jewish guests, "Now we are one family. You won't suffer any evil. My sons and I will defend you against peril at the cost of our lives." According to the daughter of another man who gave refuge to Jews, "Our home is first God's house, second our guest's house, and third our family's house. The Quran teaches us that all people, Jews, Christians, Muslims, are under one God" (Dunn 2008). Among the 22,000 non-Jewish rescuers honored by Yad Vashem are 66 Albanians.

In Belgium Catholic priests, nuns, bishops, and Protestant pastors were intensely involved in sheltering Jews, especially children. They had well-organized networks and organizations, including the Committee for the Defense of Jews, which "alerted Jews to deportations and provided money, documents and hiding places," Fogelman wrote (1994: 36). "The head of the Protestant Church in Belgium, Pastor Marc Boegner, issued clear instructions to his flock that they should help persecuted Jews, and [he] helped large numbers of Jews to find sanctuary in France," for example in an Adventist seminary near the Swiss border (Fogelman 1994: 306).

One of the most illustrious rescuers was Bishop Angelo Roncalli, later Pope John XXIII, who "interceded with King Boris III on behalf of the Bulgarian Jews, with the Turkish government on behalf of the Jews who reached that country, and he did his utmost to prevent the deportation of Greek Jews" (Fogelman 1994: 37).

In Poland and other Eastern European countries under Nazi rule, entire families, including children, were hanged in town squares for sheltering Jews. Yet despite the ubiquity of anti-Semitism, Christian individuals and networks saved Jews for religious reasons. Fogelman recounts the story of a Polish woman who decided to rescue a four-year-old Jewish girl after asking herself, "What if this was my child, my mother, or me needing shelter? What would Christ have done?" (Fogelman 1994: 173).

Of the Polish family that sheltered him for three months, Moshe Smolar said: "When I ask myself what were their motives, I can only attribute their good deeds to their humanitarian feelings originating both from their compassionate feelings toward the Jews, deep emotional empathy with the persecuted, and truly deep and pure religious feelings" (Gilbert 2003: 21).

Two social workers in Warsaw "set up a secret welfare network that forged documents to get Jews desperately needed food, medicine and clothing" (Gilbert 2003: 197). Irena Sendlerowa transformed a Jewish-Christian network into "an underground operation that smuggled 2,500 children out of the Warsaw ghetto and hid them with families in the non-Jewish part of the city." Sanctuaries in Poland included convents, orphanages, and "a trapdoor, covered with straw and manure [that] led to a tunnel that was connected to a pit, a cave-like space beneath and beyond the house, with an air shaft consisting of a hole beneath a cherry tree" where four Jews were hidden (Gilbert 2003: 6).

Varian Fry's organization, which stretched from America to France, provides a good example of a long network of rescuers. Fry and a few friends raised $3,500 in New York in June 1940 to rescue prominent European intellectuals, politicians, unionists, and artists who were trying to leave France in the wake of the German occupation. They then met with Eleanor Roosevelt and asked for help in obtaining visas to go to France to arrange for the refugees' escape. In their presence she telephoned President Roosevelt and said to him:

> If Washington refuses to authorize these visas immediately, German and American émigré leaders with the help of their American friends will rent a ship, and in this ship will bring as many of the endangered refugees as possible across the Atlantic. If necessary the ship will cruise up and down the East Coast until the American people, out of shame and anger, force the president

and the Congress to permit these victims of political persecution to land. (Marino 1999: 47)

They got their visas. Fry headed to Marseille in August 1940 with a list of 200 refugees. He intended to stay in France for three weeks and came home after 13 months. Within two weeks of arriving in France he was sending refugees (without visas) across the Spanish border on their way to New York.

In addition to Eleanor Roosevelt, Fry's network included Hiram Bingham, the U.S. vice-consul in Marseille, who hid refugees in his villa; the American Federation of Labor, which pressured the U.S. government to issue visas; a Corsican gangster in Marseille who laundered money sent from the United States; the American Friends Service Committee office in Marseille; sympathetic French mayors and border guards; and eight American and French helpers in Marseille. Each night Fry would cable a list of refugees to New York, where the Emergency Rescue Committee (ERC) would "begin to pursue the lengthy process by which the State Department would eventually transmit instructions to the Consulate at Marseille or Lyon or Toulouse, to issue the relevant visas" (Marino 1999: 124). Meanwhile Fry would distribute funds to the refugees so they could subsist. Between July and December 31, 1940, the ERC raised $100,000, a substantial sum at the time, for this and other purposes.

As the German and Spanish governments cut off escape routes, the level of danger for Fry and his confederates kept increasing. Much of what they were doing was illegal, anyway. Marino noted: "The underground work not only had to be kept utterly secret for its own sake but also to protect those in the organization who were uninvolved—and Fry still attempted to make sure he compromised as few people as possible in the execution of the illegal aspects of his work. . . . He supposed that at least they had to be shielded from the details, for by now [1941] he was openly risking the death sentence" by helping British flyers to escape from France (1999: 293). As a result he continued to make helping civilian refugees his first priority. The State Department disapproved of his actions and kept ordering him to leave France, but Fry ignored the orders. The Vichy government finally expelled Fry as an "undesirable alien" in September 1941. Although the French government gave him the Croix de Chevalier of the Legion of Honor shortly before his death in 1967, the United States did not recognize his work until 1991, when the Holocaust Memorial Council posthumously awarded him the Eisenhower Liberation Medal. In 1996 Yad Vashem named him as one of the Righteous among the Nations. But for Fry during his lifetime, virtue had to be its own reward.

From 1940 on efforts to shelter Jews went on in many parts of France. Sanctuaries included children's homes, farms, convents, schools, and private homes. Networks of rescuers included Catholic and Orthodox priests, nuns and bishops, Protestant pastors, mayors, police, peasants, and many others. For example, the bishop of Montauban, Pierre-Marie Théas, near Toulouse, issued a pastoral letter denouncing "'the uprooting of men and women, treated as wild animals,' and calling on Catholics to protect Jews" (Gilbert 2003: 267). A nun, Marie-Rose Gineste, traveled by bicycle throughout the diocese for two days, 12 to 14 hours per day, distributing the letter. It was read aloud in 40 churches the following Sunday. Resistance forces sent the bishop's letter to London, where it was broadcast to France over the BBC. Sr. Gineste continued her work by arranging safe houses in the Montauban diocese and stealing food ration cards for Jews.

In August 1942 Cardinal Pierre-Marie Gerlier of Lyon and his secretary found hiding places for 500 adults and more than 100 children threatened with deportation. This action led to the establishment of the "Circuit Garel," the first network to protect Jewish children in southern France. Both Jews and Christians participated in this network. At about the same time Germans ordered all Catholic priests who sheltered Jews to be arrested in both occupied and unoccupied France. In response Cardinal Gerlier refused to surrender Jewish children who were sheltered in Catholic homes after their parents had been deported. Eight Jesuits were arrested in Lyon and the Papal Secretary of State protested.

In Paris a Russian Orthodox nun, Mother Maria, hid Jews in her convent. She and an Orthodox priest, Fr. Klepinin, smuggled Jewish children out of the Drancy internment camp in garbage bins. They also supervised the production of false documents and made contact with rescue groups. Fr. Klepinin "issued false baptism certificates for those seeking new identities as non-Jews" (Gilbert 2003: 268). Both were arrested and died in concentration camps.

It is well known that the Vichy government cooperated enthusiastically with the Germans to round up and deport Jews to the death camps in Eastern Europe. Nonetheless, more than two-thirds of France's wartime Jewish population of 300,000 survived. Josephine Levy, one of the survivors, commented: "That could not have been done without the help of many French people, who perhaps sheltered a Jew for one night, or transmitted a message, or performed some similar act of decency" (Gilbert 2003: 292).

One French village in particular has become famous for sheltering Jewish refugees from 1940 until Liberation in 1944. Le Chambon-sur-Lignon, in a remote part of the mountainous Haute Loire region not far from Lyon, hid more than 3,000 Jewish children and adults on farms and in hostels, children's homes, and private homes.[1] Protestant pastors André Trocmé and Edouard Theis and their wives, Magda and Mildred, were honored by Yad Vashem for spearheading these efforts. Although the Trocmés and Le Chambon gained international recognition, about a dozen other communities and pastors in the region also took in Jews. These predominantly Protestant communities, descendants of Huguenots who had hidden fugitives since the 17th century, felt impelled by religious sentiment to risk their lives by helping Jews, even after the Germans took control of the area from the Vichy government.

The people of the Vivarais-Lignon Plateau and the Cévennes Mountains were mostly poor peasant farmers for whom reticence was an ingrained virtue, the result of centuries of religious persecution. In general they believed that those who did good deeds kept their mouths shut, and those who talked about what they did could not be trusted to be telling the truth. In addition, they believed that in sheltering Jews, whom they regarded as God's chosen people, they had merely done their duty. Twenty-three Protestant pastors of 13 parishes, including the former mayor of Le Chambon, Charles Guillon, coordinated and supported their efforts. A few Catholic communities on the Plateau also sheltered Jews. Historian Patrick Henry wrote: "No other communal effort on this scale ever occurred for this length of time anywhere else in Occupied Europe" (Henry 2001: 3).

The documented history of sanctuary on the Plateau went back to the French Revolution, but the area's development as a major refuge dated from well before the beginning of World War II. During World War I refugees stayed in Le Chambon. In 1938 some 2,000 refugees from the Spanish Civil War were living in a mining area nearby.

After the fall of France the Vichy government took over the southern half of the country and set up internment camps for refugees across the south. In response international organizations, such as the American Friends Service Committee (AFSC), and national groups, such as CIMADE (*Comité Inter-Mouvements auprès des Evacués*), OSE

(*Organisation de Secours aux Enfants*), and *Secours Suisse aux Enfants,* set up regional offices and began visiting the camps, providing humanitarian relief and helping some of the inmates, especially children, to escape. CIMADE, run entirely by women, started up in 1939. Philip Hallie, the best-known (though not necessarily the most accurate) chronicler of Le Chambon, wrote of CIMADE:

> At first they tried to relieve some of the suffering in the terrible, disease-ridden internment camps of southern France, and they made careful records of the horrors there in order to mobilize world opinion against them. . . . they developed a web of *équipes* (teams) in the summer of 1942 . . . and with these teams they took through the mountains of France to neutral Switzerland the refugees who were most dangerous to their hosts and most endangered themselves, the Jews. (1979: 135)

Guillon, who was part of CIMADE, brought YMCA funds to Le Chambon and facilitated the escape of Jews to Switzerland. Others involved in these efforts included Mireille Philip, Dora Rivière, Madeleine Dreyfus, and Simone Mairesse, all of whom risked their lives.

In 1940 the AFSC asked Rev. André Trocmé to help refugees in the camps, and particularly to assist children of deportees who had been sent to Germany for forced labor. Burns Chalmers, who ran the AFSC office in Marseille, encouraged Trocmé to create a "city of refuge" in Le Chambon, "a village . . . on a high plateau that was difficult to reach" (Hallie 1979: 135). Le Chambon was also a summer resort town with numerous hotels, *pensions*, and children's homes, as well as a secondary boarding school, L'ecole Nouvelle Cévenole, founded by Trocmé and his co-pastor Edouard Theis in 1938. So it had plenty of places to house refugees and educate their children. Funds to support Trocmé's work came from the AFSC, the Fellowship of Reconciliation, the Swiss Red Cross, the Swedish government, and other outside sources.

Trocmé sermonized against the Nazis indirectly and with some subtlety. On June 23, 1940, he and Theis declared from the pulpit:

> The duty of Christians is to resist the violence that will be brought to bear on their consciences through the weapons of the spirit. . . .We appeal to all our brothers in Christ that no one agree to collaborate with this violence.

... To love, to forgive, to do good to our enemies, this is our duty. ...
We will resist whenever our adversaries will demand of us obedi-
ence contrary to the orders of the Gospel. We will do so without
fear, but also without pride and without hate. (Trocmé 2004: vi)

He was more direct in refusing to cooperate with Vichy authorities. When a French police commander came to Le Chambon demanding the names of Jews he was sheltering, he replied: "I don't
know the names of those people, but even if I did have the list you're
demanding I wouldn't give it to you. They have come seeking asylum
and protection from the Protestants of this region. I am their pastor—
that is, their shepherd. It's not the place of a shepherd to give up the
ewes in his charge" (Trocmé n.d.: 365). The next Sunday he preached
to a packed church that it was the congregation's duty to hide Jews.
Vichy police took him, Theis, and Roger Darcissac to a concentration
camp, but they were released unharmed about three weeks later. In
1943–44 Trocmé and Theis became refugees themselves when they
went underground for 10 months in flight from the Gestapo.

Whether he was at home or in hiding, Trocmé's wife, Magda,
was instrumental in coordinating rescue efforts. Her daughter, Nelly
Trocmé Hewett, called her "a social service agency by herself" (interview with the author, 2007). In an interview published in 1986, Magda
Trocmé said:

> Those of us who received the first Jews did what we thought had
> to be done—nothing more complicated. It was not decided from
> one day to the next what we would have to do. There were many
> people in the village who needed help. How could we refuse them?
> A person doesn't sit down and say I'm going to do this and this and
> that. ... When a problem came, we had to solve it immediately. ...
>
> The lesson is very simple, I think. The first thing is that we
> must not think that we were the only ones who helped during
> those times. Little by little, now that we speak of these things we
> realize that other people did lots of things too. ... It is important,
> too, to know that we were a bunch of people together. ... If you
> have to fight it alone, it is more difficult. But we had the support
> of people we knew, of people who understood without knowing
> precisely all that they were doing or would be called to do. None
> of us thought that we were heroes. We were just people trying to
> do our best. (Rittner and Myers 1986: 100–107)

Many other people who sheltered Jews on the plateau still remain nameless. (In recognition of this fact Yad Vashem honored all the plateau's communities.) There was, strictly speaking, no organization, no office, no files, and no leader, but there was a network. It was simple but effective: Its members communicated at Bible study group meetings or during visits to one another's homes. Strangers would arrive and be taken in, no questions asked. A skilled refugee and several local people created false identity documents for them. Before a police raid, the telephone in the parsonage would ring, and someone—nobody was sure who—would say, "They're coming." Then someone would run out to the surrounding farms and hamlets and warn the refugees to hide in the forest for a while. One Catholic rescuer in Le Chambon remarked, "It happened by itself." Nelly Trocmé Hewett quoted her mother to the effect that "you can't plan something like that." Yet the people of the plateau managed to hide about 3,500 Jews between 1940 and 1944, and CIMADE spirited scores of them to Switzerland, 200 miles away. Thus rescue on the plateau was both an individual and a social activity.

Le Chambon still regards itself as a *terre d'asile*. A local historian told the story of a family of Iranian refugees that arrived in the village in 2005. Eventually the French government issued a deportation order for the family. But local residents spirited them away so the authorities could not find them. The village is still steeped in memories of the war years; an exhibit in the railway station documenting the wartime rescue operation is a modest tourist attraction. The local post office proudly sells first-day covers commemorating Le Chambon's recognition by Yad Vashem. A plaque donated by Holocaust survivors hangs on a wall across the street from the Protestant church where André Trocmé and Edouard Theis preached. In the village cemetery, on the top of the Trocmé family tombstones, lie memorial pebbles left by grateful Jewish visitors. At the Cévenole School founded by Trocmé and Theis, students from around the world still learn the lessons of nonviolent resistance.

Appropriately enough, Le Chambon and surrounding villages are not easy to find, hidden away on a high plateau at the end of a long journey along precipitous, winding roads. For anyone seeking to wrest positive meaning and inspiration from the horrors of the Holocaust, this remote area provides both a refuge and a proof of the enduring reality and inherent power of altruism that underlies sanctuary and asylum. The example of its heroes, who refused to consider themselves heroic, quietly renews one's battered faith in simple decency, if only for the few hours it takes to walk the well-worn village streets. Le Chambon and surrounding villages are monuments to the elemental delight of sheltering, being sheltered, and surviving.

However, some of those who survived the war in hiding could not bring themselves to go back to the places where they had hidden or even to think about what had happened there. They joined millions of other refugees, some of whom spent years in displaced people's camps, who eventually found permanent homes far from the temporary sanctuaries that had saved their lives. Many of their stories were not retold for decades, if at all. Nevertheless, by the end of the 20th century thousands of books, articles, films, broadcasts, and other accounts of the Holocaust rescuers had appeared. The rescuers became archetypal figures who would inspire people around the world to try to imitate their example. Their success restored moral authority to sanctuary and challenged governments to recognize and establish asylum as a universal human right.

CHAPTER SEVEN

The Heyday of Asylum

Any human being is a sanctuary. Every human being is
the dwelling of God. . . . Any person, by virtue of being
a son or a daughter of humanity, is a living sanctuary
whom nobody has the right to invade.

ELIE WIESEL, 1985 (MacEoin 1985: 9)

The 20th century was called "the century of the refugee,"[1] as hundreds of millions of human beings fled their homes in the wake of civil conflicts, revolutions, genocide, and total war. In 1945 an estimated 40 million people were displaced in Europe. Many spent months or years in camps, while others left for other continents. The facts of the Holocaust became widely known as the leaders of the losing side stood trial for war crimes and crimes against humanity. In response the allied nations created the United Nations as the implementer and the Universal Declaration of Human Rights as the basis of revivified international law. In the process the asylum seeker became globally recognized as a worthy subject of government protection.

Earlier international agreements had mentioned asylum seekers and refugees. In 1889 the Montevideo Treaty on International Penal Law laid down principles governing asylum in Latin America. Additional Latin American treaties on asylum were signed in 1928, 1933, and 1939. The League of Nations had set up the office of High Commissioner for Refugees in 1921, and the Convention Relating to the International Status of Refugees of 1933 established non-refoulement as a principle of international law. In this convention "signatories . . . agreed to refrain from forcibly returning individuals to their country of origin if they were likely to be persecuted there" (Bau 1985: 48).

Even so, the United States and the United Kingdom did not codify asylum in their immigration statutes during most of the 20th century. Instead they made entry as difficult as possible by relying on old restrictive laws to exclude outsiders. From 1920 on the United States kept many categories of immigrants out through quotas and other restrictions. In 1940 the Alien Registration Act required registration and fingerprinting of all aliens living in or seeking to enter the United States. Until 1950 there was no such thing as refugee status in the United States. "Any admission of refugees was made only on an ad hoc basis, under extraordinary conditions" (Bau 1985: 44). The 1950 Internal Security Act mandated the exclusion and deportation of "politically dangerous" noncitizens. All aliens were required to report their address yearly to the Immigration and Naturalization Service. However, this law also "authorized the Attorney General to withhold, or refrain from executing, the deportation of any persons who would be subjected to physical persecution in their own country" (Bau 1985: 45). Although the law did not allow for admission of refugees, but only for withholding of their deportation, this was the first time the United States recognized their need for special treatment under immigration law. In general, however, the United States did not welcome outsiders. The 1952 Immigration and Nationality Act (also called the McCarran-Walter Act) "provided that total annual immigration should not exceed one-sixth of 1% of the number of inhabitants in the United States in 1920," a very small figure indeed.[2]

On the international level the United Nations Relief and Rehabilitation Administration was established in 1943, and the International Refugee Organization was founded in 1946. Both organizations helped millions of refugees. In 1950 the office of UN High Commissioner for Refugees was established.

During the Second World War the British government closed its doors to most refugees. Nonetheless it created an official definition of refugees that found its way into later international agreements: They were "all persons, wherever they may be, who, as a result of events in Europe, have had to leave, or may have to leave, their countries of residence because of the danger to their lives or liberties on account of their race, religion or political beliefs" (Stevens 2004: 119). After the war the government accepted more than 100,000 refugees from the Eastern bloc, but "Jewish survivors of the Holocaust . . . were largely and deliberately excluded by the British authorities" (Kushner and Knox 1999: 398). Kushner and Knox observe that "belief in the fundamental justice of granting asylum to the oppressed has rarely been enough on its own to change restrictionism" (1999: 399). They attribute the British government's occasionally generous asylum policies since 1945 to guilt, economic self-interest, and the workings of international power politics.

In this ambivalent atmosphere the Universal Declaration of Human Rights was promulgated on December 10, 1948. Article 14 of the declaration simply says, "Everyone has the right to seek and to enjoy in other countries asylum from persecution." It does not give anyone the right to be *granted* asylum. Governments still saw giving asylum as the right of states in the exercise of their sovereignty. According to the UK delegation to the United Nations, "the right of asylum was the right of every state to offer refuge and to resist all demands for extradition" (Stevens 2004: 136). A historian employed by the Home Office to write its history in 1950 "refused to accept that Britain had any meaningful tradition of granting asylum or of continuous refugee presence," Kushner pointed out (2006: 30).

The resettlement or return of refugees continued to be a problem in Europe long after the end of World War II. In response the United Nations adopted the Convention Relating to the Status of Refugees in 1951. This agreement was limited to refugees displaced "as a result of events occurring before 1 January 1951" in Europe (Bau 1985: 49). Only in 1966 did the Protocol Relating to the Status of Refugees extend the convention to the entire world and declare it to be a "universal instrument" (Kushner 2006: 409). Thus Western governments could avoid addressing the refugee issues related to the massive displacement and killings of Muslims and Hindus during the Partition of India in 1947–48, for example.

Article 1(A)(2) defined a refugee as someone who,

> owing to a well-founded fear of being persecuted for reasons
> of race, religion, nationality, membership of a particular social
> group or political opinion, is outside the country of his nationality and is unable or, owing to such fear, is unwilling to avail
> himself of the protection of that country; or who, not having a
> nationality and being outside the country of his former habitual
> residence as a result of such events, is unable or unwilling to return to it. (Center for the Study of Human Rights 1992: 58)

Economic migrants, victims of natural disasters, those displaced by military or civil conflict or those judged not to have a well-founded fear of persecution were excluded from the protection of the convention. The intention of the agreement was as much to exclude as to admit people who had fled their homes.

The convention did reinforce the concept of non-refoulement in article 33(1): "No contracting state shall expel or return ('refouler') a refugee in any manner whatsoever to the frontiers of territories where his life or freedom would be threatened on account of his race, religion, nationality, membership of a particular social group or political opinion" (Center for the Study of Human Rights 1992: 65). However, article 33(2) limits the effect of the preceding article: "The benefit of the present provision may not, however, be claimed by a refugee whom there are reasonable grounds for regarding as a danger to the security of the country in which he is, or who, having been convicted by a final judgment of a particularly serious crime, constitutes a danger to the community of that country" (Center for the Study of Human Rights 1992: 65).

The drafters did recognize that those fleeing persecution might not have time to apply for a visa or take their passports with them. Article 31(1) stated: "The contracting states shall not impose penalties, on account of their illegal entry or presence, on refugees who, coming directly from a territory where their life or freedom was threatened . . . enter or are present in their territory without authorization, provided they present themselves without delay to the authorities and show good cause for their illegal entry or presence" (Center for the Study of Human Rights 1992: 65). Overall, however, as Patricia Truitt pointed out, "international refugee law turns away from the needs of the refugee and towards the sovereign interests of Western states" (Kushner 2006: 43).

The 1951 convention is a very limited and flawed document. It has no viable enforcement mechanism. It does not guarantee refugees the benefits of permanent resettlement but only says they may stay in the country of asylum indefinitely. It provides the bare minimum of protection. In many ways it is a halfway measure. The 1966 Protocol addressed some of the problems with the convention, but governments could always find ways to circumvent these and other agreements. As a result the most insistent enforcers of international law are ordinary people and organizations that pressure governments to abide by their commitments.

Nevertheless, as the Cold War became the dominant feature of postwar life, in pursuit of its interests the U.S. government found reasons to admit refugees, especially from the Eastern bloc. The Refugee Relief Act of 1953 gave emergency admission to "victims of racial, religious or political persecution fleeing a Communist or Communist-dominated country, or a country in the Middle East, as well as victims of natural calamities" (Bau 1985: 46). Up to 214,000 refugees could be admitted, and a U.S. citizen had to sponsor each one. Some 189,000 refugees were admitted under this act. With each East-West confrontation, the U.S. Congress passed special laws to admit specific groups of refugees. In 1956, for example, 31,915 Hungarians were admitted to the United States after the revolt against Soviet domination in their country. They were allowed to adjust their status after two years, but most of the refugees who came in under these laws "remained in a legal limbo, with few rights or privileges . . . , only a temporary status and an uncertain future" (Bau 1985: 47).

The British government reluctantly proposed accepting 2,000 Hungarian refugees in 1956. After much public outcry the government admitted 20,000 Hungarians (out of 200,000 who fled Hungary). Its attitude was clear in a statement by the home secretary:

> On arrival the refugees are taken to barracks. . . . At these barracks the refugees are registered by the police and provided with any necessary clothing and equipment. They are then moved to hostels in different parts of the country where every endeavor is made to familiarize them with the British way of life and to find employment for them or to place them in accommodation offered by the public. A considerable number of these refugees wish to emigrate to other countries and it is hoped that early arrangements will be made accordingly. Canada, in particular, has offered priority to Hungarian refugees. (Kushner and Knox 1999: 250)

The government provided £355,000 for the Hungarians' transportation and resettlement. A public appeal by the Lord Mayor of London raised £895,000 in a few weeks and more than £2.5 million in all. Local voluntary organizations cared for the new arrivals. But, Kushner says, all measures taken on their behalf were temporary, and many were put to work in coal mines. (The British government usually justified admitting asylum seekers and refugees during the

Cold War as a means of addressing labor shortages.) After a few years the Hungarians were forgotten, and the memory of their experience was lost. There was always a new group of refugees to become the subject of public attention, usually through negative coverage in the tabloid press and provocative statements by ambitious politicians. The experience of the despised outsiders who gradually and quietly integrated into British society was repeated many times.

In 1968, not long after the United Nations adopted the Protocol Relating to the Status of Refugees, Enoch Powell, a Conservative MP, made an inflammatory speech against immigrants that became notorious as the "rivers of blood" speech. In it he predicted a race war if "coloured" immigrants continued to arrive in Britain in large numbers. Journalist Roy Greenslade observed: "For many people there is no difference between the grandchild of a 1950s West Indian immigrant, a refugee granted permission two years ago to stay under the terms of the 1951 UN Convention or a person newly arrived and in the process of applying for asylum. All are deemed to be aliens and underpinning this viewpoint is, of course, racism" (2005: 21). At the same time as Britain and other Western nations were admitting refugees and asylum seekers from Eastern bloc countries, the press and politicians were calling for other immigrants to be expelled or refused entry. Among the results were considerable confusion about the various categories of migrants and the frequent expression of xenophobic sentiments that became commonplace and mostly unchallenged.

Nevertheless, the 1951 convention was a "powerful weapon in the Cold War armory of the Western powers," which scored many propaganda victories by giving asylum to Eastern bloc artists, intellectuals, sports stars, spies, and other famous defectors (Gibney and Hansen 2005: 503). And over time, refugee laws and policies softened somewhat. In the United States the 1962 Migration and Refugee Assistance Act allowed refugees to adjust their status after arrival and stay permanently in the country. Amendments passed in 1965 to the repressive McCarran-Walter Act abandoned national quotas in place since 1924 and ended the wholesale exclusion of Asians. Reuniting families and addressing labor shortages became the stated goals of U.S. admissions quotas.

Adjusting to the influx of refugees and asylum seekers from former colonies was difficult for the UK, however. In the late 1960s and early 1970s Parliament reacted to the arrival of 23,000 Asians with British passports who had been forced to leave Kenya by passing a law that "restricted entry to those who had a patrial connection with the UK, that is, those with a parent or grandparent born, adopted or naturalized in the UK" (Price 2007: 1). The effect of the law was to make Commonwealth citizens of color with British passports into second-class citizens. Accordingly, when Idi Amin expelled 80,000 Indians, more than half of whom had British passports, from Uganda in 1972, the UK accepted only 28,000 "with a grudging sense of political and moral obligation" (Kushner and Knox 1999: 270).

The British Immigration Act of 1971 did not include provisions regulating asylum, which was left to the discretion of the home secretary. According to Kushner and Knox, "The Uganda crisis came in a context of increasingly vocal hostility toward nonwhite immigrants and their descendants and an ongoing political campaign which used the excuse of popular antipathy to tighten immigration laws in Britain" (1999: 269). After the Labour Party came to power in 1974 the Ugandans' status was adjusted. But 15 years later British immigration officers were still making entry decisions with no knowledge of the political conditions in the countries from which asylum seekers were fleeing. No law including provisions on asylum was enacted in Britain before 1993. Until that time the government applied the Aliens Restriction (Amendment) Act of 1919, which contained no due process for asylum decisions, and generally ignored the Refugee Convention. According to Dallal Stevens, until 1993 asylum seekers who entered the UK without documents could be classed as illegal entrants and deported, in clear violation of the convention.

Another group fleeing political persecution in the 1970s tested the British government's capacity to give refuge. Between 1974 and 1979 some 3,000 Chileans arrived in the UK. In 1973, when leftwing opponents of General Pinochet sought sanctuary in the British Embassy in Santiago, the Conservative government's ambassador refused to let them in. At the time Britain was selling arms to Pinochet. The Labour government that came to power in 1974 was somewhat more hospitable but still refused to expedite entry visas for Chileans. The new government grudgingly agreed to accept "some applications on an individual basis from those who express as their first choice their wish to be resettled in the United Kingdom and who have some ties with the UK" (Kushner and Knox 1999: 294).

By 1975 about a third of the Chileans who had applied for visas had been admitted. Most were middle-class, and more than 50% were university-educated. While the government contributed only £150,000 to the UN High Commissioner for Refugees for Chilean resettlement in Britain, a Joint Working Group for Refugees from Chile set up a private resettlement program and reception centers in London and Birmingham. As with previous groups of asylum seekers, the government was reluctant to help, and a public campaign bullied it into offering scant assistance. By 1987 about 200,000 Chilean exiles were scattered around the world, along with Uruguayans, Argentineans, Brazilians, Paraguayans, and Bolivians fleeing rightwing dictatorships. Very few managed to enter Britain.

From 1975 to 1979 tens of thousands of Vietnamese, Laotian, and Cambodian refugees also sought entry into Britain. The anticommunist Thatcher government mounted "a propaganda campaign . . . to persuade people to accept them willingly" (Pirouet 2001: 19). Once again the government offered no long-term help with language instruction or resettlement. Pirouet notes: "In typical British fashion, this was left to the churches and other voluntary groups" whose efforts were "piecemeal" (2001: 19).

Thousands of refugees from the Commonwealth countries of Cyprus in the mid-1970s and Sri Lanka in the mid-1980s placed additional strains on the British government. In response Parliament passed the Carriers' Liability Act of 1987, which fined airlines or shipping companies that transported anyone without proper documents to the UK. In 1987 scores of Tamils from Sri Lanka stripped to their underwear at the airport as British authorities tried to deport them. They were detained in a disused car ferry while the Home Office processed their asylum applications. Most were deported but later quietly allowed to return to the UK. "From this time onwards, in almost every case in which a rise in asylum applications from a specific country was observed, successive Home Secretaries promptly introduced a visa requirement against the country concerned where none had previously existed" (Stevens 2004: 93).

From the late 1980s onward increasing numbers of Kurds from Iraq, Iran, Syria, and Turkey arrived in Britain seeking refuge from political persecution. The Conservative government dismissed them as economic migrants. A Labour MP denounced the "cynicism and meanness on the part of the Home Office" in its treatment of the Kurds (Kushner and Knox 1999: 342). Of the desperate Kurds who paid traffickers to smuggle them to the UK, the government said it had "no special responsibility for those people who are not refugees coming here as part of a government program," thus violating the Refugee

Convention's asylum provisions (Kushner and Knox 1999: 343). As the Thatcher government moved toward its end in 1991, Conservative MP Jeffrey Archer organized a pop concert for the Kurds, then suffering severe privation in so-called safe havens after the Gulf War. Archer said the concert had raised £57 million, but the British government still resisted resettling Kurds.[3] By the early 2000s some 20,000 Kurds, mostly from Turkey, lived in well-established communities in several British cities.

In the 1980s, although asylum applications were rising sharply in Europe, the number of asylum seekers to Britain remained relatively low. Many more people were emigrating out of the UK than immigrating into the country during that decade. Nevertheless the government held onto longstanding xenophobic policies and attitudes, continuing to ignore the Refugee Convention and other international agreements that might have eased the entry of asylum seekers.

The United States government took a more flexible approach, including the United Nations' definition of refugees in the Refugee Act of 1980 and setting a yearly quota of 50,000 refugee admissions. Subsequent immigration laws sought to control the number of asylum seekers at a relatively low level while the government selectively used sanctuary as an instrument of foreign policy. In practice asylum seekers from countries that the United States defined as enemies, such as Cuba and the Soviet Union, had an easy time gaining entry, while those fleeing friendly regimes, such as El Salvador and Guatemala, were usually denied asylum. In 1984, during the wars in Central America, 20% of all asylum applications were successful (Bau 1985: 217). Of these 60.9% came from Iran, 40.9% from Afghanistan, 32.7% from Poland, and 12.3% from Nicaragua. All these countries had governments that the United States considered hostile. Also in 1984, only 2.45% of Salvadoran applicants and 0.39% of Guatemalan applicants gained asylum in the United States, which was supporting their rightwing governments in their violent conflicts with leftwing opponents.

The U.S. government's negative attitude toward Central American asylum seekers began getting public attention in the early 1980s, as opposition grew to U.S. involvement in El Salvador, Honduras, Nicaragua, and Guatemala. But asylum was already a precarious institution. Asylum seekers lacked legal representation, were not informed of their rights, were held in remote detention facilities if they entered the United States without documents, had no access to legal materials and were not even permitted to have paper and pencils in detention. Their personal communications were routinely confiscated, and their attorneys (in the unlikely event they had them) were not notified of hearings. In subtle and overt ways authorities pressured asylum seekers to agree to "voluntary" departure. According to a series of federal court decisions in the 1980s, such practices were routine and widespread but illegal.

In 1981 Immigration and Naturalization Service (INS) agents pursued an undocumented alien into a downtown Los Angeles church, chased him down the aisle and arrested him in the loft. The negative repercussions of this incident apparently led the INS to order agents not to pursue aliens into churches, schools, or hospitals. Sanctuary would be paid lip service. At the same time, however, the Border Patrol was arresting, detaining, and deporting thousands of Central Americans who might have been asylum seekers if they had known that they could request asylum. By chance their plight came to the attention of a few good Samaritans in and around Tucson, Arizona.

One of the first to get involved in what became known as the Sanctuary Movement was Jim Corbett, a Quaker rancher in southern Arizona. One day in May 1981 a friend of his picked up a hitchhiker from El Salvador on the road to Corbett's house. The Border Patrol stopped the car and arrested both men, accusing Corbett's friend of alien smuggling. The friend told the story after arriving late for dinner at Corbett's house. A biographer later wrote: "A war was going on in El Salvador, which in itself would be reason to leave. Corbett had also read about random murders and disappearances. . . . Central American politics weren't a particular concern of his, and he didn't know too much about the causes of the war. But he did have compassion for its victims. His friend's experience affected him more than any news story he had read" (Davidson 1988: 16). The next day he "woke up knowing he had to do something" (Davidson 1988: 19).

Corbett set out to rescue the Salvadoran hitchhiker. He called the Border Patrol and the INS. When they refused to give him any information he contacted a local activist group called the Manzo Area Council. They referred him to a Catholic priest, Fr. Ricardo Elford, who was helping Salvadorans in the Tucson area. Elford and a Presbyterian pastor, John Fife, had been organizing regular vigils protesting U.S. policies in Central America since the murder of four American churchwomen in El Salvador in December 1980. Corbett was too late to find the hitchhiker, who was deported, but he did discover that many more Salvadorans were arriving in Arizona. He, Elford, and a few others began to respond to what they saw as "a deliberate effort to deny these people access to legal aid and to ship them, as quickly as possible, back to El Salvador. . . . Corbett knew that the situation required him to act. He had to try to save as many refugees as he could" (Davidson 1988: 22). He and his wife started sheltering refugees in their house. So did others in southern Arizona.

One of Corbett's friends "told . . . a story he'd heard about a planeload of deported Salvadorans who were massacred upon arrival in San Salvador. . . . It was done, he said, as an example to anyone else who might be considering leaving the country" (Davidson 1988: 18). The U.S. government denied that any deported Salvadorans were being killed when they arrived home. That year a federal district court said that the INS must inform Salvadorans in immigration detention of their right to seek asylum and found that the government was acting illegally; but the INS kept pressuring detained Salvadorans to agree to deportation. Corbett's sense of urgency grew, although he did not see what he and others were doing as a political activity. He later said the Sanctuary Movement "began as a day-to-day response to arriving refugees. None of us realized what we were getting into" (Corbett 1988: 1).

A loner, Corbett mostly worked independently on the issue. He sent "long letters to other Quakers and Quaker meetings around the country, explaining the refugees' desperate need for legal and social services. Although he did not specifically ask for money in these 'Dear Friends' letters, people sent it. Corbett used their donations to post bonds and to pay bills for the refugees staying at his house" (Davidson 1988: 28). Every day he would drive across the Mexican border, pick up Salvadorans and take them to his home. He was not afraid to break the law, his biographer wrote. His father had been a lawyer and a New York state legislator who told his children about international law and the Nuremberg trials at the dinner table.

In late 1981 John Fife read to his superiors in the Presbyterian Church a statement by Corbett. It shows the religious and political arguments that underlay the actions of the movement's founding activists.

> Because the U.S. government takes the position that aiding undocumented Salvadoran and Guatemalan refugees in this country is a felony, we have no middle ground between collaboration and resistance. . . . For those of us who would be faithful

in our allegiance to the Kingdom, there is also no way to avoid recognizing that in this case collaboration with the government is a betrayal of our faith, even if it is a passive or even loudly protesting collaboration that merely shuts out the undocumented refugee who is at our door. . . . We can take our stand with the oppressed, or we can take our stand with organized oppression. We can serve the Kingdom or we can serve the kingdoms of this world—but we cannot do both. . . . When the government itself sponsors the crucifixion of entire peoples and then makes it a felony to shelter those seeking refuge, law-abiding protest merely trains us to live with atrocity. (MacEoin 1985: 20)

Meanwhile a local grassroots group, trsg (Tucson Refugee Support Group), was already bringing Salvadorans across the border, and the Tucson Ecumenical Council (TEC), a clergy group, was trying to help Salvadorans gain refuge in the United States. By the end of 1981 TEC decided to announce publicly what it was doing, to "claim moral high ground and maybe even rally support before the INS had them all branded as alien smugglers" (MacEoin 1985: 66).

Rev. Kenneth Kennon of Tucson became aware of the situation of Salvadoran refugees in INS custody in late 1980. With several other members of TEC he visited the El Centro detention camp to interview Salvadorans. "'My God, we sent Jews back to the Holocaust. Are we doing it again?' I wondered as we talked. . . . I was stunned by their stories of systematic state terrorism, imprisonment, torture and the death of family members and neighbors at the hands of the Salvadoran military and death squads," he recalled in a 2001 memoir (30–31).

The Sanctuary activists self-consciously modeled themselves after earlier historical models such as the conductors of the Underground Railroad. In a 1991 memoir Corbett wrote: "Sometimes our neighbors count on us to obey the law rather than the government, as in the case of the efforts by the community of Le Chambon to save Jews from Vichy officials and the Nazis" (Corbett 1991: 101). Perhaps some of the activists remembered sanctuary efforts that had taken place 10 to 20 years earlier, during the Vietnam War, when conscientious objectors sought refuge in churches, divinity schools, and university student unions. For example, 10 churches in the San Francisco Bay area declared sanctuary in 1971. The next day the Berkeley City Council voted to provide sanctuary to "any person who is unwilling to participate in military action" (Bau 1985: 168).[4] Local police were forbidden to investigate or arrest sanctuary seekers. This was the first known instance since the mid-19th century of a government body offering sanctuary in the United States.

Some of the Tucson activists, such as Gary MacEoin, had helped Chilean refugees during the 1970s, and several local churches had "established a support network for them" (Cunningham 1995: 15). MacEoin told Hilary Cunningham that this support system "became the infrastructure for the Sanctuary Movement" and the model for its operation in Arizona.

At the suggestion of a Lutheran pastor in Los Angeles, in early 1982 John Fife proposed to his congregation that the church serve as a sanctuary for Central Americans. TEC asked other churches around the county to sign a declaration of sanctuary, and Fife wrote to the U.S. attorney general that his church would "publicly violate the Immigration and Nationality Act, Section 274(A)" (Crittenden 1988: 74). On March 24, 1982 (the second anniversary of the assassination of Salvadoran Archbishop Oscar Romero, who, like Thomas Becket, had been killed at the altar of the national cathedral), Fife, Corbett, Elford, and others publicly announced their intention to offer sanctuary to Central Americans. A rabbi quoted Leviticus: "If a stranger lives with you in your land, do not molest him. You must count him as one of your own countrymen. Love him as yourself, for you were once strangers yourselves, in the land of Egypt." Churches in five U.S. cities also announced their intention to provide sanctuary. The press conference on the steps of Southside Presbyterian Church received national coverage. The INS sent undercover agents to the press conference, a procession and an ecumenical service that day.

Fife later said:

> We couldn't stop. We'd already made the decision when we got involved in that whole effort that the life-and-death needs of the refugees overrode any other set of risks that we might encounter here in the United States. The conclusion we came to is the only other option we have is to give public witness to what we're doing, what the plight of the refugees is, and the faith basis for our actions. (Bau 1985: 11)

"Sanctuary activism in Tucson did not start out as a coherent, ideologically motivated movement," Cunningham wrote (1995: 187). She pointed out that Sanctuary Movement theoreticians such as Jim Corbett cited the separation of church and state to justify offering sanctuary on religious grounds and claimed that giving sanctuary was part of the right to free exercise of religion guaranteed in the U.S. Constitution. Corbett and others also claimed that the U.S. government was violating national and international law by refusing to grant asylum to Central Americans. In 1985, when the Sanctuary Movement was at its height, Bau commented: "The contemporary invocation of sanctuary is not simply a legal or a political phenomenon but rather the revival and continuation of an ancient tradition" (1985: 124).

Typically, sanctuary activists would drive about 10 hours into Mexico to pick up refugees from a church with which they were in contact. They would drive the refugees to the Mexican side of the border with the United States, give them Mexican clothing and instruct them to identify themselves as Mexicans if caught, so they would not be deported to Central America. Once the refugees had crossed the border they would go to a nearby church and wait to be picked up. A sanctuary worker would take them to Tucson on back roads where there was less chance of being intercepted by the Border Patrol. Sometimes sanctuary workers would hike with the refugees through the Sonoran desert.

Soon not just dozens but hundreds and then thousands of Central Americans were arriving in Tucson and other cities near the U.S.-Mexican border. By December 1982 Southside Presbyterian Church had given refuge to 1,600 Salvadorans. What had started as a cottage industry became an industrial operation. Overwhelmed, Corbett and other Arizona sanctuary workers asked for help from contacts around the country.

Between 1982 and 1987, some 400 to 500 churches decided to offer sanctuary to Central Americans. They provided legal services, social services, transportation, and resettlement help. The churches were equipped for such work because many already fed and housed the homeless or helped legal refugees through church-related agencies. To shelter undocumented people they had to redefine their mission and priorities. "There is a new urgency about being a genuine community; the person in the next pew is no longer a stranger but now a potential co-felon," Bau observed (1985: 15). Some churches did not actually take in refugees; they provided other services. And some took in refugees without publicly declaring themselves sanctuaries.

In 1982 Rev. David Chevrier, pastor of Wellington Avenue United Church of Christ, a sanctuary church in Chicago, remarked: "This is

1. Asylee in Toryglen housing estate, Glasgow. Photo by Linda Rabben © 2008.

2. "Be welcome," Ticuna indigenous village, Brazilian Amazon. Photo by Linda Rabben © 1993.

3. Alabaster carving, 15th century: Martyrdom of Thomas Becket. © Trustees of the British Museum.

4. The 19th century's most notorious asylum seeker, Karl Marx.

5. Principal routes of the Underground Railroad. James Oliver Horton and Lois E. Horton. *Hard Road to Freedom: The Story of African America.* Copyright © 2001 by James Oliver Horton and Lois E. Horton. Reprinted with permission of Rutgers University Press.

6. Trocmé family tomb with remembrance stones, Le Chambon-sur-Lignon, France. Photo by Linda Rabben © 2007.

7. Hungarian refugees boarding train to asylum in Switzerland after unsuccessful uprising, 1956. UNHCR/32/UN 52161/1956–1957.

8. Panel from "The St. Louis Refugee Ship Blues," by Art Spiegelman, originally published in *The Washington Post*, copyright © 2009 by Art Spiegelman, reprinted with permission of The Wylie Agency LLC.

9. Asylum seekers and volunteers at Crossroads Women's Centre, London. Photo by Linda Rabben © 2007.

10. "Solidarity with the Sans Papiers, demonstration," Nantes, France, 2010. http://nantes.indymedia.org/article/19493, downloaded October 2010.

11. Humane Borders volunteers provide water for migrants in the Sonoran Desert, Arizona. Photo by Linda Rabben © 2008.

the time and we are the people to reinvoke the ancient law of sanctuary, to say to the government, 'You shall go this far and no further'" (Bau 1985: 9). But Bau cautioned: "While it is inevitably a political act to break the law—an act of civil disobedience—law-breaking is not the primary motivation for sanctuary." He quoted a sanctuary church member who said, "By offering sanctuary, we can at least stop supplying these death squads with their victims" (1985: 20).

A network of church members, clergy, lawyers, and social workers coordinated the movement, but there was no defined hierarchy, organization, or rules. The churches did not join a formal structure— they simply declared themselves to be sanctuaries. Bau called it a "profoundly democratic movement" of people transporting, housing, feeding, and assisting refugees.

In 1982 Corbett visited the Chicago Religious Task Force on Central America, which was trying to lead a nationwide movement against U.S. policy toward the region. He asked the Task Force to undertake coordination of the burgeoning Sanctuary Movement. The Task Force agreed, but its priorities and philosophy were fundamentally different from Corbett's. He saw his mission as humanitarian rescue; it saw sanctuary as a political tactic in the larger struggle to change U.S. foreign policy. The Task Force wanted the refugees to become public figures in the antiwar movement, but the Arizona people opposed "using" the refugees, especially if their public appearance could endanger them. On one occasion the Task Force sent a mentally ill refugee back to Tucson because sanctuary workers could not cope with him, infuriating the Arizona activists. The Chicago churches did not have the resources to provide private sanctuary, said Michael McConnell, who managed the Task Force from 1984 to 1988 (interview with the author, 2007). They believed it would help more people to send refugees out into the community as witnesses and victims to inform the public about the real nature of the Central American wars. Cunningham pointed out that the Task Force was "dominated by Catholic clerics, nuns and lay persons" and wanted to set up a more centralized structure for the movement, whereas the Tucson activists were Quakers and Presbyterians "whose traditions rejected overarching creeds, doctrine and hierarchical decision-making structures" (1995: 42).

The Task Force and the Arizona activists clashed when the Task Force refused to give Corbett its mailing list. Thereupon Corbett wrote a report in which he backed away from "an active role in shaping the future of the movement," in Bau's words (1985: 30). The movement and its politics got in Corbett's way, it seemed. He continued to work with a few friends and organizations in southern Arizona. "The Tucson sanctuary groups discussed each case individually and had to agree unanimously to render aid" (Davidson 1988: 82). They did not base their decisions on the refugee's political ideology but on their definition of need and their interpretation of the 1966 Protocol Relating to the Status of Refugees. Meanwhile, in Chicago, the Task Force was organizing antiwar marches, demonstrations, canvassing, and other public actions that often featured refugees who told stories of persecution, torture, murder, and genocide.

By 1983 some 30,000 Salvadorans had been killed and 1 million displaced, of whom one-third to one-half were said to be in the United States (Davidson 1988: 76). U.S. military assistance to the far-right Salvadoran government totaled $500 million per year. In Guatemala, which received much less public attention, tens of thousands were dead, and 200,000 had fled to the United States or refugee camps in Mexico. A 1984 Supreme Court decision refused to define "a well-founded fear of persecution" in deportation cases, so the INS continued to deny asylum to Salvadorans and Guatemalans. In 1985, 1,000 refugees were being deported to Central America each month. A Congressional bill to grant extended temporary departure status to Salvadorans languished in committee.

By 1983 "it became clear that the INS was not planning to arrest members of sanctuary-providing communities," making it easier for churches to decide to give refuge to undocumented refugees (Davidson 1988: 75). During 1983 and 1984 the movement grew steadily across the country. The Conservative Rabbinical Council of the United States passed a resolution: "Whereas millions of Jews were murdered by the Nazis because nations, including the United States, would not open their gates, the National Assembly endorses the concept of sanctuary and urges the government of the United States to grant extended voluntary departure status to those fleeing the violence in Central America" (Bau 1985: 187). Progressive Catholic bishops and the National Assembly of the Conference of Major Superiors of Men endorsed the movement, as did Rev. Jesse Jackson. Some conservative Catholic bishops opposed it, and the National Association of Evangelicals refused to endorse it, but "some 75 other American and Canadian churches . . . sought to create an 'overground railroad' to help Central American refugees get to Canada" (Bau 1985: 188). When the Canadian government began deporting Guatemalan refugees, a United Church of Canada congregation in Quebec declared sanctuary, and the government stopped the deportations.

As the movement grew, local groups struggled to coordinate their efforts. Gary MacEoin put together a guidebook for local sanctuary providers. MacEoin instructed:

> Selection of an appropriate refugee family should begin as soon as the decision to declare sanctuary has been made. The role of this family will involve active and continuing dialogue with the host community, educating as many North Americans as possible about the situation in Central America, about the plight of the refugees there and here, and about U.S. policy toward Central America and toward refugees from Central America. (1985: 202)

A committee of six to 10 people, at least one of whom should be fluent in Spanish, was to coordinate sanctuary provision and facilities. During the first two weeks of the refugees' stay, "monitors must be continuously present on the church premises." Then the refugees should be moved to a house or apartment. He quoted Rev. David Chevrier's recommendation that volunteers spend six to 10 hours per week for the first two months "on coordinating, food, furniture, clothing and monitoring." The sponsoring congregation was to be responsible for the refugee family until it became "economically and emotionally independent." But community support was to decrease after three months. MacEoin's instructions resembled the policy the federal government took toward the refugees it brought to the United States: "It is important to avoid the development of dependency by not providing anything the refugees are able to provide for themselves," he wrote. But it was difficult to insist that traumatized torture survivors, peasants who spoke no English, and small children become self-sufficient in a matter of months.

Who carried out all this work? According to Robin Lorentzen, "A striking feature of the movement is that women outnumber men by about two-thirds on all levels of the organization." The workers were mainly "housewives and nuns . . . volunteers who mobilize family, church and community resources to reconstruct refugees' lives" (1991: 3). Women not only organized local sanctuary provision, they also participated in advocacy, outreach, and direct action, including travel to Central America on fact-finding missions. They saw the church as women's territory and themselves as part of a venerable religious tradition that stretched from ancient and medieval sanctuary to the Underground Railroad and Holocaust rescuers. During their travel to Central America they discovered that the Catholic Church played an important role in the liberation movements targeted by repressive governments, they picked up the rhetoric of liberation theology, and they saw themselves as allies of Third World movements in their defiance of U.S. policy.

By the mid-1980s, Lorentzen wrote, about 2 million Central Americans had fled their home countries; "an estimated 42,000 Americans had pledged to resist U.S. policies in Central America, and sanctuary had become the largest grassroots civil disobedience movement in North America since the 1960s" (1991: 14). The movement spanned 34 states. At least one state (New Mexico), 12 to 27 cities, 500 churches and synagogues and "thousands of organizations" declared themselves sanctuaries. Eventually participants numbered about 70,000 North Americans and 2,000 to 3,000 Central Americans out of the 500,000 who were entering the United States each year.

For a time the U.S. government chose not to prosecute the principal figures of the Sanctuary Movement. The INS seemed to be following the advice of the undercover agent who attended the March 24, 1982, launch of the movement in Tucson:

> It seems that this movement is more political than religious but that a ploy is going to be Border Patrol "baiting" by that group in order to demonstrate to the public that the U.S. government via it's [sic] jack-booted Gestapo Border Patrol Agents think [sic] nothing of breaking down the doors of their churches to drag Jesus Christ out to be tortured and murdered. I believe that all political implications should be considered before any further action is taken toward this group. (Crittenden 1988: 75–76)

The Border Patrol arrested a few activists while they were transporting Salvadorans in Texas in 1984. Then the FBI sent professional human smugglers to infiltrate the movement, tape sanctuary meetings, and provide evidence that participants were breaking the law. Corbett claimed the government launched the operation under pressure from Arizona Senator Barry Goldwater, "who was outraged that

60 Minutes, People magazine, *USA Today,* and numerous documentaries, newspaper series, and TV news reports were covering my border crossings, with no apparent intervention or deterrence by the government" (Corbett 1991: 166).

According to Kennon:

> Our witness provoked a governmental attempt to repress us. It engaged in intimidation, clandestine infiltration, electronic surveillance, and finally, federal prosecution. To their chagrin, these tactics did not diminish the movement. On the contrary, they spurred us on. In holy defiance of outrageous policies, hundreds of religious congregations across the nation publicly declared themselves sanctuaries for Central American refugees, as did colleges and universities, cities, and even states. (2001: 33)

In January 1985 the government's undercover campaign (called "Operation Sojourner") against the movement reached its climax with the indictment of 16 activists, including Jim Corbett and John Fife, for smuggling illegal aliens and conspiracy, which were federal felonies. The defendants included two Mexican nationals who had helped Central Americans in Mexico; they voluntarily traveled to Arizona to participate in the trial. Several of the defendants made deals with the prosecutors or had charges dropped. Eleven stood trial: two Catholic priests, one nun, a Presbyterian minister, a Methodist missioner, a Catholic director of religious education, the director of TEC's refugee services, a Unitarian volunteer, a Mexican lay worker from Nogales, and two Quaker volunteers. There were also scores of "unindicted co-conspirators," and 55 Guatemalans and Salvadorans were subpoenaed as prosecution witnesses.

On the same day the indictments were issued, the Border Patrol arrested undocumented Central Americans in Phoenix, Seattle, Philadelphia, and Rochester. None was in a church—according to one Sanctuary Movement activist, no refugee in sanctuary in the 1980s was ever arrested. Also on that day an international symposium on sanctuary convened at a Tucson synagogue. More than 1,300 people attended. They took the opportunity to discuss legal and fundraising strategies for the upcoming trial.

"The arrests breathed new life into the movement," Davidson wrote (1988: 96). Numerous church groups, Catholic bishops, the Presbyterian Church, the American Baptist Church, the Mennonite

Central Committee, the American Friends Service Committee, the National Council of Churches, the Rabbinical Assembly, and many other organizations spoke publicly in support of the defendants.[5] Meanwhile, at a U.S. Senate subcommittee hearing in April 1985, Reagan administration official Elliott Abrams insisted that Salvadorans were economic refugees. There was no evidence that they had been persecuted, he said, and asylum decisions were fair and impartial. In his testimony the INS commissioner raised the specter of a refugee "invasion" from Central America.

The Sanctuary trial began in federal court in October 1985, lasted six months, and cost the government about $1.2 million. It was a circus. Almost every defendant had his or her own lawyer, and the defense strategies sometimes clashed. At the beginning of the trial the judge prohibited the defense from mentioning conditions in Central America, international law, human rights, or religious or political reasons for giving sanctuary. As a result the defendants did not gain the jury's sympathy, and the defense rested without presenting any case. Defense attorneys did manage to discredit one undercover witness for the prosecution and force the government to withdraw taped evidence. In addition, the government presented almost no evidence against the pivotal figure in the case, Jim Corbett.

In his instructions to the jury the judge said:

> Good motive is not a defense to intentional acts of crime. So, if you find beyond a reasonable doubt that the acts constituting the crime charged were committed with the intent to commit the unlawful act and bring about the prohibited result, then the requirement that the act be done knowingly and willfully as defined in these instructions has been satisfied, even though the defendant may have believed that his conduct was politically, religiously or morally required, or that ultimate good would result from such conduct. (Davidson 1988: 146)

Perhaps the jurors were mystified by this instruction, since the judge had forbidden the defendants from explaining their motives. They deliberated for nine days, finally finding eight of the 11 defendants guilty of one felony or another. Jim Corbett was among the three who were acquitted of all charges.

After the trial the INS commissioner said: "Above all, this case has demonstrated that no group, no matter how well-meaning or highly motivated, can arbitrarily violate the laws of the United States" (Davidson 1988: 154). But some jurors said they did not feel good about the verdict. One commented, "I didn't want to do it but we had to." Another explained, "We followed the [judge's] instructions to the letter."

Arizona Senator Dennis DeConcini and 47 members of the House of Representatives wrote to the judge in support of the sanctuary workers. Amnesty International promised to designate the defendants as prisoners of conscience if they were sent to prison. The judge might have disappointed the government when he sentenced all the convicted defendants to five years' probation in May 1986. He demanded that the defendants sign a statement agreeing to stop their sanctuary activities, they refused, and he dropped the statement as a condition of probation.

In his sentencing statement John Fife declared:

From the Declaration of Independence to the trials at Nuremberg, our country has recognized that good citizenship requires that we disobey laws or officials whenever they mandate the violation of human rights. A government agency that commits crimes against humanity forfeits its claims to legitimacy. . . . Sanctuary depends . . . on the capacity of the human spirit to respond to suffering. (Davidson 1988: 154)

Perhaps as a result of his leading role in the Sanctuary Movement, Fife was elected moderator of the General Assembly of the Presbyterian Church (USA) in 1992. He was still helping sanctuary seekers in Arizona in 2008.

After the trial Corbett "routinely informed the INS that undocumented people were coming in from the border to apply for asylum. The Tucson INS office accepted these asylum requests without arresting the applicants," (Davidson 1988: 160). In mid-1987 four sanctuary workers—Rev. Kenneth Kennon, a rabbi, a Presbyterian elder, and a Lutheran layman—were apprehended as they shepherded refugees across the border, but the Border Patrol let them go. "As long as sanctuary operated without a lot of publicity, the government seemed content to look the other way" (Corbett 1991: 160). Kennon reported that he coordinated sanctuary efforts from 1986 to 1989 without hindrance and "participated in the ongoing sanctuary work in a variety of regional and national forums, speaking tours, educational engagements and church-related groups. I also continued my involvement in sanctuary border work assisting refugees to arrive safely in Tucson, get legal representation, apply for asylum and make contact with family members" (2001: 36).

Corbett wrote in his memoir: "Since [1986], there has been no further challenge by federal officials to our practice of sanctuary in Tucson. The Border Patrol has agreed not to pursue suspected 'aliens' into a place of worship" (1991: 177).

But at about the same time in Manchester, England, Viraj Mendis, a Sri Lankan human rights activist and failed asylum seeker, lost his final appeal against a deportation order after 13 years' residence in the city and marriage to a British citizen. "This time," Winder recounted, "he decided on a publicity stunt. With the support and blessing of Fr. John Methuen, a fellow peace campaigner, he took refuge in the [Catholic] Church of the Ascension in Hulme." Reporters interviewed him in sanctuary. On January 18, 1989, more than 50 police raided the church and "smashed their way in before dawn, with drills and rams." Mendis, who was wearing pajamas at the time, was handcuffed to a radiator. Soon after he was deported to Sri Lanka. British MPs exchanged angry words over the invasion of a church at dawn to roust an asylum seeker. Later Mendis gained asylum in Germany, where he worked for an international human rights group (Winder 2004: 412).

Some historians of the U.S. Sanctuary Movement have written that the guilty verdicts caused the movement to decline, but the number of churches giving refuge to Central Americans actually increased after the 1986 trial. Cunningham wrote:

> The courtroom drama . . . heightened public awareness of the Sanctuary ministry and prompted several hundred churches, a few synagogues and 22 city councils to declare themselves public sanctuaries for Central American refugees. . . . by 1987–88 there were three semiautonomous Sanctuary Movements—in South Texas, southern Arizona and southern California. . . . Each of these groups established its own independent network of church groups and funding resources. . . . Each region also developed its own style of sanctuary. . . . several Salvadorans formed their own sanctuary communities (mainly in San Francisco and New York). . . . (1995: 62)

Meanwhile, public opinion gradually turned against the Reagan administration's "Contra War" in Central America, especially after the

Iran-Contra Affair in 1987 and the murder of six Jesuits in El Salvador in 1989. As a result the incoming G. H. W. Bush administration began backing away from overt involvement in the region. In 1990 Congress stopped deportations of Salvadorans already in the United States and granted temporary protected status to them. At that time an INS official stated: "If sanctuary is feeding and clothing persons in distress, then the INS does that. The immigration service feeds more and clothes more Salvadorans than anybody in the Sanctuary Movement" (Cunningham 1995: 35–36). Corbett concluded: "In effect, we'd won" (1991: 181). By 1993 "Central American refugees and human rights organizations were no longer contacting the Sanctuary underground for assistance" (Cunningham 1995: 189). Almost 20 years later millions of people who had fled Central America in the 1980s were still living in the United States.

A civil suit, *American Baptist Churches v. Thornburgh*, brought during the Sanctuary trial and decided in 1990, established the ABC Agreement, an important precedent in U.S. asylum law. According to Corbett,

> Because there was "a real and immediate threat of prosecution of sanctuary providers," the court had ruled that the plaintiffs had standing to bring the suit. . . . to avoid having the evidence of federal violations of refugee law presented in court, the Department of Justice agreed to halt the deportation of in-country Guatemalans as well as Salvadorans and to re-adjudicate any Guatemalan or Salvadoran political asylum application that had been rejected during the 80s. At least 500,000 undocumented Salvadorans and Guatemalans would be eligible for temporary safe haven, and more than 100,000 asylum cases could be re-adjudicated under new, reformed procedures. (Cunningham 1995: 181)

To Corbett, however, ABC was "just an agreement signed by a government that continues to sponsor gross violators of human rights in Central America and that routinely violates its own statutes and treaties." He considered "the sanctuary movement's real victory" as "the development of sanctuary as an enduring institution. . . . For these churches, synagogues and meetings, providing sanctuary has become integral to being faithful" (Cunningham 1995: 182). From the beginning of his involvement in 1981 until his death in 2001, Corbett was faithful to his conception of sanctuary as a religious institution first, and what he called a "civil initiative" second. His legacy is a faith-based sanctuary movement that continues to operate quietly in Arizona and beyond.

The women activists whom Lorentzen interviewed believed that the Sanctuary Movement had been successful and credited it with preventing a U.S. invasion of Nicaragua. They also saw their resistance to the Central American wars as part of a long-term struggle against U.S. imperialism that they expected to continue for many years. One said, "Sanctuary was fighting for 'the salvation of the soul of America'" (Lorentzen 1991: 199).

Although the Sanctuary Movement presented itself as religious in character, it operated in the public realm, and it used political strategies to gain political objectives. Even Corbett sought to do something much more ambitious than sheltering individuals fleeing from persecution. Challenging the inequitable implementation of asylum policies, he called upon the U.S. government to live up to its obligations under the Constitution and international law. The churches and faith-based organizations that supported the Sanctuary Movement not only offered refuge, they also advocated for the human rights of asylum-seekers, refugees, and immigrants by carrying out a variety of public activities, pressuring the government, bringing legal actions, organizing local and national groups, and building coalitions.

Placing the movement in historical context, Rosser wrote: "Unrecognized by the law, the modern sanctuaries owe the grudging respect with which they have been viewed by public authority largely to the strength of community feeling. . . . neighborhood action clearly retains a potential independent force as a mitigator or critic of the policies of government" (1996: 79). Since the 1980s sanctuary activists in the United States and other parts of the world have used similar strategies to defend and advance the right to asylum wherever it is threatened. And without a doubt it *is* threatened.

CHAPTER EIGHT

Asylum Now: Canada, Australia, and the USA

History teaches us that when human beings feel impelled
to migrate, there is little that states can do to prevent it.

DALLAL STEVENS (2004: 436)

In 2004 alone 250 people took refuge in Canadian churches. That year
"Sanctuary Week" was commemorated across the country after police
raided a church to seize an Algerian who claimed to fear torture in
his home country. In his book on Canadian sanctuary, Lippert wrote
that the government tried to make a secret agreement with churches
to speed consideration of immigration cases, but the churches insisted on their right to give sanctuary. Apparently refuge in churches is
customary in Canada, and in recent years it has "taken the form of
groups of churches and communities harboring individual migrants
or migrant families threatened by imminent arrest and deportation
by federal immigration authorities" (2005: 4). Lippert also found cases
of church sanctuary of refugees in Germany, France, Belgium, the
Netherlands, Norway, Switzerland, and Australia from the 1980s to
the present. In 1986, soon after the Sanctuary Movement trial in the
United States, an international conference convened in Holland on
"Sanctuary: The Congregation as a Place of Refuge." Sanctuary workers from the United States and Western Europe attended.

Lippert did not see sanctuary in Canada as similar to the institution in the United States, where the division between church and

state is more clear-cut. "Sanctuary in Canada was . . . a collection of local incidents that were disconnected socially and geographically from one another, temporally limited, and surprisingly, often not primarily religious in orientation" (2005: 13). Nonetheless, incidents keep happening in which churches proclaim publicly that they will shelter migrants. Local groups have taken it upon themselves to hide migrants from police, but according to Lippert these actions do not constitute a coordinated movement.

Asylum seekers have tended to stay in churches for about five months, but some remained for more than a year. The longest recorded incident that Lippert found lasted 630 days. There were three usual outcomes: the asylum seeker gained legal status, went underground, or surrendered for deportation. Sometimes lawyers, politicians, television talk-show hosts, and even police officers suggested that migrants take shelter in a church; at other times the migrants themselves came up with the idea. In 27 of 36 incidents that Lippert investigated, the churches did not initiate sanctuary; they responded to urgent pleas. Decisions to give sanctuary were ad hoc, with no coordination among congregations.

Sanctuary providers were predominantly middle-class, middle-aged, white Canadians. "Care for migrants in sanctuary was carried out mostly by women, whereas media relations and other efforts to expose the plight of migrants were handled mostly by men" (Lippert 2005: 32). Clergy were seldom heavily involved. Community members "regularly visited migrants in sanctuary, provided material support such as food and furniture, organized fundraising events, became centrally involved in visible protests, marches and vigils, and met with immigration officials to discuss alternatives to deportation," Lippert wrote (2005: 34). Public reaction to church sanctuary was overwhelmingly supportive, and usually the local press covered the incident sympathetically.

More than 260 migrants gained sanctuary in the 36 incidents that Lippert recorded. These incidents involved both individuals and families, including children. Asylum seekers came from 28 countries. All had tried to gain legal status via official procedures but had been denied humanitarian waivers. They sought sanctuary when all other means had been exhausted. As in medieval times, church sanctuary gave time to the authorities to reconsider their decision, the community to raise support, and lawyers and officials to negotiate. In most cases the migrants gained legal status or "long-term permission to remain in Canada" (Lippert 2005: 40).[1] In addition the government responded to public outcry by staying deportation orders of some 2,000 asylum seekers from Guatemala, Turkey, and Algeria.

Perhaps these incidents were the means by which the public civilly protested or appealed the restrictive immigration policies the government had introduced in the 1980s. It was clear that the authorities wanted to avoid deporting massive numbers of migrants and the political embarrassment such outcomes might bring. Canada wanted to keep its international reputation as a compassionate shelter for persecuted people (and a welcoming haven for hard workers) while responding to U.S. pressure to keep out dangerous strangers. Especially after 9/11 this balancing act became more difficult.

Pressure on sanctuary providers increased after 9/11, too. Tax authorities told church administrators that their tax exemption could be taken away for the "political activity" of sheltering asylum seekers. Some sanctuary workers made sure the church was always unlocked, so the police would not have any excuse to break in to apprehend migrants. One worker said: "If Immigration's decided that they wanted to come pick her up, they [can] just tell us. We'll hold the door. . . . We aren't going to stand in the way of an actual apprehension, but we are also going to grant her sanctuary" (Lippert 2005: 146). For Lippert, the ritual of sanctuary provides a means for citizens to resist governmental power and readjust the government's relationship with them. In the process the refugee is redefined as a potential citizen with a face, a story, and a self. In Canada sanctuary is a last resort in exceptional cases, when the government oversteps its moral, if not its legal, boundaries.

Although the two countries are similar in some ways, Australia's asylum policy stands in sharp contrast to Canada's. Like Canada, "Australia has developed a proactive approach to immigration—actively recruiting and selecting prospective newcomers. Immigration has been utilized as a mechanism of nation-building by successive governments" (Tazreiter 2004: 126). The result was that by 2001, a quarter of Australia's population was foreign-born. But Australia kept in place its 1901 Immigration Restriction Act, which excluded nonwhites from the country, for 70 years. Despite its adoption of multiculturalism in the 1970s, the government's recent policy of mandatory, nonreviewable detention of mostly nonwhite or nonwestern asylum seekers echoed older racist attitudes and actions toward Aborigines, the original inhabitants of the country.

Since the 1990s Australia has had quotas for admission of asylum seekers, reserving 12,000 places for humanitarian cases and women at risk. When the number of accepted asylum seekers increases, admissions of other humanitarian cases decrease. In contrast, Canada, whose population is one-third higher than Australia's, admits about 50,000 asylum seekers per year.

As it became increasingly difficult to gain asylum in Australia and other countries in the 1990s, desperate people fleeing persecution, civil conflicts, and genocide began paying smugglers to transport them to safety. Human trafficking and smuggling now constitute a huge global industry worth $12 billion to $30 billion annually. Caroline Moorehead gave an example of an Iraqi-Iranian Christian family that fled religious persecution in the Middle East. The smugglers they hired gave them no choice of destination, sending them to Australia via Malaysia. The Australian press contemptuously referred to such people as "queue jumpers," because they entered the country without visas. The Australian government's response was to try to exclude asylum seekers summarily on arrival. Those who did manage to land had difficulty finding legal advice or other assistance if they decided later to apply for asylum. They had to wait six months before becoming eligible for help from the Immigration Advice and Application Assistance Scheme, administered by the Red Cross. All sorts of restrictions and deadlines tended to exclude many asylum seekers from consideration.

Australia's asylum policy was fraught with contradictions. During the 1990s refugees from nearby East Timor had considerable difficulty in obtaining asylum in Australia. The Australian government was trying to deport them to Portugal, which had controlled East Timor until 1975. In response a sanctuary movement developed among Australian Catholic organizations. "A network of some 15,000 people around Australia evolved with a large number of 'safe houses' which could be activated in the case of an imminent deportation" (Tazreiter 2004: 147). Finally, in 1999, after Indonesian troops and their collaborators ravaged East Timor and thousands of Australians demonstrated in support of its independence, the Australian government gave temporary safe haven to Timorese refugees. Also that year the government transported 4,000 refugees from Kosovo at a cost of $100 million while trying to prevent 10,000 Asian boat people from landing. Although they warmly welcomed the Kosovars, "the public response to other asylum seekers, particularly those arriving by boat, was markedly negative" (Tazreiter 2004: 148).

From 1992 on the government passed increasingly restrictive laws to prevent asylum seekers without documents from arriving in the country. Meanwhile the media exposed sensational cases of inhumane conditions in immigrant detention centers or instances of refoulement. For example, in 2000 the government deported a Chinese woman who was 8 1/2 months pregnant after her asylum claim was denied. On arrival in China she was forced to undergo an abortion.

In the 2001 *Tampa* incident, 433 asylum seekers rescued from a sinking boat by a Norwegian container ship were denied entry to Australia. Most were sent to the independent island nation of Nauru, which Australia paid to detain them. (New Zealand granted asylum to 149 of the refugees.) To gain public support for their actions in this case, government officials made the false claim that Iraqi refugees on the *Tampa* had thrown their own children overboard. Parliament then passed laws that seemed to repudiate Australia's responsibilities under the 1951 Refugee Convention. From 2001 to 2003 the government spent more than $500 million on offshore refugee detention, which it called the "Pacific Solution." The mandatory, indefinite detention of asylum seekers, both offshore and in remote locations in Australia, continued until 2008, when the newly elected Labor government ended the policy. Even so, the government found it difficult to abandon offshore detention of asylum seekers who sought to enter Australia by boat.

For more than 15 years Australian nongovernmental organizations worked closely with the government while protesting its asylum policies. Church and other groups provided services to torture survivors, visited asylum seekers in detention, and published reports about detention conditions while receiving government funds to provide social services to immigrants. In 1996 the Asylum Seekers' Centre set up a forum for refugee organizations to coordinate their activities and meet with government agencies and the UNHCR. The forum, called "Interagency," had more than 100 member groups, an international e-mail network, and an e-mail newsletter. But its effectiveness was constrained by its members' ties to the government.

At the same time community organizations, such as Rural Australians for Refugees and Chilout (Children Out of Detention), advocated on behalf of asylum seekers. Residents of outback towns near a desert detention center visited detainees weekly. In the late 1990s the Refugee Action Collective, a grassroots group, and

Australians for a Fair Australia, which included prominent public figures and ordinary citizens, conducted information campaigns and convened university study groups on behalf of asylum seekers. In 2001 and 2002 a network of activists gave sanctuary to asylum seekers who had escaped from detention facilities, risking a 10-year prison sentence for "acts against the state" (Tazreiter 2004: 183).

The Professional Alliance for the Health of Asylum Seekers and Their Children, composed of 50,000 physicians and health workers, "the largest alliance ever formed on a single social issue in Australia's history," issued reports documenting cases of posttraumatic stress disorder among detained children (Moorehead 2005: 119). The Australian Catholic Social Justice Council called detainees' treatment torture, the World Council of Churches protested against detention practices, and the president of the Australian Medical Association spoke out on public radio about the damaging effects of detention on asylum seekers. Various reports by the United Nations and NGOs such as Amnesty International accused Australia of violating international human rights standards and the Refugee Convention in its treatment of asylum seekers.

Surprisingly, reports by Australian government agencies made the same charges. The Human Rights and Equal Opportunity Commission of Australia declared that detention of asylum seekers should be used only as a last resort and was "particularly undesirable for vulnerable individuals such as single women, children, unaccompanied minors, or those with special medical or psychological needs" (Tazreiter 2004: 204).

Moorehead commented that the government's Pacific Solution was "an immense sledgehammer to crack a very small nut" (2005: 128). In 2001, the year of the *Tampa* incident, 1,640 asylum seekers arrived in Australia, while about 50,000 overstayers, who had arrived legally from Europe and the UK but remained after their visas expired, were living quietly, unmolested, in the country. Despite the expense and opprobrium its asylum policies caused, the rightwing government of John Howard repeatedly fomented a moral panic among Australia's citizenry, manipulating fears of an "invasion" of desperate or terroristic Asian hordes, to win election three times over an 11-year period. And yet, each turn of the political screws generated more public opposition to those policies. A sanctuary movement without a name insistently challenged the government in the name of Australian values, basic fairness, and human decency. Finally, in mid-2008, the new government announced a more humane asylum policy:

Australia will no longer lock up asylum seekers on arrival in the country. The new immigration policy will put an end to the tough measures in place since 1992, in which all migrants who arrive without proper travel documents were immediately detained until they were granted a visa or deported. Immigration Minister Chris Evans announced that the government will also stop detaining migrant children and their families. Migrants who do not pose a threat to the community will now be able to remain until their status is resolved. (Panos Institute 2008: 1)

After trying out pilot programs modeled on Sweden's asylum system, which emphasizes case management, alternatives to detention, and work rights for asylum seekers, Australia's government announced in May 2009 that it would reform the asylum system across the entire country. It remains to be seen if other governments will follow the examples of Australia and Sweden. In light of recent history, it is difficult, but not impossible, to hope that they will.

Like the other receiving countries the United States increasingly resorted to detaining asylum seekers and other immigrants after the end of the Cold War. For most of the 19th century entry into the country had been "regulated by local jurisdictions. Most immigrants arrived at major ports, and decisions about how to handle them were made by the port commissioners" (Dow 2004: 6). Only at the end of the century did the federal government create administrative structures to carry out immigration policies. Ellis Island, the government's reception center in New York for immigrants from Europe, opened in 1891, and its detention facilities were notoriously bad. Between 1891 and 1930 some 3,000 detainees committed suicide there. From 1930 until it closed in 1954 it became what its official history called "a grim detention center." In 1953 a Supreme Court justice called it an "island prison." After Ellis Island closed the Immigration and Naturalization Service abandoned detention in most cases until the 1980s. During that period undocumented immigrants including asylum seekers were usually paroled pending administrative proceedings.

The Illegal Immigration Reform and Immigrant Responsibility Act of 1996 made it much more difficult to gain asylum in the United States. "Congress barred asylum for most persons who did not apply for it within a year of entering the United States. It also created a new system of 'expedited removal,' under which airport immigration inspectors (and, later, land border officials) could summarily deport, without hearings, many foreign nationals who arrived in the United States without valid passports or visas" (Kenney and Schrag 2008: 3). Under the 1996 law it is possible for an asylum seeker to gain "relief from removal" if he or she establishes a "credible fear" of persecution in the home country. But at least 60% of asylum seekers in the United States do not go on to gain asylum (Acer and Chicco 2009).[2]

Asylum seekers are now in jeopardy as soon as they set foot in the United States. Threatened by gangs in the Haitian slum where he had his church, 81-year-old Rev. Joseph Dantica fled to the United States in October 2004, while United Nations forces were occupying Haiti.[3] Although he had a valid multiple-entry visa and passport, Rev. Dantica asked for asylum at Miami Airport. He was arrested, detained, and placed in expedited removal proceedings. In the middle of the night his niece, the novelist Edwidge Danticat, received a phone call but could not reach the phone in time because she was heavily pregnant. A U.S. Customs officer left a message on her voicemail: "Ms. Danticat, we have your uncle here. He's requested asylum and we're completing his paperwork." The officer left no telephone number. When Edwidge Danticat called Customs at the airport, the man who answered said Rev. Dantica and his son had had no papers (which was untrue) and hung up on her.

Edwidge Danticat tried to gain access to her uncle at the airport, but officials told her she could not see him. They said he would be taken to Krome Detention Center. "My heart sank," Danticat wrote in her memoir about her uncle, *Brother, I'm Dying*. "The year before I had been to Krome Detention Center as part of a delegation of observers organized by the Florida Immigration Advocacy Center." There she had seen adolescent detainees classified as adults; the authorities had determined their ages by examining their teeth. "I couldn't escape this agonizing reminder of slavery auction blocks, where mouths were pried open to determine worth and state of health," she wrote.

Apparently the basis for Rev. Dantica's detention was an administrative mix-up, but it took his niece many months to find that out, and by then it was too late.

After an uncomfortable night on a cement bed at the airport, Rev. Dantica was taken to Krome along with his son, who was handcuffed. The officer "agreed not to handcuff my uncle but told [his son] to tell my uncle that if he tried to escape he would be shot." The elderly, chronically ill man spent the weekend in detention without his medications, which had been taken from him.

During the immigration interview at Krome the following Monday, Rev. Dantica had a seizure and started vomiting violently. A nurse and a medic arrived about 15 minutes after the seizure started. "I think he's faking," the medic said. Dantica's lawyer replied, "You can't fake vomit. . . . This man is very sick and his medication shouldn't have been taken away from him." The medic insisted again that Dantica was "faking," because he kept fixing his gaze on the medic. Finally Dantica was taken to the clinic at Krome and the immigration interview was cancelled. Sometime later he was transferred to a hospital "with shackles on his feet."

Rev. Dantica did not see a doctor until 24 hours after his arrival at the hospital emergency room. He died Tuesday night in the hospital after two days' acute illness. Edwidge Danticat was not allowed to see her uncle in the hospital, even after he had died. The authorities at Krome denied her access to him. An autopsy determined that he had suffered from acute and chronic pancreatitis, "for which he was never screened, tested, diagnosed, or treated while he was at Jackson Memorial Hospital."

At least 100 other stories could be told about immigration detainees, including asylum seekers like Rev. Dantica, who have died in custody since 2003 (Bernstein 2010). This one may not be the worst. Surely Jason Ng's months-long ordeal, recounted in Chapter One, was more atrocious, because the abuse, neglect, and cruelty he suffered and the pain he endured went on so much longer.

These horror stories highlight the punitive nature of immigration detention in the United States. Detention centers, jails, and prisons are built and run according to a correctional model, in defiance of the Refugee Convention. It could be said that immigration detainees are treated even worse than criminals, since most have not been charged with a crime, do not understand why they are detained, have no idea how long they will be held or what will happen to them after detention ends. Frequent transfers to facilities far from families or lawyers, lack of medical attention or treatment for chronic or serious conditions, isolation from fellow language-speakers, and lack of recreation or organized activities make detention a hellish experience, especially for traumatized survivors of torture, war, or civil conflict.

It is easy to conclude that the purposes of detention include coercing asylum seekers into abandoning their claim and returning to their home country, as well as sending a warning to anyone thinking of seeking asylum in the United States. As long ago as 1981 then-Attorney

General William French Smith said: "Detention of aliens seeking asylum was necessary to discourage people like the Haitians from setting sail in the first place" (Dow 2004: 7).

Especially since the 9/11/01 attacks the United States has expanded detention for more and more immigrants. The yearly number now surpasses 300,000, the vast majority of whom are undocumented migrants, overstayers, and foreign-born criminals who have served their sentences and are awaiting deportation. About 10,000 per year are asylum seekers. From 2003 to 2009, Human Rights First estimated, the U.S. government spent about $300 million to detain some 48,000 asylum seekers. Although much cheaper alternatives, including electronic monitoring, are available, the federal government pays more than 350 local jails and prisons an average of $95 per head per day to hold immigrants while their cases are being decided, to the benefit of the localities where they are kept.

For example, York County, Pennsylvania, was able to reduce its local property tax as a result of receiving federal payments for detaining undocumented migrants and asylum seekers. A county jail superintendent in New Hampshire told Dow, "I simply have an opportunity to make use of available beds that exist within my facility to reduce the burden on my local taxpayers by creating a revenue to offset the operating expenses" (2004: 229). In addition, the "prison industrial complex" of private prisons and detention centers, which hold both domestic and foreign inmates, has become a major industry in the United States. Thanks to construction of six large, privately run facilities, the number of detention beds increased by 78% between 2005 and 2008.

Border security has been a particular focus of federal attention. By 2007 it had a budget of $10.4 billion, some of which went to build new detention facilities, including the Pearsall Immigration Detention Center, a complex of giant, tentlike, windowless structures that resembled a concentration camp. Located in a cow pasture in a remote part of south Texas, it held more than a thousand detainees, including asylum seekers.

Immigration offenses, such as entering the United States without a visa or valid passport, are not classified as crimes under federal law. Thus detained immigrants and asylum seekers are "civil detainees held pursuant to civil immigration laws," covered by the Fifth Amendment of the Constitution, which protects any person in U.S. custody "from conditions that amount to punishment without due process of law" (Patel and Jawetz 2007: 2). For these reasons those accused of such offenses, as well as those in expedited removal proceedings, are supposed to be detained apart from criminals. However, "simply by renaming imprisonment 'administrative detention,' the law denied to immigration detainees all . . . Constitutional protections" (Alaya et al. 2007: 11). Administrative detention has become a parallel system, "outside of the guarantees of the criminal justice system." Although ICE has promulgated detention "standards" that are supposed to be applied in jails, prisons, and private facilities, these standards are not mandatory. As a result abuses are common.

Numerous reports by advocacy organizations have told stories of asylum seekers—including children, torture survivors, disabled and elderly people with chronic health problems—housed with convicted felons or in overcrowded conditions, denied emergency medical treatment, abused physically and psychologically by guards, punished for calling attention to abuses, transferred in the middle of the night without notice, and incarcerated after being granted asylum, in violation of federal court decisions, federal statutes and regulations, and international law. Many stories highlight the problems plaguing the U.S. asylum system. For example, the New Jersey Civil Rights Defense Committee reported that a diabetic detainee was abused in one jail after another that refused to treat his medical condition. When he was in isolation the guard threw his food away, saying, "I don't care if you die" (Alaya et al. 2007: 11). He was finally released after nine months of mistreatment.

Mentally ill or traumatized detainees have especially difficult experiences. If they seem suicidal, have an anxiety attack, or break down, they may be segregated in solitary confinement cells instead of receiving treatment. A report by the Justice Department's Inspector General said that four of five audited detention facilities did not comply with suicide watch standards. As a result a number of detainees have committed suicide.

Despite the UNHCR's clearly stated position against detention of immigrant children, they are kept in prison-like facilities for short or long periods. The inappropriately named T. Don Hutto Residential Center in Texas received considerable attention in 2007 after an advocacy organization, the Women's Refugee Commission, published a highly critical report about conditions there, and the ACLU sued ICE over conditions at the facility. The government was paying $2.8 million a month to the Corrections Corporation of America to manage the former medium-security prison, which housed immigrant families in cells, kept them under 24-hour surveillance, forced even children and babies to wear uniforms, threatened children with separation from parents if they did not behave, and did not provide adequate schooling, recreation, or medical care. As a result of the lawsuit conditions improved somewhat at Hutto, but the Women's Refugee Commission continued to campaign for an end to the detention of children. In August 2009 ICE announced that families would no longer be detained at Hutto, which would become a detention facility for women.

Parole from detention has become increasingly hard to get. Human Rights First pointed out that "decisions to release asylum seekers on parole are entrusted to ICE, which is the detaining authority, rather than to an independent authority or court" (Acer and Chicco 2009: 32). Recently asylum seekers have had to pay bonds as high as $5,000 to be paroled, and since many are destitute they end up remaining in detention for months or even years, making a mockery of the term "expedited removal."

Restrictive regulations, often promulgated in the name of efficiency or to reduce backlogs and case loads, have abridged asylum seekers' human rights to an alarming degree. Probably in reaction to the 9/11 attacks, in 2002 then-Attorney General John Ashcroft "directed the [Board of Immigration Appeals] to stop writing opinions in most cases" and issue summary judgments. He "directed the board to dispose of its 55,000 cases within 180 days" (Martin and Schoenholtz 2006: 169–70). The consequences included David Ngaruri Kenney's long-running ordeal, summarized in Chapter One.

Asylum seekers who are not detained may be allowed to work or receive welfare benefits only at the discretion of the attorney general during the entire appeals process, even if it takes years. Detained or not, they must pay for legal representation or find pro bono assistance. "The American government does provide free legal help to indigent persons who are accused of crimes, even misdemeanors and juvenile offenses, but it does not provide lawyers for indigent asylum applicants who face possible deportation. To the contrary, Congress has prohibited the federally supported neighborhood offices sponsored by the Legal Services Corporation from representing asylum applicants" (Kenney and Schrag 2008: 315). Some asylum seekers who do not gain asylum are granted "withholding of removal," which is "something like asylum, because the respondent who wins it is not deported. However, it is not as good as asylum, because the person whose removal is withheld may not become a permanent resident or a citizen. If conditions ever change for the better in the respondent's country, even decades later, after the person has established a new life in the United States, he or she can be deported at that time" (Kenney and Schrag 2008: 105).

Studies of immigration judges' decisions have found that "more than 200 immigration judges in the United States grant asylum at widely differing rates, even to applicants from the same country and in the same time frame" (Kenney and Schrag 2008: 307). For example, law professor Philip Schrag discovered that judges' asylum approval rates for Kenyans in Arlington, Virginia, ranged from 0% to 67%. The judge who rejected the asylum petition of Schrag's client and coauthor, David Kenney, gave the lowest number of positive asylum decisions in the entire district—17%—in contrast to more than 30% by other judges. "Among nondetained asylum seekers . . . those who have representation in their immigration court proceedings are nearly three times as likely to win asylum as those who are unrepresented . . . and detained asylum seekers are six times more likely to win if they are represented" (Kenney and Schrag 2008: 315). At least a third of asylum seekers are not represented and do not have knowledge of complex immigration law or access to law books so they can represent themselves. Thus asylum has become a lottery, rigged to make sanctuary least available to the people who need it most.

Many asylum seekers get lost in the system for years or even decades. Tam Tran, a 24-year-old graduate student at UCLA, and his family were arrested and detained by ICE in October 2007, five months after he testified before the U.S. House of Representatives Immigration Subcommittee about the plight of undocumented immigrant students.[4] The subcommittee's ranking member, Rep. Zoe Lofgren, called the arrests intimidation, but ICE claimed they had not known about Tran's congressional testimony when they stormed the family's home in a predawn raid. The family members were arrested because they had lost their asylum appeal in 2001 and received a deportation order at that time. The Trans were lucky, however, because after only one night in custody they were released with electronic monitoring devices attached to their bodies.

The family had been in transit since 1980, when they fled Vietnam and went to Germany, where they tried and failed to apply for resettlement in the United States. Tam was born in Germany during their six-year stay in that country. In 1989 they arrived in the United States and applied for asylum. At the time it was possible for asylum seekers to obtain work permits, so they were able to establish themselves as taxpaying, law-abiding residents. Every year they would renew their work permits as required. Nobody appeared to deport them until after Tam became visible by testifying publicly.

In 2001 the Board of Immigration Appeals had rejected their asylum claim despite their legitimate fear of persecution in Vietnam. The court ruled that the family should be deported to Germany, a "safe third country" under international agreements, but Germany refused to accept them, because they had been absent from that country for more than six months. U.S. officials insisted they would keep seeking travel documents for the Trans to return to Germany, or perhaps even to Vietnam. However, at that time Vietnam had no repatriation agreement with the United States. So the Trans waited in legal limbo for resolution of their case. Meanwhile Tam graduated cum laude from UCLA and went to work part-time to pay for his graduate studies in American literature.

What would be the point of deporting this hard-working, upstanding family? Did the government merely want to show that it could? Perhaps the answer may be found in U.S. authorities' tendency to see asylum seekers as potential terrorists, ever since the leader of the 1993 World Trade Center bombing, Ramzi Yousef, entered the United States legally as an asylum seeker in 1992. The inclusion of expedited removal and mandatory detention of most asylum seekers in the 1996 immigration law may be attributable to that rare attempt to subvert the asylum system.

In 2007, the same year the Trans were detained, the Canadian Federal Court ruled "that the United States was not a safe third country for refugees because the United States does not comply with international standards for the protection of refugees" (Qazi 2008: 19).

Even asylees who have gained refugee status cannot rest easy. In *American Gulag*, Mark Dow recounted the story of Hanwa Saro-Wiwa, widow of the world-famous Ogoni environmental activist Ken Saro-Wiwa, who was executed in Nigeria in 1995. After fleeing Nigeria with her infant son, she was granted asylum in the United States.

> Then, in September 1999, she was stopped for a routine traffic violation in San Pablo, California, and local police handed her over to the INS. She was detained in the Marin County Jail for six days. It turned out to be an administrative mix-up, but

for days the INS refused to explain why it was holding her. She was freed through the intervention of attorney Sarah Jones and [Congressional] Representative Tom Lantos but only after she agreed to sign an order of supervision. Saro-Wiwa noted on the form that she was signing under duress and that she had been refused access to her attorney. . . . When Saro-Wiwa told an INS officer that she worked as a teacher, "he was a little taken aback." The officer seemed to have "a perception of me being a criminal or . . . a layabout." . . . Jones added that the case was plagued by "the assumption that because [Saro-Wiwa] was from Nigeria, that she was lying about everything. . . ." INS officials in San Francisco were "gung-ho" to deport Saro-Wiwa, she continued, and because they had never heard of her husband they had no idea why so many people were volunteering to help her. "They thought it was just another African—why is the media involved?" (Dow 2004: 337–38)

The local police handed Saro-Wiwa over to the INS under a provision of the 1996 immigration law; she was denied access to her attorney, because under that law she was not entitled to one. The INS officer shared the "culture of disbelief" that is entrenched among immigration authorities around the world. His stereotyped assumptions about her are also commonplace.

Such attitudes have worsened since 2001, as the immigration system has become increasingly militarized and politicized. Among the federal measures instituted after 9/11 were the Absconder Apprehension Initiative, "the widespread arrest and detention of members of the Arab and Muslim communities under the cover of immigration enforcement investigations" and Operation Liberty Shield, which included "automatically detaining and interrogating asylum seekers from 34 countries designed as terrorist host countries" (Barry 2009: 1). Dow pointed out that these initiatives "did not come out of nowhere" but rather were offshoots of the mandatory detention system established for undocumented migrants and asylum seekers in expedited removal under the 1996 immigration law.

Asylum seekers, most of whom committed no crime except the civil violation of entering the United States without a valid visa or passport, were swept into the post-9/11 maelstrom along with undocumented migrants and other detainees. In 2003 the ICE Office of Detention and Removal published a 10-year plan called "Endgame," to "remove all removable aliens" from the United States by 2012 (United States Department of Homeland Security 2003). These "removable aliens" included people such as Mary and Jason Ng, the asylum seekers whose stories were told in Chapter One. Mary was subject to a deportation order she knew nothing about, issued because she did not attend a hearing her lawyer did not tell her about. Estimating that 500,000 people are "ignoring" such orders, ICE has been trying to deport them all as fast as it can. It is unlikely to accomplish this goal and has made plenty of mistakes in the process—arresting and even deporting U.S. citizens for nonexistent immigration violations, breaking up families with U.S.-citizen children, sedating deportees with powerful and inappropriate drugs, and breaking international laws and agreements against refoulement.

The new Obama administration promised to introduce immigration reform legislation in 2009, and early that year the new secretary of homeland security appointed a special adviser to review immigration enforcement measures. However, that year the U.S. government deported almost 400,000 undocumented people, more than ever before. In late 2010 it was still unclear what the consequences of "Endgame" would be for asylum seekers caught in the system that has been reinforced by the draconian and punitive policies of the past dozen years.

For years numerous community and nonprofit advocacy groups have been pressuring the government for reform of the system. In the mid-1990s a coalition of advocacy organizations started meeting regularly with federal officials, trying to persuade the INS to make detention standards legally binding on the hundreds of jails, prisons, and private facilities that were holding thousands of undocumented migrants and asylum seekers. As of 2009 the groups still had not succeeded in this effort. But they seemed to be making some headway on the issue of medical care for detainees, which came to the attention of Congress in 2008, after several damning reports of deaths in detention appeared in the media. Neither the INS nor ICE had implemented earlier federal court decisions in favor of detainees, so it seemed that a law or laws would be necessary to reform the detention system. In 2009 and 2010 a number of bills on this and related issues were under congressional consideration.

Meanwhile 10 voluntary agencies, or VOLAGs, were managing resettlement of thousands of refugees in the United States with federal funding from the Office of Refugee Resettlement, based in the

Department of Health and Human Services.[5] The VOLAGs helped refugees and asylees (but not asylum seekers, who were ineligible for such government support) to find housing, schooling, employment, training, medical care, and very modest financial assistance for a maximum of eight months. Some of these agencies had advocacy offices that produced or endorsed campaigns, reports, letters, and statements supporting the human rights of asylum seekers and calling for the improvement of detention conditions, enforcement of nonbinding detention "standards" or the end of detention of children, asylum seekers, and other vulnerable people. But as with the Australian refugee assistance organizations, their effectiveness as advocates was limited by their close relationship with the government whose punitive immigration policies they were seeking to change. Their limited budgets, which the government had not increased for many years, made their resettlement work increasingly difficult as economic crisis took hold in the late 2000s.

Even so, the VOLAGs were in the forefront of efforts not only to shelter but also to integrate persecuted outsiders into U.S. society. Asylum and sanctuary may be conditional and temporary according to law and custom, but integration is an enduring form of welcome and acceptance, the greatest hope of those with no place to go back to and nowhere else to go.

CHAPTER NINE

Asylum Now: Europe and the United Kingdom

Still Human Still Here

BRITISH CAMPAIGN ON BEHALF OF DESTITUTE ASYLUM SEEKERS

Asylum claims rose sharply from the 1980s on, especially in European Union states and the UK. The increase became acute at the end of the Cold War. Before then, asylum seekers mainly moved from East to West and South to North. Afterward France, Britain, Belgium, and the Netherlands became major destinations of African and Asian asylum seekers, many of whom were from those nations' excolonies. Germany, Austria, and Switzerland received asylum seekers from farther east, especially when the Balkans exploded in war in the late 1980s and early 1990s. Because of its liberal asylum policies, put in place after World War II, West Germany received more asylum seekers than any other Western European country. Its Basic Law of 1947 gave persecuted persons the right to *gain* asylum, unlike other countries, where the state reserved the right to *grant* asylum. Other factors encouraging asylum seekers to pick certain countries included the proximity or accessibility of the destination; "economic, political and cultural connections and linguistic bridges from colonial history" (Bade 2003: 264); well-established migration routes; ethnic and labor networks; and family reunification possibilities.

As early as 1974, however, Western European countries had "stopped labor recruitment and redefined themselves as 'zero immigration countries.' . . . People who had previously been admitted as workers now had to claim asylum" (Borjas and Crisp 2005: 41). Even at that time "there was a growing presumption that refuge was sought under false pretenses and that the true reasons were in fact not political but economic and social" (Bade 2003: 270). In 1980 more than 150,000 people were seeking asylum in Europe; by 1992 the figure had jumped to 690,000. As the number of asylum applications increased, the percent granted decreased.

Even West Germany became less generous in giving asylum. Because the West German government did not recognize torture as a form of political persecution, it did not constitute sufficient grounds for asylum (Bade 2003: 271). Even so, almost two-thirds of all asylum petitions filed in Europe in 1980 were in West Germany. As they became increasingly unwelcome in that country, asylum seekers went to France, Switzerland, the Netherlands, and Belgium. After the end of the Cold War those countries passed restrictive laws and signed international agreements to limit entry of asylum seekers. As a result of the restrictive Schengen Agreement of 1985 and the Dublin Convention of 1990, asylum seekers became "refugees in orbit." And the more asylum seekers were excluded, the more illegal immigration and human smuggling increased.

Meanwhile, war, ethnic conflict, and genocide created millions of refugees and internally displaced people in Somalia, Sudan, Sierra Leone, Angola, Bosnia, Iraq, Afghanistan, Colombia, and other countries during the last decade of the 20th century and the first decade of the 21st. In response the European Union states and other receiving countries traded strategies for avoiding their obligations under international law and preventing asylum seekers from arriving and gaining refuge. Since 1985 members of the Intergovernmental Consultations on Asylum, Refugee, and Migration Policies in Europe, North America, and Australia, known as the IGC, have met periodically, in secret, to exchange information and policy ideas (Tazreiter 2004: 185). Their publicly expressed goal is to "harmonize" asylum policies. Hatton wrote:

> Some observers believed that the process of harmonization would produce a set of policies that would be more generous to refugees, at least for the countries with the toughest pre-existing policies. These hopes seem to have been dashed as those countries have exerted pressure to bring what were initially more generous

proposals for harmonized policies more in line with their own. (2005: 110)

Repeated calls for a "common European asylum policy" therefore bode ill for asylum seekers.

Governments usually say they are driven by the force of public opinion to limit all kinds of immigration, including asylum, and

> surveys of public opinion typically find that most voters do not want to see immigration increased. . . . those who are most vulnerable to labour market competition from immigrants, or who are most likely to bear the fiscal costs, are more inclined to be against immigration. . . . But there is often an element of racism towards non-white immigrants. . . . Attitudes towards immigrants are more negative the larger the share of immigrants in the population. (Hatton 2005: 113)

In fact, in many receiving countries, including the UK, Ireland, Italy, Holland, and Spain, the foreign-born make up 10% or less (in Italy and Holland, less than 5%) of the national population. However, they are often numerous in large cities and conspicuous in small towns or rural areas (where they may be detained in prison-like establishments). Most people are unaware of the distinctions in status among legal immigrants, undocumented migrants, refugees, asylum seekers, and asylees, tending to lump together all foreigners (but especially people of color) as unwanted, illegal intruders. In the 1990s newly reunified Germany seethed with xenophobia, scapegoating of and violence against foreigners. Neo-Nazi groups were on the rise, especially in eastern Germany, where fire bombings of immigrant hostels resulted in dozens of deaths and hundreds of serious injuries. In Germany and across western Europe, "both [asylum seekers] with genuine claims for protection and others who were said to have economic motives came to be part of a negative stereotype associated with a drain on state resources and became associated in popular discourse with criminal activities," Tazreiter wrote (2004: 106–07).

Politicians have long used negative attitudes toward foreigners to get elected and push anti-immigrant laws through Parliament or provincial legislatures. In Italy, for example, after his election as prime minister in 2001 Silvio Berlusconi introduced legislation extending detention of "illegal" entrants (including asylum seekers) to 60 days.

A dozen prison-like detention centers for 60 to 400 inmates were set up to hold allegedly illegal entrants. Sometimes they were kept in freight containers, "unbearable both in summer and winter" (Welch and Schuster 2005: 343). Médecins sans Frontières physicians visited several of the detention centers and found deplorable conditions, including excessive administration of tranquilizers and painkillers, no physical exercise, inadequate medical care, and lack of mental health services.

After their release, while awaiting decisions on their asylum claims—which could take a year or more—many asylum seekers were destitute. As recently as 2006 Italy had no asylum law, and only 5% to 10% of these entrants were recognized as refugees under the 1951 Convention. The rest were deported, left the country, or went underground. In 2001 Italy reportedly had 1.5 million legal and 1 million illegal immigrants. The head of the rightwing Lega Nord expressed a common sentiment when he declared that "cannons should be set up on Italy's coasts to deter would-be asylum seekers" (Moorehead 2005: 63). Meanwhile, despite paying lip service to "harmonization," the European Union has looked the other way.

Other receiving countries also have an underground of undocumented migrants and asylum seekers. In Germany and the United Kingdom it is said to consist of 400,000 people or more. "In the OECD countries somewhere between 50 and 70% of asylum seekers receive neither refuge nor a non-Convention status but nonetheless remain," often with limited or no access to social services (Borjas and Crisp 2005: 74). Since the late 1990s asylum seekers in EU countries have not been permitted to work for pay while awaiting a decision on their claim, and failed asylum seekers can work only illegally. Thus they are integrated into the labor market in dead-end, usually temporary, jobs and are paid substandard wages for dangerous, unskilled, or soul-destroying work.

As Borjas and Crisp pointed out, "legal, moral and practical restraints mean that only a fraction of asylum seekers whose applications are rejected are returned; expanded deportation for unsuccessful claimants is thus not an effective way of dealing with the challenges associated with making asylum regimes more effective" (2005: 71). But the system does function in a perverse fashion: states consistently respond to increased numbers of asylum seekers through draconian strategies of prevention, deterrence, restriction, and management. They try to prevent asylum seekers from entering their territory in the first place; to deter them from claiming asylum by making procedures complicated, time-consuming, and expensive; to limit their stay through restrictions and deportation; and to manage their movement inside the national territory through dispersal, detention, or registration. Mistreatment, abuse, and neglect could be added to this list. Application of these strategies may have led to a reduction in the number of applications for asylum but has not resulted in a reduction in the number of people fleeing from persecution. They keep arriving and staying, because the conditions that led them to flee persist or worsen.

"While it may be in the short-term interests of Western governments to reduce the number of asylum seekers they receive, their actions can have hidden costs both for other actors and, in the long term, for themselves. . . . policies that deflect or contain refugees can generate regional instability or corrode international norms on refugee protection by creating great inequalities in the burdens between states," Borjas and Crisp observe (2005: 87). Not only that; these repressive policies do not work. They do not produce the desired outcome of asylum seekers returning in short order to their own countries. Instead they consume financial resources that could be used for more constructive purposes and contribute to the perpetuation of a destitute underclass in the host country.

At least one European government seems to have recognized the wastefulness and ineffectuality of punitive asylum policies. In 2007 the Netherlands proclaimed an amnesty for more than 25,000 asylum seekers who had applied for refuge before April 2001 and stayed in the country while awaiting a decision or after being rejected. Under the previous government 11,000 asylum seekers had been rejected or deported, and 4,200 had been expelled by force. New arrivals had been "confined in 'departure centers' while their applications [were] processed" (under the obvious assumption that they would be denied) (*Associated Press* 2007). The change "marked an easing of policy in a country which has imposed some of Europe's toughest migration and integration laws" (*Sydney Morning Herald* 2007: 1).

Some observers consider Sweden to have the most enlightened asylum system in Europe. The government generally takes "a social service approach" to the treatment of asylum seekers, keeping them for a strictly limited time in administrative detention or reception centers that are not prisons or placing them under supervision without incarceration (Global Detention Project 2009). Red Cross volunteers visit the detention centers weekly. "Sweden received a favorable review of its detention infrastructure, which has led to its characterization as a European role model. . . . There were no allegations of abuse and . . . detention center staff were sufficient in number and skills. . . . Material conditions . . . were of a very high standard," the European Committee for the Prevention of Torture and Inhuman or Degrading Treatment or Punishment reported in 2009 (Global Detention Project 2009).

Tens of thousands of Iraqis, Somalis, Serbians, and others have gained asylum in Sweden over the past five years. In late 2008 some 24,000 asylum cases were pending, and only 1,645 people were detained that year. Even so in 2008 "the number of Iraqis granted residency dropped dramatically after the Swedish Migration court ruled that Iraq is no longer a war zone" (Global Detention Project 2009). Apparently some localities where Iraqis had settled felt overwhelmed by their presence, and a far-right political party elected representatives in municipal elections.

Ironically in view of the European obsession with limiting entry, eight of the top 10 refugee destinations in 2000 were outside Europe. They were Pakistan, Iran, Germany, Tanzania, United States, former Yugoslavia, Guinea, Sudan, Democratic Republic of Congo, and China. Asylum seekers and refugees in each of these countries that year numbered in the scores or hundreds of thousands.

During the Iraq War, which started in 2003, millions of Iraqis fled, but most went to neighboring or nearby countries such as Jordan, Syria, and Egypt; relatively few—tens of thousands—have managed to arrive in Western countries with the help of the UNHCR. Other Iraqis who tried to enter the European Union via Greece or Turkey found themselves stuck in a revolving door. According to a 2008 Human Rights Watch report, Iraqis who enter Greece "can't move onward because EU asylum law . . . normally requires asylum seekers to lodge their claims for protection in the first EU country in which they set foot and they also can't move back home because of fear of war and persecution." Greek police then expel them into Turkey, where border authorities subject them to "inhuman and degrading conditions of detention. . . . Once detained, such migrants have no meaningful opportunity to seek asylum or other forms of protection and are often held indefinitely until family or friends are able to provide them return tickets." Turkey's government recognizes only Europeans as refugees, and so the authorities forcibly return Iraqi refugees to Iraq without considering their appeals for asylum (Human Rights Watch 2008: 4). This is a classic example of refoulement.

In any case, "refugees are overwhelmingly concentrated in the poorest countries," and most people who flee from persecution never leave their own country but instead are internally displaced (Human Rights Watch 2008: 42). That is as far as they can afford to go. Only asylum seekers with sufficient resources to pay thousands of dollars in smuggling fees or plane fares manage to reach Europe, Britain, the United States, or Australia. First World nightmares of desperate millions invading from Bangladesh as it sinks under the waves or from North Africa as the desert encroaches are politically potent but highly unlikely.

It is true that hundreds of thousands of desperate people, including economic refugees, political refugees, and asylum seekers, set out for richer countries every year, smuggled or stowed away in boats or trucks or on foot. They are usually intercepted, although an unknown number succeed in arriving or die in the attempt to escape untenable situations at home. Many are detained for short or long periods and then deported. Only a few apply for asylum. According to the UN High Commissioner for Refugees, 383,000 applications for asylum were received in 51 countries in 2008, an increase of 12% over 2007. Asylum seekers' top five countries of origin were Iraq (40,500), Somalia (21,800), Russian Federation (20,500), Afghanistan (18,500), and China (17,400). The main receiving countries were the United States (49,000), Canada (36,900), France (35,200), Italy (31,200), and the UK (30,500).

Asylum seekers who manage to arrive in the UK, France, other European countries, and the United States receive a cold welcome. Detention and deportation are important features of asylum policy and practice in all the major receiving countries. In France, for example, a 1945 law limited detention of foreigners to the time necessary to arrange for their departure. It was for 48 hours only, renewable for five days and renewable again for urgent reasons. This law may have been part of a reaction against the notorious internment and transit camps of the wartime Vichy regime, through which hundreds of thousands of Jews and other enemies of the Nazis were funneled on their way to Auschwitz.

Over time and under the pressure of thousands of refugee arrivals, the number of days allowed for detention in France increased to 32, the time thought to be necessary for issuance of travel documents for expulsion. Under the law, if expulsion is impossible, detainees must be released unless they have resisted deportation. Although this regulation pays lip service to the 1951 Refugee Convention and human rights law, conditions in French detention centers are "among the worst in Europe" (Welch and Schuster 2005: 340). Sometimes detainees have even been kept in windowless, unheated shipping containers. Violence against detainees by border police is common, especially at Charles de Gaulle Airport, where 95% of undocumented migrants are held. Officials often refuse to allow detainees to apply for asylum and do not provide information on human rights. Refoulement occurs, and the authorities restrict NGO access to the detention centers.

Access to German immigration detention centers is also difficult, although some NGOs do manage to monitor conditions there. Two forms of detention exist in Germany: "preparation," for a maximum of six weeks, and "secure," for those who can be deported within three months, if the detainee is considered likely to abscond. Detention may be extended for an additional 12 months if the detainee refuses to sign travel documents. Undocumented migrants aged 16 to 65 may be detained. They are kept in barred cells in 45 detention centers and prisons, and their guards are police. They may have one hour's exercise per day. No work or vocational training is provided. Detainees must pay for legal representation, and "money and possessions are taken from the detainees on arrival, and any money put towards the cost of detention" (Welch and Schuster 2005: 341f). Often they cannot keep personal possessions or reclaim them when released. Only pregnant women detainees get some relief from this harsh treatment— they are sent to a hospital six weeks before their due date and allowed to stay there for six weeks after the birth.

Advocacy groups in the UK have reported mistakes in the practice of detaining suspected illegal migrants, including asylum seekers without visas or passports, on arrival in the country. Reginald Kargbo, a 34-year-old, native-born British citizen, told a harrowing story about his return to London from a visit with relatives in Sierra Leone. He was suing the Home Office, because he was detained at Heathrow Airport on suspicion of being an illegal migrant. He presented his UK passport to the immigration official, "who claimed it was false and . . . began 'ripping at it'" (*New Londoners* 2007: 1). Then he was taken to a secure room and searched "under suspicion of having an 'invalid document.'" Despite presenting a copy of his British birth certificate, he was told he would be deported to Sierra Leone. A security van took him to Campsfield Removal Centre, where he was detained for a weekend. Yet the identification card they issued him declared him to be a British national.

Unlike most immigration detainees, Kargbo managed to contact a lawyer, who threatened legal action to gain his release. When he was taken to the airport he thought he would be deported anyway, but officials released him late Monday "on condition that he return back to the airport." Two weeks later he received a message that he did not have to report to the airport after all. The Home Office offered no apology but told him he would have to apply for a new passport, because the old one was damaged (by the immigration officer who had torn it).

Kargbo offered a rare glimpse of conditions at Campsfield, which he described as substandard: unwashed sheets on beds in tiny rooms, tasteless food. He told an interviewer: "Many of the people in the detention center seemed to be mentally disturbed because they had been there for so long. Some had asked to return home but had been refused, had been there for six months or a year. When I arrived the supervisor asked me if I wanted medication."

There are several reasons that some who had asked to return home had been refused:

- Some governments decline to provide passports or other travel documents to citizens scheduled to be deported from other countries;[1]
- The home country is unsafe;
- It is difficult to transport deportees to a place where the airport is not operational;
- Deportees are too ill to travel or unable to obtain medical attention in the home country;
- It is impossible to trace their parents if they arrived as unaccompanied minors.

Finally released after months or even years in detention, failed asylum seekers disappear into the destitution underground. As of May 2004, from 155,000 to 283,500 of them were awaiting removal from the UK (Amnesty International 2006: 5). More recent estimates have gone up to around 500,000. At a cost of £11,000 for each deportation, it would take 10 to 18 years to get through the backlog. In its report on the destitution underground, Amnesty International UK concluded: "For the foreseeable future thousands of rejected asylum seekers in the UK are condemned to live in abject poverty, stripped of their dignity and relying on others to subsist. Sometimes they go hungry and sleep in the streets. All avenues to a normal life are blocked. . . . the whereabouts of many rejected asylum seekers are unknown" (Amnesty International 2006: 5). La Beninoise, whose asylum hearing is described in Chapter One, and her British baby may be two of the disappeared.

Presumably the British government set up its asylum policies with the intention of fulfilling its obligations under international law, but it often seems as if its real intention is to make it as difficult as possible for asylum seekers to gain asylum. Since 1993, when the Refugee Convention was incorporated into British law, at least five statutes have regulated and limited asylum. The 1993 law instituted "fast-track" procedures to deal with asylum applications that had "no foundation." Asylum seekers were to be fingerprinted and detained during the decision process. The 1996 Asylum and Immigration Act established a "white list" of countries that the British government considered "safe," where nationals were thought to be at little risk of persecution. The fast-track system was expanded to include more groups of migrants. In addition, the government adopted the "safe third country" rule from the Dublin Convention of 1989, allowing it to deport an asylum seeker to a "safe" country if the asylum seeker has already landed there.

The 1999 law expanded the definition of deception in immigration cases. Asylum seekers could claim they had had good cause to enter the country illegally only if they presented themselves to the authorities without delay. It also set up an agency to provide financial assistance to asylum seekers and to arrange for their dispersal throughout Britain. The 2002 law set up "accommodation centers," which were to provide educational and health services to asylum seekers. It mandated an asylum registration card containing biometric data. If an asylum seeker from a "safe" country presented a "clearly unfounded" case, he or she could appeal a negative decision only after being deported. Asylum seekers, their parents, and spouses were denied permission to work while they waited for their claim to be processed, putting them on the road to destitution.

The 2004 law made it a crime, punishable by two years in prison, to enter the UK without a "reasonable excuse" for not having a passport. It established credibility tests to be administered by immigration officers and courts. Refused asylum seekers' families were denied financial support. If the refused asylum seeker did not agree to leave the country voluntarily, financial support would be stopped. Accommodation of asylum seekers was to depend on their participation in community activities. Electronic monitoring of asylum seekers was instituted. The 2006 law established penalties for employers of illegal workers. It set up a three-day period for fingerprinting of asylum seekers and rules for accommodation of asylum seekers by local authorities. It mandated inspection of detention facilities by the Chief Inspector of Prisons. The "New Asylum Model" was put into operation in 2007 but it remained unclear if its modest reforms had any positive effects.

In 2010 a British high court ruling lifted a work ban on 45,000 asylum seekers. In reaction the UK immigration minister announced that the Home Office would allow asylum seekers to "apply only for vacancies among 400,000 skilled jobs in shortage occupations. . . . Asylum seekers would have to be qualified maths teachers, chemical engineers, high-integrity pipe welders or even experienced orchestral musicians or ballet dancers. . . ." The Refugee Council replied that "the shortage occupation list is not designed for asylum seekers but rather economic migrants needing sponsorship to come to the UK" (Travis 2010). The new policy seemed to be a transparent attempt to prevent asylum seekers from escaping from destitution while they waited for their claims to be decided.

On and on rolled the rules and regulations, seemingly disconnected from the realities of asylum seekers' situations. For example, according to Anthony Good, the UK Border Agency (UKBA) "expects 'genuine' applicants to declare themselves on entry" into the UK. "They may be wholly unfamiliar with the UK—indeed, may not even know it *is* the UK—and are often exhausted and terrified, yet any delay in claiming asylum is seized on by the Home Office as undermining their credibility" (2007: 99). Asylum law, Good says, "occupies a solipsistic parallel universe" (2007: 96). The judicial system rigidly construes words and narrows the application of sanctuary to a few highly circumscribed types of entrants. Casuistic interpretation of the law severely limits access to asylum. In the UK, Good concludes, authorities systematically use the Refugee Convention to exclude people from asylum.

One of the ways of ensuring that "too many" people do not seek asylum is to make the application procedure as complicated and time-consuming as possible. In the UK, for example, most "asylum applicants are required to fill in a Statement of Evidence Form (SEF) to set out the claim for asylum. This 19-page form must be completed in English and submitted to the Home Office within 10 working days of the date of the claim" (Shaw and Witkin 2004: 6). If the form does not arrive by the deadline it is rejected for "noncompliance"; this happens in 15% of Home Office cases. After they make a statement at an asylum interview, asylum seekers are "expected to sign an interview record in a language they do not understand, without having the opportunity to read it" (Shaw and Witkin 2004: 6). No other area of the British legal system allows this sort of procedure.

The Home Office does its own assessments of political, economic, and social conditions of countries for use in asylum cases, and nongovernmental experts say most are of poor quality. The Home Office makes asylum decisions assuming that "the majority of asylum claims have no factual basis," and so the country assessments take information from government and other sources out of context to make the situation look more positive than it actually is (Shaw and Witkin 2004: 9). Here again is the "culture of disbelief" in action. Amnesty's report on asylum decision making gives examples of denials of asylum claims in which the Home Office accepted at face value a foreign government's claim that it did not allow torture or abuse. Even countries such as Algeria or Iran, where Amnesty has documented systematic torture and other human rights violations, received the benefit of the doubt, while asylum seekers did not.

Amnesty comments:

Many asylum seekers flee countries where any expression of opinion in opposition to the existing regime is banned and perceived dissidents are ruthlessly punished. . . . Nonetheless . . . exceptional individuals continue to strive for political change in such countries, despite the threat to their lives or the lives of their families. This quality is applauded when it is presented in a biographical film, book or TV documentary but appears to be entirely misunderstood when presented in the form of an asylum claim. The Home Office makes assumptions about asylum applicants that reveal a total lack of understanding of how people live under restrictive regimes—and the strength of their political motivation when their rights to freedom of expression are threatened or denied. (Shaw and Witkin 2004: 23)

A particularly callous and obtuse denial of a 2001 petition by an Iranian asylum seeker sneered:

When describing your mistreatment in prison you refer to being subjected to activities of a tortuous nature such as food deprivation, suspending upside down and daily beatings, yet you claim that you were able to prevent your captors sexually abusing you by denying them, although "they tried." The Secretary of State is aware of the harsh conditions that exist in Iranian detention centers and rape is known to have been inflicted on inmates. He cannot accept that rape and sexual abuse are regarded as a matter of the inmate's choice in the manner that you have claimed and must therefore conclude that you have, at best, exaggerated your account. (Stringer and Lumley 2006: 10)

Another denial letter, received by a 14-year-old asylum seeker in 2006, scolded:

The Secretary of State . . . is of the view that you were aware of the plot to overthrow the legitimate and democratic government of [your] country [and should not have participated in this unlawful activity]. . . . He is of the view that you did not stop to think that as a child you should not take part in such activities and neither should you be handling a gun. (Stringer and Lumley 2006: 10)

The UK ratified the Optional Protocol to the Convention on the Rights of the Child on the Involvement of Children in Armed Conflict in 2003. Denying asylum to a child soldier on the grounds that he or she should have known better, attributing to children a sense of responsibility that by definition of the Protocol they do not have, requires a twisted and perverse interpretation of British responsibility under international law.

The most vulnerable asylum seekers, including children, torture survivors, and rape victims, seem to have the greatest difficulty in establishing their claims. UKBA caseworkers sometimes do not try to obtain "independent, corroborative medical evidence" of torture or give the applicant time to obtain it (Shaw and Witkin 2004: 31). In cases in which the caseworker has failed to seek information about torture, the Home Office has used the lack of such information as a reason to deny asylum. Caseworkers may use asylum seekers' inability to obtain treatment as a reason for denying their claim.

According to Home Office guidelines authorities are to refer torture survivors to the Medical Foundation for the Care of Victims of

Torture for evaluation and treatment. In 2006 the Foundation received 2,145 asylum seekers from 86 countries. Males constituted 56% of the clients, women 35%, and children 9%. The Medical Foundation says all asylum seekers should be treated as possible torture survivors. Yet despite the inclusion of the Medical Foundation in the asylum process, medical evidence of torture is often "downplayed, ignored or disputed" (ICAR 2007d: 21). And in some cases, even after presenting documented evidence of torture the asylum seeker is still rejected.

Until the mid-1990s British authorities often ignored or misconstrued the special problems of women asylum seekers. After all, the words "sex," "gender," and "rape" did not appear in the Refugee Convention or UNHCR guidelines. Although the UN passed the Convention on the Elimination of All Forms of Discrimination against Women (CEDAW) in 1979 and the UK ratified it in 1986, British immigration judges often did not recognize rape as grounds for asylum. They seemed to see sexual aggression as a private act of lust rather than a political act of violence. One judge denied asylum to a 50-year-old woman saying, "Without wishing to appear unchivalrous, we have to say that there can be no significant risk of rape at her age" (Good 2007: 95). Some judges apparently discriminated against women asylum seekers on the basis of ethnic or national stereotypes, finding rapes of Bosnian women to be acts of "politically motivated ethnic cleansing" while denying that Tamil women in Sri Lanka were raped for political reasons (Good 2007: 95). Women's reluctance to talk about rape or their failure to discuss it immediately was used to discredit them. Instead of investigating cases of trafficked women, authorities detained them and placed them in fast-track removal proceedings.

Landmark legal cases were supposed to change treatment of women in the asylum system. In *Fathi and Ahmady* (1996), "refusal to conform to gender norms in Iran was seen as a political act within the definition of the Convention at the appeals stage" (ICAR 2007d: 11). In the *Shah and Islam* case of 1999 "the appellants, both Pakistani women, had suffered domestic violence and were at risk of being accused of adultery, with all its consequences, if returned to Pakistan" (Stevens 2004: 329). On appeal the House of Lords found that under the Refugee Convention, "women, who share an immutable characteristic, can constitute a social group if they face persecution in a country for being a member of that group" (ICAR 2007d: 11). These decisions led to the issuance of Gender Guidelines in 2000 by the Asylum and Immigration Tribunal (AIT). The 2005 *Fomah* decision by the House of Lords reinforced them by finding that women in Sierra Leone constituted a social group under the terms of the Refugee Convention because of their perceived inferiority and subjection to male domination.

The Gender Guidelines declare that "rape and other forms of sexual violence clearly amount to persecution in the same way as do other acts of serious physical abuse" (BWRAP 2006: 7). They also point out that women may delay in reporting rape in their asylum applications. Nevertheless, "despite all the gender guidelines . . . judges often start from the position that a woman is lying," a former AIT member said. "They demand a much higher degree of proof from women. The idea that they wouldn't tell their husbands or family members about a rape, for example, is regarded as absolutely implausible" (BWRAP 2006: 7). (In the UK only 5.3% of reported rapes result in conviction.) In 2006 the AIT's deputy president said: "The 'Gender Guidelines' are not, and have never been, the policy of the AIT" (BWRAP 2006: 37).

The Black Women's Rape Action Project concluded:

- 88% of Home Office asylum decisions dismissed asylum seekers' reports of rape;
- Women presenting experts' reports corroborating their accounts of rape were six times more likely to win their case than those without such documentation;
- 71% of requests for more time to gather evidence of rape were denied;
- In appeals where rape was not accepted as grounds for asylum, 43% of judges found that rape did not constitute a form of persecution. (BWRAP 2006: 7)

In response to pressure from women's groups and Parliament, the Home Office established the Poppy Project to assist trafficked women and collect evidence for prosecution of traffickers. Asylum Aid looked into the results of their asylum claims and found that none of the 32 trafficked women who sought asylum during a two-year period gained it initially, but 25 of them received refugee status or humanitarian protection on appeal. This finding is much better than 2004 statistics indicating that 3% of asylum applicants were recognized as refugees, 9% were granted humanitarian protection or discretionary leave to remain, and 88% were rejected in the first instance. Nineteen percent of applicants gained asylum on appeal.

According to a 2007 ICAR report, Lesbian/Gay/Bisexual/ Transgender (LGBT) asylum seekers are classified as members of a persecuted social group as a result of the *Shah and Islam* decision, but the Home Office insists that applicants prove their sexual orientation or claims that it can be hidden to avoid persecution. Applicants must present sexual partners to testify on their behalf or prove their participation in LGBT organizations. Homosexuals who establish heterosexual relationships are not considered genuine, although homosexuals in many societies have such relationships to hide their true sexual orientation. Homosexuals unlucky enough to come from countries on the Home Office's "white list" (such as Jamaica) are unlikely to obtain asylum, even though Amnesty International and other human rights organizations have shown that they are persecuted there.[2]

Many asylum seekers have Kafkaesque experiences as they try to navigate the British system. They enter a seemingly endless labyrinth at a Dickensian building called Lunar House, the UKBA headquarters outside London. A report published in 2005 by South London Citizens, a community group, documented conditions there. At the rear of the building asylum seekers waited outside in long queues for hours with no awnings to shelter them from the weather, hemmed in by railings as if they were cattle.[3] Immigrants had the privilege of waiting outside in front of the building. Waiting times averaged four to six hours. Portable toilets at the front of the building were dirty and smelly, and there were no toilets at the back of the building where the asylum seekers waited.

A social worker accompanying an asylum seeker wrote an indignant letter about their experience waiting outside Lunar House: "I joined the queue on behalf of my client at 10 A.M. and counted approximately 45 people in front of me; nearly seven hours later still standing and with little progress made, we were asked to leave, there were still approximately 35 people in front of me in the queue" (Back, Farrell, and Vandermaas 2005: 125).

Inside the building only one counter might be open, and there was no service during the lunch hour. No cell phones were permitted, and the temperature inside was inhospitably cold. Metal chairs, bolted to the floor, were placed too far from the counter for the petitioner to sit comfortably. "The only chance of communication was when your body is tilted strongly forward and you sit on the edge of the bench. People slightly shorter than me would not be able to speak to the officer and sit at the same time," a foreign student reported (Back, Farrell, and Vandermaas 2005: 21).

The asylum unit had "pig-pen" metal railings inside the building. Women stood with crying babies in their arms for hours, and no baby-changing facilities were provided.

Refreshments were available but too expensive for destitute asylum seekers. "We spent the whole day there without having anything to drink or eat after days without food and didn't have any money," an asylum seeker said (Back, Farrell, and Vandermaas 2005: 27). No water fountains could be found. Inside there were only pay toilets. The community group "heard from several women victims of rape who had been poorly treated during their interview at Lunar House. Despite clear grounds for complaint, none of the women had felt able to report mistreatment by staff or to question their experience at the time. One of these women had been sent out of the building without first aid while miscarrying" (Back, Farrell, and Vandermaas 2005: 29).

Lost documents and delayed decisions were common. Ten percent of petitioners reported their original documents had been lost; 50% reported delays, ranging from six days to eight years, in the return of their documents. The average delay was one year. Delays and losses of documents went unexplained. Usually they were sent to the wrong address. In 2003 "an MP stood in line at Lunar House to retrieve a constituent's passport . . . but was told the passport was not with [UKBA] and could not be handed over. Two years later . . . the passport was returned to the constituent without explanation" (Back, Farrell, and Vandermaas 2005: 37).

In some cases asylum seekers arrived at Lunar House to sign on for welfare benefits while awaiting a decision on their case, only to be arrested and detained on the spot. The result was that asylum seekers became too fearful to report to the authorities and disappeared into the destitution underground.

The report found that interviewers were sometimes angry or rude; they took down information incorrectly and refused to change it; they would not give a copy of interview notes to the petitioner; or they failed to record the interview. Rape victims had a particularly difficult time in interviews. They lacked privacy, and no women interpreters might be available. Despite Britain's ratification of the Council of Europe Convention on Action against Trafficking in Human Beings, officials did not seem to consider trafficking as grounds for asylum. (The 2007 case of La Beninoise, recounted in Chapter One, is an example.) Children were usually not believed, and adolescents were often considered to be adults, even if they provided documentary evidence of their age. Decisions coming out of Lunar House were based on "poor questioning, inappropriate reasoning and speculation, poor country-of-origin knowledge, poor application of human rights law, inadequate knowledge by interviewers," Good wrote (2007: 53).

A political asylum seeker told the Lunar House report's authors: "I shouldn't have been allowed in the country to keep my life on hold for seven years. My case was refused with unsatisfactory arguments and has gone twice to appeal. All the time I have not been able to work. There is no accountability. I have been fobbed off, sent back and forth, no decision ever made. No one wants to take responsibility. I feel I have no human rights" (Back, Farrell, and Vandermaas 2005: 54). At least he was not in detention for all of that time.

Immigration detention was introduced in Britain in the 1920 Aliens Act and expanded in the 1971 Immigration Act. It was rarely used until it became an "integral part of immigration procedures" in the early 1990s, when Britain felt overwhelmed by refugees from all parts of the world (ICAR 2007a: 2). A 2002 government white paper reaffirmed detention as an "essential element" of immigration control; yet the Home Office's Enforcement Instructions and Guidance say detention should be used only as a "last resort" for the shortest possible time. Instead it has become a major industry, with operations contracted out to private, profit-making corporations (Bacon 2005).[4] According to Amnesty International, undocumented immigrants, immigrants convicted of criminal offenses, refugees, and asylum seekers are detained because beds are available in so-called removal centers, not because they pose a flight risk.

Refused asylum seekers scheduled for "voluntary" removal are required to obtain travel documents from the government they might have fled. Often the foreign government refuses or fails to provide such documents, and the UK government then detains them for an indefinite period—sometimes years. Detention, Amnesty International maintains, "is an extreme sanction for people who have not committed a criminal offense. It violates one of the most fundamental human rights protected by international law, the right to liberty." In many cases it is "inappropriate, unnecessary, disproportionate and, therefore, unlawful" (Amnesty International 2005: 6). The Parliamentary Joint Committee on Human Rights expressed concern in 2004 that "a relatively significant number of potentially vulnerable people, who are either unconvicted or have completed any sentence of imprisonment, are being held in an inappropriate prison environment" (Amnesty International 2005: 34).

Amnesty and other human rights organizations have visited the removal centers, as have delegates from the UK Inspectorate of Prisons. They reported lack of recreation activities, overcrowding, mistreatment by staff, long periods in cells, lack of privacy, visiting restrictions, limits on making and receiving telephone calls, lack of 24-hour medical provision, no facilities to treat serious illnesses, transfers without warning, and insufficient interpretation services. The Prison Inspectorate delegation found a detainee "literally lost inside the system, three months into what was supposed to be an overnight stay in prison" (Medical Justice Network 2007: 2).

Members of the Medical Justice Network, a small organization of healthcare professionals, reported that they had seen 20 detainees who showed signs of torture. "In no case were these patients aware of any effort by the Home Office to investigate this, even when it had been appropriately reported to Home Office officials and doctors" (2007: 1). A lawyers' group that monitored detention conditions found women who had been detained for as long as two years after living in the UK for periods ranging from two weeks to 14 years.

NGOs have collected many stories of inhumane treatment. Amnesty reported in 2005 that police had raided the home of a West African woman and took her and her British-born, six-month-old baby to a removal center. She was told they would be deported the following day, but the flight was cancelled. During detention of more than six months, the woman and her baby were moved between a removal center in Scotland and one in London several times. Eventually the story reached the newspapers, and a member of the House of Lords helped the mother and child obtain legal help. The Home Office rejected her application for asylum, but she managed to get bail. She gained asylum on appeal when the child was a year old. Britain is the only European country that detains children involved in asylum cases. "About 2,000 asylum-seeker children are detained every year" (*Community Care* 2008: 2).

The Children's Commissioner for England visited the Yarl's Wood Removal Centre and spoke with children detained there: "Not one of these children had any clear idea or, in the case of some children, any idea at all, of why were detained at Yarl's Wood. Neither had the children any knowledge of how long they would be there and what was likely to happen to them" (New Philanthropy Capital 2007: 16).

Some did not know what country they came from, and one said her mother was from London. "Many of the children clearly saw themselves as English children." In August 2008 the Chief Inspector of Prisons expressed "serious concerns" about the lack of health care for children and the length of time they were detained at Yarl's Wood—as long as 275 days.

In November 2008 the British government finally "lifted its reservation to the application of the United Nations Convention on the Rights of the Child to asylum-seeking children" after 17 years of pressure by children's campaigners (*Community Care* 2008: 2). Early in 2010 detainees at the facility went on hunger strike for six weeks to protest conditions for families there. Meanwhile, a report by Refugee and Migrant Justice claimed that "child asylum seekers arriving at the United Kingdom Border Agency in Dover [were] being denied rest, food and medicine until they [had] completed interviews." The March 2010 report "accused UK authorities of disregarding children's welfare and failing to provide them with legal or adult support" (Panos Institute 2010). In July 2010 the new Tory–Liberal Democrat government announced that families would no longer be detained at Yarl's Wood, but by late September it seemed to be backing away from that commitment.

Adults were still being held indefinitely. An Indian asylum seeker detained for more than six years was released in 1997 after the European Court ruled his deportation illegal. In 2009 a failed asylum seeker who had committed minor crimes, such as shoplifting, was deported after spending a total of eight years in immigration detention (Phelps et al. 2009: 33). The majority of detainees are released eventually, "either because they cannot be removed because of conditions in the country of origin, because travel documents for the persons to be removed cannot be issued, because they are allowed to appeal, because they are released on bail, because they are granted leave to remain on compassionate grounds or because their claim for asylum is eventually allowed" (Welch and Schuster 2005: 339). Meanwhile thousands of detainees, including pregnant women, HIV-positive individuals, torture victims, and mentally ill people, languish in custody. The 1999 Immigration and Asylum Act promised automatic bail hearings for detainees, but this provision was repealed in 2002. They "now have to request a bail hearing and many are unaware of this possibility" (Welch and Schuster 2005: 339). It is especially difficult for those detained upon arrival in the UK to find sureties (bail guarantors).

A small nonprofit organization called Bail for Immigration Detainees (BID) sends lawyers to removal centers to inform detainees of their rights. In June 2007 I accompanied one of BID's lawyers to Yarl's Wood Removal Centre, which houses women and families, on the barren site of a World War II air force base in Bedfordshire. We drove up to low boxlike buildings surrounded by 20-foot-high razor-wire fences.

Most of the 26 women waiting in the meeting room were black; a few were Asian. They looked tired, red-eyed, as if they had been weeping for a long time. The woman detained the longest had been in the center for eight months; the others had been there for three or four months. Several detainees could not attend the workshop, because they had chicken pox, which had spread rapidly through the building. Some who could not speak or understand English attended the meeting just to have something to do.

BID's lawyer explained how to apply for bail and urged those who already had applied to do so again. They should apply repeatedly to make a record of their detention, because the government denies that people are being held for long periods against their will. Applying for bail again and again belies the government's claims, the lawyer said. One of her clients applied 12 times before an immigration judge finally gave her bail. As I left the meeting room, one of the detainees slipped me a note complaining about the conditions. Among other things, the note said: "Women have been here for six months or more. Escort taking women to the airport, have been beaten, broke their fingers. Women with medical problems like blood pressure, diabetic, asthmatic have not been treated, no medication, never take you out of this place for hospital treatment. Some women were pregnant when they were arrested, they lost their babies, no medical attention."[5] Back in the car the lawyer told me she was quitting, burned out after months of giving the same presentation again and again to little effect.

A pamphlet picked up at a protest march in London quoted Ruth Williams, who had been detained at Yarl's Wood for almost six months: "We are women like other women, who have suffered and been forced out of our countries by killing and other violence. We have committed no crime but are locked up without rights and terrorized by threats to send us back to the horrors we fled. We want our human rights" ("Action alert" 2007).

Detained asylum seekers at Yarl's Wood and other removal centers are subjected to so-called fast-track procedures that were established to decide their cases within a month. Immigration judges hold hearings on site. Although the asylum seekers are supposed to be provided with legal representation, in practice they have difficulty obtaining a lawyer. The Legal Services Commission (LSC), an independent body, has set up rigid rules for determining whether lawyers will be paid to represent asylum seekers. If there is less than a 50% chance of success (as in the overwhelming majority of cases), the LSC will not pay. It is inconvenient and time-consuming for pro bono lawyers to travel to far-off detention centers, and difficult for their clients to obtain evidence of torture, their legal status, or other documentation. Amnesty International expressed the opinion in 2005 that "the time constraints imposed within the super fast-track procedures . . . make it impossible for the procedure to be a fair one, and therefore . . . adherence to such a strict timetable, in and of itself, represents a denial of justice for the individuals concerned" (Amnesty International 2005: 65).

In mid-2010 the new government delayed payments to Refugee and Migrant Justice (RMJ), the principal nonprofit legal-advocacy group providing representation to detained asylum seekers, and the organization had to close. The government's cutbacks in legal aid were expected to leave "hundreds of thousands of the most vulnerable people including asylum seekers and victims of domestic violence, without access to advice" (*Guardian* 2010).

At three removal centers surveyed in 2007, judges refused 94% to 99% of fast-track asylum petitions and allowed 6% to 11% of cases to be appealed (ICAR 2007a). In contrast, at the Asylum and Immigration Tribunals, about 20% of appellants gain asylum (Home Office 2008). Just because the legal proceedings at removal centers are rushed, that does not mean that refused asylum seekers are expeditiously deported. They may remain in detention for months or years while the British government tries to arrange their removal.[6] The fast-track system exists, BID believes, "for the administrative convenience of the state," not for the sake of justice (2006: 36).

Asylum seekers who are not detained, who have been released from detention, or whose applications have been rejected are eligible to receive very limited financial assistance and accommodation from the National Asylum Support Service (NASS), part of the UKBA. However, to receive this help rejected asylum seekers must sign a statement that they will leave the country "voluntarily." Some forgo the aid, because they are afraid of coming to the attention of the authorities or losing custody of their children. They "face a choice between homelessness and destitution here [in the UK], or persecution or even death in their country of origin" (Refugee Council 2007b: 5). A refused asylum seeker said, "People kept asking me to sign. But I said no, I can't do that. To do so would be to sign my death warrant" (Still Human Still Here 2007a: 3).

The financial assistance from NASS hardly seems worth the risk. For several years it was stuck at £35 per week, "calculated nicely at 70% of what is deemed the minimum necessary for a decent life, and therefore not a sum to be envied," Moorehead wrote (2005: 132). According to the British, Scottish, and Welsh Refugee Councils:

> Failed asylum seekers at the end of their process who cannot
> be returned home but are complying with reporting require-
> ments are able to obtain very limited help from the Home Office.
> This support is known as 'Section 4' or 'hard case' support and
> is in the form of accommodation and weekly vouchers worth
> £35 which can only be used in certain stores and on particular
> essential goods. In many cases, vouchers cannot be used to buy
> clothes, shoes, nappies [diapers], sanitary items, pens, aspirin,
> paracetamol [acetaminophen] or to get a haircut. As of September
> 2008, just over 10,000 asylum seekers were receiving Section 4
> support. There are many thousands more who receive no sup-
> port at all. ("Joint Parliamentary Briefing" 2009: 7)

Asylum seekers and asylees may be "dispersed" to cities far from relatives, friends, and work in London. Asylum seekers are not allowed to apply for a work permit until they have been in the UK for a year. Their housing is sometimes classified as unfit for human habitation. Refused asylum seekers have no right to public housing, are not legally permitted to work, cannot claim government benefits or tax credits, are not eligible for most NASS support, and cannot receive routine medical treatment at a hospital. A 2009 study by a community organization in Leeds found that some refused asylum seekers, who were afraid to apply to NASS, were barely surviving on £5 per week (Taylor 2009). Several cases in which NASS denied assistance to destitute asylum seekers went to the courts, which found that the denials had violated the European Convention on Human Rights.

Asylees and other immigrants can take English courses at colleges, refugee organizations, and private language schools but may be asked to prove their immigration status in order to enroll. Unemployed refugees receive free tuition, but asylum seekers must pay for the course at the overseas student rate, even if they are destitute or receiving NASS support. They are not eligible for any support if they attend university classes. In 2007 the government sought to cut back provision of ESOL by laying off teachers as a cost-saving measure, making access to English language instruction harder than ever.

These mean-spirited policies have severe consequences for vulnerable people. A Zairean asylum seeker asked: "Is it a crime to be an asylum seeker in the United Kingdom? I am saddened and powerless in the face of the situation in a civilized country where human rights are respected. I have suffered and I continue to suffer psychologically and mentally" (Kushner and Knox 1999: 382). A Congolese asylum seeker living on the street told an interviewer: "I have lost myself. I came to the UK for safety and protection and to fulfil my right to live with dignity and liberty. Now, though, I feel as if I'm being morally tortured instead. . . . If I am sent back to my country, I will be killed" (*New Londoners* 2007: 7).

In 2007 the Parliamentary Joint Committee on Human Rights declared: "The government is practicing a deliberate policy of destitution. . . . We believe that the deliberate use of inhumane treatment against asylum seekers is unacceptable and falls below the requirements of the common law of humanity and of international human rights law" (Still Human Still Here 2007a: 3).

The intention of destitution policy seems to be to convince the asylum seeker to give up the search for sanctuary and "voluntarily" leave the UK. At £11,000 per removal and with a backlog of more than 400,000 cases, it seems unlikely that the government can carry out enough deportations to rid the country of all its failed asylum seekers anytime soon. In 2001 then-Home Secretary Jack Straw promised that 30,000 failed asylum seekers would be removed by the end of the year, but the Home Office had to back away from this goal, because it was impossible. Removals reached a yearly peak of 18,235 in 2006.

Forced removals have a way of going wrong, precipitating unwanted publicity. In some cases in Europe, "people have been bound, gagged and even injected with sedatives. Some have died of asphyxiation" (Stevens 2004: 312). Most removals are carried out by private contractors and take place on scheduled commercial flights.[7] If the deportee protests or resists, the pilot may refuse to transport him or her. As a result the Home Office began shipping failed asylum seekers out on charter flights—more than 75 flights in 2006–07. Destinations included Eastern European countries, Iraqi Kurdistan, Democratic Republic of Congo, and Vietnam. Governments resist spending the time and money to monitor returned asylum seekers, so some human rights groups have tried to investigate the fates of deportees. A 2002 report by Pro Asyl, a German organization, found that 40 returnees to Turkey had been "subjected to arrest and detention, with some tortured again before managing to return to Germany" (ICAR 2007c: 24).

Feeling under pressure to carry out Straw's removal policy, in 2002 the British government instituted dawn deportation raids, especially but not exclusively in Scotland, where thousands of asylum seekers had been "dispersed" starting in 2000. Taken by surprise, asylum seekers had no time to call a lawyer or gather their personal property. There were "no Home Office guidelines stipulating that asylum seekers must be given enough time to wind up their affairs before being removed," nor was there time to challenge their imminent deportation (ICAR 2007c: 23).

When their neighbors were taken away at dawn, people in Scotland became distressed and began to protest. A student wrote: "The government had started to deport a lot of families and it was a big shock because nearly everyone in our school lost a friend. . . . It just didn't seem right how they can just come to your house at late hours or early in the mornings and get you without anyone knowing that you've gone because they didn't even let people to pack [*sic*] their stuff or say their goodbyes" ("Dawn raids" 2007: 2). In response students at Drumchapel High School in Glasgow circulated petitions, organized demonstrations, and contacted their Member of Parliament.

Saida and her family had lived in Scotland for five years as asylum seekers, so she was very affected by the raids:

> I was quite worried and at the same time very angry. I was worried because most of us have no status and demonstrating against the deportation system was not that easy for me. Although I was not alone I still had the fear that this demonstration may cause us to face problems in the future. And I was angry because I have been living here for nearly five years but we are living with this sense of fear that my family would be deported next. I have seen my friends who have gone through this and I really don't want my family to suffer from this humiliation. This sense of fear is killing us. We die each day. All we want from them is to let us live in peace. . . . ("Dawn raids" 2007: 6)

Durr-e Maquoon, a student who was deported with her family to Pakistan, wrote to her classmates in Scotland. The family was detained while registering weekly at the Home Office. The following Monday her class was informed of her situation. "Our first thought was 'why'? After all, Durr-e hadn't done anything wrong," a classmate wrote ("Dawn raids" 2007: 9). After a few days their teacher let them telephone her at the detention center. Officials hung up the phone during the conversation. "We found this pathetic that we couldn't have a conversation with our 14-year-old friend" ("Dawn Raids . . ." 2007: 9).

According to Durr-e, the family's arrest "was really shocking to us. We were terrified" ("Dawn Raids . . ." 2007: 11). Her five-year-old sister was especially affected. During the trip to the detention center they had no food for six hours. After a weekend at the Scottish detention center, Dungavel, the family was sent about 350 miles south to Yarl's Wood. The journey took eight and a half hours in a sealed van with no ventilation.

Late that night they were transported to the airport. Durr-e's mother asked for a lawyer, saying their deportation violated the law against refoulement. "They said if we refuse to go they will put handcuffs on us and drag us. They also said that they will split the children from the mother." The next morning the whole family was put on a plane. At Lahore, Pakistan, officials questioned Durr-e's mother for hours; "they were really rude with her" ("Dawn Raids . . ." 2007: 12).

At every stop the authorities "searched us like we were some criminals. . . . We don't have any house or property. We are living in someone else's house right now. We are really worried" ("Dawn Raids . . ." 2007: 13). Their anxiety stemmed from the fact that they were members of the Ahmadiya Muslim community, persecuted in Pakistan. A few months before their return to the country, masked gunmen had invaded an Ahmadiya mosque, killed eight worshippers, and wounded 20. Durr-e's story ended abruptly there.

After repeated outcry from Scottish and English citizens and the Scottish National Party government, the Home Office suspended dawn raids in Scotland in early 2008 but resumed them later that year. This obdurate insistence on continuing to implement harsh policies, despite high court decisions and years of advocacy on behalf of asylum seekers by community organizations and NGOs, has driven many campaigners to despair. One told me that she had long since given up hope of persuading the government to treat asylum seekers humanely, but she kept working for reform of the system out of a deep sense of obligation to denounce what she was witnessing. Some had hoped that Tony Blair's New Labour government, in office from 1997 to 2007, would institute new policies in line with Britain's obligations under international law, but they were bitterly disappointed when it continued or even hardened the anti-immigrant policies of the previous Conservative regime.

For example, "Jack Straw, when foreign secretary, suggested that Britain might decide not to reaffirm its commitment to the 1951 [Refugee] Convention. Britain thereby became the first government to threaten to pull out" (Moorehead 2005: 148). As home secretary, Straw proposed that asylum seekers be sent to offshore processing centers on the fringe of the European Union or in the regions they came from, perhaps in imitation of Australia's Pacific Solution. In 2004 the Blair government even proposed to pay Tanzania £4 million in aid in exchange for taking in the UK's refused Somali asylum seekers. Tanzania declined (Moorehead 2005: 149).

The Labour government of Gordon Brown did little to ameliorate asylum seekers' living or detention conditions, despite some change in public attitudes. A 2007 poll "revealed that over two-thirds of the British public would favor asylum seekers being allowed to work" (Still Human Still Here 2007b: 7). Perhaps the public recognized that if asylum seekers could work legally, they would pay more than 1 billion pounds in taxes. However, Brown's promise that he would create "British jobs for British workers" only stoked anti-immigrant sentiment as economic conditions worsened in 2008 and 2009, and legal workers from new European Union countries kept arriving in the UK. As ever, asylum seekers were handy scapegoats, easily blamable for the government's failure to provide adequate services, housing, health care, and other social benefits.

Xenophobia has been customary in Britain for hundreds of years, but asylum seekers (especially Jews) first seem to have become the targets of powerful newspaper publishers in the 1930s, when anti-Semitic sentiment was openly expressed. In his study of the British media's portrayal of asylum seekers, journalist Roy Greenslade pointed out that they "have been made into scapegoats for a variety of society's current ills, or alleged ills, such as the level of crime, the liberalism of the welfare state, the housing shortage and an apparently overcrowded island" (2005: 5). They are "cast as interlopers who have little or nothing in common with settled migrant communities. But, despite editors' success in having demonized the concept and practice of asylum-seeking, and turning the very phrase into a term of abuse, the casual misuse of terminology reveals an underlying anti-immigrant mindset. . . . in reality, popular newspapers remain opposed to all immigration."

The principal purveyors of anti-asylum seeker sentiment, Britain's four top-selling tabloid newspapers, *The Sun, Daily Mail, Daily Express,* and *Daily Star,* sell an average of some 7,500,000 papers per day. It is estimated that three people read each purchased copy of the tabloids, so that some 22 million people—more than one-third of the country's population—read the four top papers per day. As a result the tabloids are tremendously powerful formers of public opinion. The more respectable papers tend not to challenge the tabloids, and even the BBC repeats some of their claims without challenging them. The tabloids have been waging a campaign against asylum seekers for more than 20 years, and as a result the public is negatively disposed toward them.

Stevens pointed out in 2004 (261–62):

> There has been a tendency to categorize asylum seekers—tacitly by the government, explicitly in the tabloid press—as "bogus refugees," "scroungers," "economic migrants," even "criminals" and "terrorists." Seldom a day passes at present when "asylum" does not receive media coverage. . . . There is constant talk of fraudulent claims, illegal entrants playing the system, "floods" of asylum seekers, the trafficking and smuggling of asylum seekers by ruthless gangs, the ineffective removals system, and the financial burden on the UK taxpayer. Little wonder, then, that a beleaguered government promises greater restriction and turns to the law for assistance.

By the late 1980s, Greenslade wrote, intolerance and reckless disregard for the truth in the tabloids "tipped over into an aggressive and unpalatable nastiness" (2005: 10). Even after the establishment of a Press Complaints Commission, the tabloids continued to stoke moral panics about asylum seekers and illegal migrants. In 2004 the *Express* carried on a vicious campaign against the Roma, forecasting a "huge gipsy invasion" from Eastern Europe.

"These stories led to *Express* journalists taking the unprecedented step of writing to the Press Complaints Commission to complain about being put under pressure by their senior executives to write slanted articles," Greenslade wrote. "The paper's union members had previously complained, in August 2001, about their paper's 'sustained campaign against asylum seekers in pursuit of circulation.'" The PCC had refused to intervene on that occasion "because it dealt with public complaints, not journalists." In another instance an independent journalist investigated one of the tabloids' wilder stories and found it to be a fabrication. Months later the paper published a "clarification" of the story on page 41 after the PCC declared it to be false.

Greenslade concluded: "People want to believe what they are reading because it confirms their prejudices. . ." (2005: 29). Politicians cite these prejudices as justification for their draconian policies against asylum seekers. So the cycle goes, on and on, feeding on itself. In this context it is all the more remarkable that community groups throughout the country have campaigned to keep asylum seekers from being detained and deported.

A story about such a grassroots campaign was published in the liberal *Guardian* in April 2009. When Tony Lola, a nine-year-old Congolese boy, and his mother were threatened with deportation, children and teachers at his school in Didsbury, near Manchester, "organized a petition that collected thousands of signatures and the children urged the home secretary to reverse the decision to deport Tony" (Carter 2009: 1). His mother had been an activist in an opposition political movement in the Democratic Republic of Congo. After she fled to the UK, leaving then-six-year-old Tony with relatives, "he was arrested and held in Congolese police custody." His family later sent him to join his mother in England.

Tony's teacher said: "When we were told the [deportation] letter had come, I had to explain about it to the whole class and they were stunned into silence. The next day they started asking questions and the class said they wanted to talk about it. It brought a lump to my throat thinking about the impact, not just on Tony but on his peers." One of the teachers who led the campaign commented: "The community in Didsbury has become part of their extended family. It is a white, middle-class area. When [Tony's mother] first came here, some people were suspicious, as they didn't have experience of asylum seekers. But she has won everyone over." As a result of the campaign and the *Guardian*'s coverage, the immigration minister granted the boy and his mother leave to remain in the UK. In this case the community, not the government, gave sanctuary to people fleeing persecution.[8]

As heartwarming as such stories may be, the official system that makes public campaigns necessary remains firmly in place.

Thousands of asylum seekers languish in removal centers; tens of thousands are deported to the deadly situations they fled; hundreds of thousands struggle to survive in destitution; and hundreds of millions of pounds are spent on the manufacture and maintenance of cruelty and suffering. What then does asylum mean?

CHAPTER TEN

Asylum vs. Sanctuary

We are not in hiding. We have come out into the daylight.

SANS-PAPIERS MANIFESTO, 1997 (Hayter 2004: 143)

In 2007 the Independent Asylum Commission organized a series of events around Britain to gather evidence about the situation of asylum seekers. These public hearings featured testimony by asylum seekers and their supporters, as well as representatives of the UK Border Agency, police, local authorities, and pressure groups hostile to immigration, as part of a comprehensive review of the UK's asylum system. The commission published three reports about its findings in 2008. The final one included the results of a survey by the Public Attitudes Research Project on asylum and sanctuary (Hobson, Cox, and Sagovsky 2008d: 15). The survey found:

- People do not share a common understanding of the term "asylum" or "asylum seeker" and do not strongly associate it with people fleeing persecution;
- People view "asylum" as an overwhelmingly negative term with associations including mental illness, oppressive and disordered institutions, criminality, terrorism, benefit fraud, and "bogus" foreigners. They cannot relate the term "asylum" to their own lives, except in a few cases negatively, citing places of stress and oppression as "my asylum";
- People are not able to distinguish accurately between the different meanings of the term "asylum" or "asylum seeker"

and "economic migrant," "refugee," and "irregular or illegal immigrant";

- People have a strong perception that "asylum" is bad and has a negative impact on their local area.

In sharp contrast, the survey also found:

- People share a common understanding of the term "sanctuary" as a safe, secure place in which someone can take refuge;
- People view sanctuary as an overwhelmingly positive word and can relate the concept to their own lives positively, many even citing their home, bedroom, the countryside, or a spiritual retreat as examples of their own personal sanctuary;
- People also understand and accept that sanctuary can refer to a place of safety for those from abroad who are fleeing persecution;
- People believe strongly that it is a good thing that the UK provides sanctuary to those fleeing persecution.

Consequently the IAC decided to stop using the word "asylum" and start referring to sanctuary in all its publications and presentations. It seems like such a simple solution to two decades of scapegoating, abuse, and exclusion. Would changing the name of the institution really change anything for the strangers who seek shelter, the hosts who provide it, and the members of the public who stand by and watch, walk by and do not notice, or shake their fists in anger and rejection?

The history of sanctuary and asylum shows that the two things are not the same. So merely changing the name might help a little but not enough to solve the problems of 500,000 failed asylum seekers and undocumented migrants in Britain's destitution underground. Since the 17th century, when the British Parliament formally abolished it as a legal institution, sanctuary has remained a morally and religiously based phenomenon that often takes place outside or against the law. Meanwhile asylum has become a formal category in international and national law, distinguishing the treatment and status of one kind of person (the asylum seeker) from other kinds (the refugee, the immigrant, and the undocumented migrant). The word has been used to exclude and discriminate as much as to include and welcome. As a legal institution asylum is provisional, temporary, and often grudging, hedged by rules and restrictions, whereas sanctuary is an act of hospitality, generosity, and compassion. Like mercy, to which it is closely related, sanctuary's quality is not strained: "It droppeth as the gentle rain from heaven / Upon the earth beneath." As a form of reciprocal altruism, sanctuary "is twice blessed / It blesseth him that gives and him that takes."

Those who seek and give sanctuary operate in a separate realm, far from the hearing room where asylum is granted or denied (usually denied, in most places). And even when the authorities grant asylum, real, enduring sanctuary—in the form of integration into the host society—may be difficult or impossible to obtain. For every ballet dancer who leapt over the Iron Curtain to freedom and acclaim, thousands of unknown refugees have struggled and often failed to establish themselves in the new country or to reclaim the kind of life they left behind when they fled their native land. Sanctuary can compensate for but cannot reconstitute what has been lost. True integration often has to wait until the next generation, and sometimes it does not come even then.

Those who seek sanctuary or asylum suffer from what the sociologist Erving Goffman called spoiled identity; they are stigmatized by their flight and their outsider status. Reconstructing their dignity can take decades. In the meantime they may be treated as nonpersons, herded into "pig pen" enclosures in front of Lunar House, detained for months in windowless tents in Texas, shackled on their way to hospital, disbelieved when they tell their story in court. And yet they sometimes manage to transcend and defeat the stigma.

For example, in 2007 Rotimi Adebari was elected mayor of Portlaoise—the first black mayor in Irish history. Forced to flee Ogun State, Nigeria, by religious persecution, he took his wife and two children to Dublin in 2000. He was one of 30,000 asylum seekers to arrive in Ireland since the mid-1990s. Between 1997 and 2007 Ireland's foreign-born residents increased from 1.5% to 10% of the country's population.

As an asylum seeker Adebari was not allowed to work for pay, so he set up a support group for the unemployed, then earned a master's degree in intercultural studies at Dublin City University. He eventually went to work for the Laois County Council "on an integration project for new immigrants" (Bowcott 2007). He was gracious enough to say that only individuals were prejudiced, not society as a whole. "The immigrant community has to come out of its shell and the local community has to accept them. They need to meet in the middle. Immigration is never going to go away," he said, calling Ireland "home."

Perhaps even more extraordinary is the story of the Sans-Papiers [Without Papers], undocumented migrants and failed asylum seekers who created an independent, radical movement in Paris and other French cities in the mid-1990s. They became visible in March 1996, when 324 African migrants occupied the Church of St. Ambrose in Paris. Evicted after a few days, they moved on, starting hunger strikes in Paris, Lille, and Versailles and setting up 25 collectives around the country. In August 1996,

> 300 undocumented African women, children and men were violently evicted by police from the St. Bernard Church in Paris, where they had taken sanctuary for several months. The Sans-Papiers of St. Bernard have organized several occupations, gone on hunger strikes and toured France in a caravan to mobilize support against deportations. They demand papers for all, an end to detention and deportation, the return of all deportees, and the repeal of all immigration laws. (Cissé 1997: 1)

After the incident at St. Bernard, 20,000 protesters marched in solidarity with the Sans-Papiers in Paris. In 1998 Sans-Papiers occupied Notre Dame de la Gare and St. Jean de Montmartre churches in Paris in response to passage of repressive anti-immigrant laws. In 1999 the Sans-Papiers National Coordinating Committee convened a large demonstration in Paris to call for regularization of all the undocumented migrants in Europe. One of their leaflets said: "To accept the Europe as conceived by states and governments, both of the right and of the left, means to accept the vision of a world where inequality and misery reign while a minority which monopolizes all wealth protects itself by every means possible. . . . To tolerate this situation means to tolerate apartheid on a world scale" (Hayter 2000: 146).

The Sans-Papiers' first visible leader was the outspoken Madjiguene Cissé of Senegal. In a booklet published in the UK, Cissé wrote:

> There were organizations which came to support us and which were used to helping immigrants in struggle. They were also used to acting as the relay between immigrants . . . and the authorities, and therefore more or less to manage the struggle.

They would tell us, "Right, we the organizations have made an appointment to explain this or that"; and we had to say, "But we can explain it very well ourselves." If we had not taken our autonomy, we would not be here today. . . . (Hayter 2004: 146)

According to Helene Trauner, "What stands out is the strong presence of women and families within the movement and mobilizations, resisting police forces, holding sit-ins and strikes or occupying public spaces" (2005: 232). Women constituted more than 30% of participating adults in the Sans-Papiers movement.

Over time the Paris group split over disagreements about tactics and alliances with political parties. But they were back in the headlines in April 2008, when, with the help of the General Confederation of Labor (CGT), about 1,000 Sans-Papiers launched strikes and occupations in the cleaning, construction, retail, security, and catering industries where they worked. The government responded by offering to legalize 1,000 undocumented workers out of the estimated 400,000 in France. In May the Sans-Papiers occupied CGT headquarters in Paris after the CGT would not allow them to submit their own applications for legal residency to the local government. One member of the group declared: "The CGT has taken the Sans-Papiers movement hostage. We are taking the union hall hostage" (Ira and Lerougetel 2008: 1). They were still occupying the building a month later.

Yiribou, an Ivoirian who had lived in France for nine years before being "regularized," told an interviewer:

The worst thing about not having papers was always being afraid, hiding from the cops, knowing that at any moment they could come and say, 'You, show me your papers.' But all the same you had to go out every day and work to feed your family, in spite of the risk. . . . To get your papers, you've got to go and make your request in a big, big group. If you go alone, they mess with you. . . . If you go in a large group, they know you can't be fooled, and it's harder for them to arrest you. But you have to fight for your papers. You can't just go and make the request, because the government is against you. You have to fight. (Maltby 2008: 3)

In the venerable style of French labor militancy, the Sans-Papiers do not request; they demand. They seek not only sanctuary but visibility, and they act unhesitatingly, sometimes at great risk, to secure it for themselves. Their classically French discourse expresses their claim to national identity:

> We came to France with the intention of working here and because we had been told that France was the "homeland of the Rights of Man"; we could no longer bear the poverty and the oppression which was rife in our countries, we wanted our children to have full stomachs, and we dreamed of freedom. . . . The prime minister of France had promised that families would not be separated: we demand that this promise finally be kept and that the principles of humanity often proclaimed by the government be implemented. We demand that the European and international conventions, to which the French Republic has subscribed, are respected. (Hayter 2004: 143)

The Sans-Papiers defy the definition imposed on them as nonpersons by standing up to defend their interests. In acting politically they reconstruct their dignity. As Paulo Freire would put it, they become the subjects, not the objects, of their own history.

In Germany opposition to restrictive asylum policies has taken a different form. As in other European countries, "public opinion polls indicate that over 60% of Germans want immigration stopped or reduced, and confirm a wide-held belief that at least some of the foreigners living in Germany will return to their country of origin" (Tazreiter 2004: 91).

Even so, German NGOs and the Green Party quietly but firmly question these attitudes. The Berlin Green Party monitors immigration detention conditions and informs NGOs of detention practices. The Greens also publish a newsletter on immigration issues. In addition, the Organization against Deportation started in Berlin to coordinate campaigns, disseminate information, and provide legal representation to immigration detainees. Some 70 members "meet on a regular basis to discuss individual cases, organize visits to detention facilities and plan public action" (Tazreiter 2004: 180).

The best-known NGO working on asylum issues in Germany is Pro Asyl, founded in 1986 to do public education and lobbying. Major political parties called it "radical and extremist" in the mid-1990s because it strongly criticized government policies. Since 1998 Pro Asyl has operated a legal center at Frankfurt Airport, where detained asylum seekers were going on hunger strike and attempting suicide in significant numbers. Pro Asyl makes 50 lawyers available to advise arriving asylum seekers of their rights.

Other German organizations doing refugee work have included the Red Cross, the Trade Union Federation, Catholic and Protestant churches, and religious charities such as Diakonie and Caritas. In general, Tazreiter wrote, German NGOs work on individual cases, understanding that narrow definitions of refugees exclude some who need humanitarian protection. The Jesuit Refugee Service, an international organization operating in Germany and other receiving countries, goes somewhat further by helping undocumented migrants who are afraid to return home.

When they learn that a detainee is about to be deported, German NGOs often intervene. They even give pamphlets to passengers boarding international flights, asking them "to draw the attention of the captain and crew to the involuntary and violent nature of the deportation" and "to protest until the detainee is allowed to disembark from the plane prior to departure" (Tazreiter 2004: 181).

In the early 1990s a church sanctuary movement sprang up in Germany. Thirty-three Catholic, Protestant, and Independent churches and convents in Bavaria gave sanctuary to undocumented migrants between 1989 and 1996. "The decision to give an asylum seeker the protection of a church or parish is an unambiguous statement that the state has failed in its obligation of protecting those fleeing political persecution" (Tazreiter 2004: 182). In a small number of cases church sanctuary has led to legal appeals and granting of refugee status.

In Munich in the mid-1990s, in an effort to draw public attention to the plight of asylum seekers,

> a group of local organizations who worked with asylum seekers primarily as volunteers, together with the Munich Refugee Council, erected a shipping container in . . . the central shopping district of Munich, to demonstrate the living circumstances of asylum seekers. Containers were regularly used as hostel-style accommodation. The containers were filled with all sorts of goods—food and clothing, which were made available for the asylum seekers to buy, most often with the use of coupons. The food and clothing were of inferior quality, and it was not uncommon for food items . . . to have expired use-by dates. Yet prices of these items were often higher than in regular shops. . . . This campaign drew a significant response from the public of Munich. (Tazreiter 2004: 179)

It is difficult to determine the long-term effects of such actions on public opinion. Nonetheless, local groups and NGOs continue to assist asylum seekers, express their opposition to government policies, and try to educate the public in Germany and other countries. Regional organizations, such as the European Council on Refugees and Exiles (ECRE), maintain networks and coalitions that publish reports on asylum policies and practices, develop analyses and positions on issues and laws, and lobby politicians and policymakers. With 69 institutional members from 30 countries, ECRE "aspires to influence the European agenda and to promote the protection and integration of asylum seekers, refugees and internally displaced people" (ECRE 2009). However, because decision making on asylum policy takes place in obscure offices or secret intergovernmental meetings, far from public view, organizations such as ECRE have little apparent effect. Their measured, well-mannered advocacy gains scant public attention.

Some organizations operate behind the scenes. For example, the Medical Justice Network (MJN), composed of 150 former detainees, physicians, and health professionals in the London area, lobbies "to end medical abuse in immigration detention centres" (2007). Not a registered charity, the MJN is not allowed to give immigration advice and cannot treat patients. Its objectives are to

- give a voice to those in immigration detention;
- publicize inadequate medical care and the damaging psychological effects of indefinite detention;
- take action to secure health care in detention centers;
- pressure for implementation of Home Office regulations prohibiting detention of torture survivors, the mentally ill and children.

It carries out no public activities; instead its members work in their professional capacity to try to influence policy makers and implementers.

Another organization working behind the scenes is Bail for Immigration Detainees (BID), which has nine paid staff, 24 volunteers, and three offices in London, Oxford, and Portsmouth. BID attorneys run bail workshops at detention centers, submit bail applications, provide free legal representation at the Asylum and Immigration Tribunals, do research for campaigns, and "document and publicize injustices." On a very modest budget of £150,000 they help thousands of detainees each year. Their activities in 2005–06 included presenting written evidence to parliamentary inquiries and oral submissions to a House of Lords committee; meeting with the immigration minister; pressuring the Legal Service Commission to provide advice to detainees; holding a public meeting in London on deaths and forced removals of detainees; and presenting papers at meetings and conferences.

One of BID's most compelling cases involved a failed Iranian asylum seeker who finally received bail after 23 months in detention. He could not be deported, because the Iranian government refused to provide him with travel documents. Three months after his release on bail, he was re-detained "while reporting to an immigration enforcement unit" (BID n.d.). BID found him a lawyer who challenged his detention and gained bail for him again.

Periodic initiatives aim to affect public opinion. In the 1990s local people launched the Campaign to Close Campsfield (a removal center located near Oxford). For years they held a monthly vigil outside the center, and in 1995 they camped on adjacent land owned by the defense ministry for weeks until they were evicted. Large numbers of Oxford University faculty members signed letters to the prime minister calling for an end to the detention of asylum seekers. Local campaigns against detention also sprang up in Kent, in Cambridgeshire, and near Heathrow Airport. Ethnic community organizations representing Algerians, Zaireans, and Kurds have campaigned on behalf of asylum seekers. Many nongovernmental organizations, including the Campaign against Racial Discrimination, the Joint Council for the Welfare of Immigrants, the Institute of Race Relations, the British Refugee Council, Asylum Aid, and the Churches' Commission for Racial Justice, have organized and participated in campaigns or published reports exposing the plight of asylum seekers in Britain.

Other UK initiatives included Citizens for Sanctuary (CS), which came into being to implement the recommendations of the Independent Asylum Commission. In 2009 CS local groups persuaded the UKBA to transform the squalid reception area of Lunar House into a Welcome Centre; set up internships for refugees and asylum seekers in England and Wales; demonstrated around the country in support of asylum seekers who had to travel long distances at their own expense to report weekly to the police; and persuaded Manchester Metropolitan University to offer five places to young asylum seekers.

The national Still Human Still Here campaign started in late 2006 with the backing of nongovernmental and religious groups. A few months later a large march through central London streets and a rally at Trafalgar Square expressed the campaign's concerns. Speakers, including bishops and MPs, called on the British government to

- end the threat and use of destitution "as a tool of government policy against refused asylum seekers";
- "continue firm support and accommodation of refused asylum seekers as provided during the asylum process and grant permission to work" until they leave the UK or receive leave to remain;
- provide full access to health care and education to failed asylum seekers and their families.

Thirty-nine organizations, from Amnesty International UK to the Welsh Refugee Council, supported the campaign, which was still going on two years later. It seemed that the government and most of the public did not want to hear their pleas.

Historians Tony Kushner and Katharine Knox have pointed out that "governments and their state apparatus have often been too eager to satisfy negative sentiment and too willing to dismiss alternative voices calling for more generous refugee policies. . . . anti-asylum and anti-immigration laws have only legitimized and increased hostile sentiment." Nonetheless, they emphasize "the vital role played by ordinary people in not only caring for refugees locally but also in campaigning for their well-being at the level of national and international politics" (1999: 402). The Still Human Still Here campaign might not have attained its objectives in the short term, but it bore witness to the plight of 500,000 destitute asylum seekers, and its cosponsors persisted in speaking out and working on their behalf.

Events in Scotland show the importance of local people in providing something more than temporary refuge to asylum seekers. In 2000 the Home Office dispersed asylum seekers to various cities far from London. As Stevens recounted,

Perhaps the most notorious case of ill-conceived dispersal was organized by Glasgow City Council, which accommodated more than 2,000 asylum seekers in one of the city's most deprived [public housing] estates. . . . In August 2001, tensions between local youths and young Kurdish asylum seekers reached a peak, resulting in a fatal stabbing. This incident helped publicize one of the worst aspects of the system: the "dumping" of asylum seekers in rundown and unsuitable properties. (2004: 252)

A survey by the housing NGO Shelter found that 26% of dwellings set aside for asylum seekers were unfit for human habitation, and 86% were unfit for the number of occupants housed; more than 80% posed a fire hazard.

Ahlam Souidi, an Algerian asylum seeker, told me in 2008 how shocked she had been by the house she was sent to in Glasgow. Classified as unfit for habitation, with no heating, it had stood empty for decades. The next-door neighbor harassed her and her family during their first night in the house, but authorities did nothing to stop the harassment. One of her children contracted chronic eczema from the dampness. They stayed for four years before the house was demolished and they were resettled in better accommodation.

Ahlam started to hate Glasgow and Glaswegians and became severely depressed. Her health suffered, and she found it difficult to learn English. She and her family worried constantly about being deported. They watched as Iraqi neighbors were taken away in handcuffs during dawn raids and children were separated from their parents. On one occasion UKBA agents and police broke down the apartment door of a Kurdish asylum seeker family. The father threatened to jump from a 20-storey window, and his wife had a heart attack. Protesters gathered for four hours until the father surrendered and was taken to jail. On another occasion a father threatened to throw his child out the window, and authorities stopped the raid.

At first Ahlam's petition for asylum was denied, and the family could see no future but detention. "But we are lucky to have local people and organizations to support us. We are very grateful to them," she said (interview with the author, January 2008). She is convinced that such pressure resulted in her family finally receiving indefinite leave to remain after about seven years of waiting. The local people who helped said they did not want to see asylum seekers treated unfairly in Scotland. They told her they were ashamed of government actions such as dawn raids.

Eventually Ahlam took English classes at the YMCA and began to feel better. She was the first member of the Framework for Dialogue, a committee that liaised with local officials, and she became active in the Scottish Refugee Council. Unable to work legally while she waited for her asylum case to be decided, she taught French at a local school as a volunteer. She joined the Scottish Refugee Policy Forum, a group of asylum seekers and refugees that met regularly with government agencies and policymakers. "We built a very strong bridge with the Home Office," she said. She also testified before a parliamentary human rights commission about the situation of asylum seekers in Glasgow.

Ahlam pointed out that Scotland's population was aging and declining; the country needed new workers. As more asylum seekers and refugees arrived, the economy improved, and so did local attitudes. The organizations she joined continue to campaign on behalf of asylum seekers, sponsoring visits to schools to talk about their situation and taking other actions to change public opinion.

Unable to return to Algeria, Ahlam said she no longer felt like a foreigner in Glasgow. Her youngest child was born in Scotland, and her oldest felt Scottish. Her life and the lives of her children were there. Still, she identified with new arrivals and was ready to help them. She and other members of the Refugee Policy Forum were seeking to turn it into an independent nonprofit organization, and she hoped to have a paid job there.

Through her activism Ahlam became integrated in the local community and made it her own. She had found—and achieved—enduring sanctuary.

Eveline Louden was one of the Scots who helped people like Ahlam. A longtime resident of the Toryglen public housing estate in southern Glasgow, she began doing volunteer community organizing there in the early 1990s. Developed in the 1950s and 1960s, Toryglen is a rundown settlement located on barren marshland. Contractors found asbestos buried there when a "regeneration" project started in the mid-2000s. The site's former use as a dump might explain the high level of environmentally caused health problems from which residents suffer. Eveline pointed to a high chain-link fence that circled the entire estate during the redevelopment project and said it did not feel good to be surrounded in that way.

After the sudden arrival of hundreds of dispersed asylum seekers on the estate in 2000, Eveline became involved in efforts to help them. Now she manages Integrating Toryglen Community Ltd, a project funded by the Glasgow government, at Toryglen Community Base, an outwardly shabby but inwardly tidy and lively oasis in a row of boarded-up shops. In conjunction with nearby Langside College its Integration and Orientation Programme offers dozens of classes and workshops in everything from money management and home safety to health care and English as a Second Language. Life is still not easy for the residents of Toryglen, but they are working to make it better by helping asylum seekers integrate into the community.

A few miles away at Eastwood Parish Church, Rev. Moyna McGlynn was managing an asylum center in the parish hall. Started with seed money from eight churches, funded by the Glasgow government and staffed by about 20 volunteers, it served more than 200 families. The center provided a free shop, child care, help with housing, and health care and support for detainees. Rev. McGlynn said she would not want to persuade anyone to stay illegally in the UK, but she had helped people who were destitute. She did not ask them about their immigration status. "That's not our concern; our concern is humanitarian," she said (interview with the author, January 2008). Although there had been talk of giving sanctuary in churches to refused asylum seekers, she did not think her congregation could cope with it. But overall, she concluded, integration has worked in Glasgow.

Activists in Glasgow were the only ones I encountered in Britain who expressed optimism about the prospects of asylum seekers. They phrased their opinions in practical and pragmatic terms. For example, Rev. McGlynn suggested that the British government was unlikely to change its punitive immigration policies until it acknowledged that it would be impracticable to deport all the undocumented people, so adequate provision would have to be made for those in destitution. She and others pointed out that Britain would need to admit millions of young immigrants in the coming years to care for its aging population and replace older workers as they retired.

Why are things better for asylum seekers in Glasgow? The reasons are mainly political. Scottish asylum advocates told me that nationalists had gained ground after the British government devolved authority for local lawmaking to Scottish, Welsh, and Northern Irish Parliaments in 1997. In 2007 the Scottish National Party, which seeks independence for Scotland, won control of the Scottish Executive. Soon afterward it began jousting with London for greater control over immigration policies—protesting dawn deportation raids, detention of immigrant families, denial of some social welfare benefits to asylum seekers, and especially measures that negatively affected the children of asylum seekers. The Scottish government also pressed

London to grant amnesty in so-called legacy cases of asylum seekers such as Ahlam Souidi who had been waiting years for decisions on their claims. It made life easier for them by furnishing services and benefits that London refused to provide, such as access to higher education.

The first sentence of its 2006 action plan for refugees was "The Scottish Executive is committed to the integration of refugees" (Scottish Executive Equality Unit 2006). To that end it proposed to address refugees' housing, health, justice, employment and training, community development, and children's welfare. It organized a "One Scotland" campaign, encouraging schools to use advocacy organizations' materials containing accurate information on refugees and asylum seekers. It sponsored the Framework for Dialogue with the Scottish Refugee Council, the Glasgow City Council, and 10 refugee organizations. In addition, the Scottish Executive and local authorities allocated funding to grassroots projects and initiatives to help asylum seekers.

In Scotland, a smaller political arena than England, it is easier for asylum advocates to make and keep in contact with authorities at the local and regional level. Since most asylum seekers in Scotland live in Glasgow, community activists have one place on which to focus their efforts and thousands of potential activists to enlist. For all these reasons Scotland could provide a model for successful integration of asylum seekers, refugees, and immigrants throughout Britain—if the government and lawmakers could move beyond a punitive system based on fear and exclusion. Even if the government cannot bring itself to make changes in the short term, citizens and asylum seekers have shown that they can join together to challenge the system constructively and effectively.

In the United States asylum seekers and their advocates receive little public attention, which tends to focus on so-called illegal aliens who are thought to enter the country for economic reasons. But asylum seekers are detained in substandard conditions along with undocumented workers and criminal aliens awaiting deportation. As a result advocacy groups that have tried to inform the public about asylum issues have found themselves challenging the entire detention system. For example, the New Jersey Civil Rights Defense Committee's principal goal was to expose the illegality of immigration detention, not just abusive conditions. It used tried and true strategies to reach the public. A committee report described "holding community meetings and rallies, distributing flyers, issuing press releases, sending letters and stories to the press, and circulating a newsletter to detainees" (Alaya et al. 2007: 39–40). Citizen activists described detention conditions and read statements from detainees at county meetings. The response of elected officials was "hostility," but they could no longer plead ignorance. The Passaic County sheriff, whose jail was holding immigration detainees, blamed cancellation of the detention contract the county had with the federal government "on activist protests, and specifically on protests organized spontaneously inside and outside the facility." The committee commented,

> We think he was right. The decision came after several years of tireless activism on both sides of the prison wall, and shortly after the detainees circulated a petition demanding cancellation of the ICE contract. Our experience is that such coordination starts with local public protests demanding termination of ICE contracts and explaining the unconstitutional nature of the detentions. It is important to reach out to detainees, visit them, speak to the relatives and collect descriptions of how these severe hardships have impacted them and their families. (Alaya et al. 2007: 40)

One of the committee's informants was Farouk Abdel-Muhti, a stateless Palestinian who was detained for 23 months, eight months of which he spent in solitary confinement. Three months after his release he died of a heart attack at age 57 while speaking about detention. In jail "he fought against illegal and unconscionable detention by organizing the detainees." He organized meetings and helped detainees obtain legal representation. In retaliation ICE repeatedly transferred him, transforming him into what the New Jersey committee called "a political prisoner" (Alaya et al. 2007: 40).

Many local groups have sprung up to help immigration detainees. The Interfaith Coalition for the Rights of Immigration Detainees and the Families, a New Jersey grouping of about 20 organizations, sponsored vigils at the Bergen County jail. One of the participating groups, Families for Freedom, came into existence in September 2002 to fight secret detention and deportation of undocumented migrants, deportable criminal aliens, and unsuccessful asylum seekers after thousands of Arab males were arrested in the wake of the 9/11 attacks. Others included venerable faith-based organizations such as the American Friends Service Committee, ethnic community groups, and rights organizations such as the American Civil Liberties Union Prison Project, Human Rights Watch, and Human Rights First.

Some of the local and regional groups considered themselves part of the New Sanctuary Movement, described by the religionlink.com website as follows:

> Launched in 2007, the New Sanctuary Movement stretches from Massachusetts to Washington state, with 35 different networks in at least 10 states. The Associated Press estimated earlier this year [2008] that there are at least 13 undocumented immigrants currently receiving physical sanctuary at congregations around the country. Thousands more immigrants—illegal and legal—have been aided by the movement with clothing, food, money and legal counseling. Among the movement's main goals is a more compassionate U.S. immigration policy. (religionlink.com 2008)

The name of the new movement pays homage to the 1980s Sanctuary Movement, but it is decentralized, operating on the local level with no national coordinating body or visible leaders. In 2009 the New Sanctuary Movement's website was blank and the domain name was up for sale; but by 2010 several websites had sprung up, recording the activities of local sanctuary groups from Oregon to Pennsylvania.

For example, the New Sanctuary Movement of Philadelphia described itself as "an interfaith coalition of immigrants, congregations and individuals dedicated to taking a public stand for immigrant rights" and "part of the National New Sanctuary movement based in congregations around the United States which are connected to immigrant families who are facing the possibility of separation through deportation." The Philadelphia group started in summer 2008, when a synagogue "became the first officially affiliated New Sanctuary Movement congregation in Philadelphia" (New Sanctuary Movement 2010). As of 2010 three religious congregations—two Christian and one Jewish—had joined the local movement, which was staffed by two young people, including a Catholic Worker. The group visited immigration detainees, assisted families of detainees, attended deportation hearings, did outreach to community groups and congregations, conducted "Immigration 101" educational workshops at congregations, and conducted "Know Your Rights" training workshops with immigrants.

The New York City New Sanctuary Coalition posted a pledge on its website:

> The New Sanctuary Movement is a coalition of interfaith religious leaders and participating congregations, called by our faith to respond actively and publicly to the suffering of our immigrant brothers and sisters residing in the United States.
>
> We acknowledge that the large-scale immigration of workers and their families to the United States is a complex historical, global, and economic phenomenon that has many causes and does not lend itself to simplistic or purely reactive public policy solutions.
>
> We stand together in our faith that everyone, regardless of national origin, has basic common rights, including but not limited to: (1) livelihood; (2) family unity; and (3) physical and emotional safety.
>
> We witness the violation of these rights under current immigration policy, particularly in the separation of children from their parents due to unjust deportations, and in the exploitation of immigrant workers.
>
> We are deeply grieved by the violence done to families through immigration raids. We cannot in good conscience ignore such suffering and injustice.
>
> Therefore, We Covenant To:
>
> - Take a public, moral stand for immigrants' rights.
> - Reveal, through education and advocacy, the actual suffering of immigrant workers and families under current and proposed legislation.
> - Protect immigrants against hate, workplace discrimination and unjust deportation. (New York City New Sanctuary Coalition 2010)

Like many immigrant advocacy groups, these new sanctuary organizations did not distinguish between asylum seekers and undocumented immigrants. Nor did they mention offering sanctuary in places of worship or homes. They seemed to stay within the bounds of secular law.

In Arizona, where the 1980s Sanctuary Movement began, a number of groups began providing humanitarian aid in 2000 to undocumented migrants who were crossing the Sonoran Desert. Since 1994 the number of migrant deaths in the desert had been climbing after the Border Patrol made it impossible for them to cross the border in more accessible areas. The *Arizona Daily Star* was publishing reports of migrant deaths that moved veterans of the Sanctuary Movement to take water, food, and clothing to places in the desert where border-crossers were known to rest.

In March 2001 a new group, Humane Borders, placed 65-gallon water barrels on public and private land, and dozens of volunteers drove trucks out to the desert to refill the barrels. Pennants with the group's logo waved above the barrels. The logo consists of the North Star and the Big Dipper pouring water; it is based on "the code signals used during the Underground Railroad to ferry slaves away to the North" (Cook 2007: 5). Rev. Robin Hoover of Tucson's First Christian Church emerged as the group's leader. He sought permission from local, state, and federal agencies to maintain the barrels and insisted that he had no intention of violating any laws. He even obtained an annual grant of $25,000 for Humane Borders operations from the Pima County Board of Supervisors, which reasoned that "saving lives would save the city some of the $300,000 annually it had been costing to pick up, identify, autopsy, store, and bury bodies found in the desert" (Cook 2007: 12).

Other groups undertook humanitarian efforts in the desert—the Samaritans and No More Deaths. The Samaritans formed in 2002 to send out "voluntary patrols that would travel known migrant paths in the desert looking for people in need of water, food, or medical care" (Cook 2007: 5). They went beyond Hoover's approach by not asking permission to carry out rescue missions. No More Deaths (NMD), formed in 2003, "represented an escalation of aid to migrants in that it was to establish a permanent presence in the desert through camps, from which patrols would go in search of migrants in distress. It also broadened the campaign in favor of humanitarian aid (and against U.S. border policy) by creating a space and an activity that could chan-nel donations and volunteers from across the country." Both groups deliberately operated in the "grey area of legality" (Cook 2007: 5).

Other Tucson organizations focusing on border issues, many with overlapping membership lists, included Derechos Humanos, the Border Action Network, BorderLinks, the American Friends Service Committee of Arizona, and the American Civil Liberties Union. They carried out community organizing, public educational campaigns, lobbying, and monitoring of Border Patrol operations. Most of these groups were faith-based: "Religion provided the frame, cultural and symbolic resources and justification for . . . direct action" (Cook 2007: 9). Rev. John Fife and Fr. Ricardo Elford, two of the founders of the 1980s Sanctuary Movement, were intensely involved in their efforts.

Although the government and numerous immigration opponents insisted the migrants were economic rather than political, the new sanctuary groups drew implicit parallels with the situation in the 1980s, when "the United States was complicit in the torture, disappearances, and killings of tens of thousands of people in the region, and responsible for the welfare of those fleeing the violence and repression." Over time, "sanctuary movement veterans, as well as new adherents to the humanitarian aid groups, adjusted their diagnostic frame to justify support for economic migrants and not just political asylum seekers" (Cook 2007: 7). They contended that they had a moral obligation to help the innocent victims of NAFTA and globalization.

In mid-2005 Border Patrol agents arrested two young NMD volunteers, who had driven three migrants from the desert to a Tucson clinic, for "transportation in furtherance of an illegal presence in the United States" and conspiracy—felonies with maximum sentences of 15 years (Cook 2007: 18). A vocal campaign erupted in southern Arizona on the volunteers' behalf with the slogan "Humanitarian Aid Is Never a Crime." At about that time NMD made an agreement with the state of Sonora, Mexico, to operate a shelter there for returning migrants. From mid-2006 to mid-2007 NMD helped 136,000 migrants at two stations in Mexico. The group also set up a "mobile base camp" in the desert south of Tucson, "sending patrols out twice a day to walk, bike, or drive trails" in search of migrants needing assistance (Cook 2007: 20). In September 2006 the government dropped the charges against the volunteers.

However, in 2009 the federal government charged 18 NMD members with littering after they left bottles of drinking water on migrant trails inside the Buenos Aires National Wildlife Refuge near the Arizona–Mexico border. Sixteen of the charges were dropped, but two of the activists were convicted of the federal charges. Dan Millis appealed, and the U.S. Ninth Circuit Court of Appeals overturned his conviction in September 2010. The court said "that the clean bottles of drinking water placed on known migrant trails could not be considered 'garbage' due to their intended purpose of preventing death by exposure" (No More Deaths 2010).

Claiming to obey a higher moral law, "the frontline advocacy groups . . . were doing more than saving lives. They were simultaneously engaged in a struggle with officials over the permissibility and legality of humanitarian assistance" (Cook 2007: 21). Over time, an uneasy collaboration developed between the humanitarians and some government officials in the name of saving lives. John Fife told a *New York Times* reporter about a conversation he had had with the Border Patrol chief in southern Arizona: "You know I'm not going to turn over anyone I find to Border Patrol for deportation. He told me, 'If I find you reverting to your old ways, I'm going to put the cuffs on you myself'" (Goodstein 2001). Fife continued his involvement with the new movement and was not arrested. Meanwhile, in 2005 Congressman James Sensenbrenner sponsored legislation that would have criminalized both migrants and any organizations or individuals that helped them, but after an outcry by nonprofit groups his bill failed to pass.

Desert deaths continued to rise as migrant smugglers developed new and more remote routes in the continuing effort to evade capture. Border Patrol raids increased, and eventually numbers of migrants crossing the southern border fell as economic conditions in the United States became less accommodating to undocumented workers. Even so, Humane Borders, No More Deaths, Samaritans, and other groups continued providing humanitarian assistance to migrants in the desert. When I visited Tucson in 2008, as we drove from one water station to the next in the unforgiving April heat, volunteers pointed out migrants' personal effects recently abandoned on the side of the path. The *Daily Star* continued to print stories of their deaths in the desert. Along the highway I glimpsed a migrant weeping as she sat on the ground next to the bus that would deport her and dozens of others to Mexico. Fifty miles from the border the Border Patrol stopped every vehicle at a checkpoint, demanding identification. The ceaseless war against the undocumented continued, no matter how much water the volunteers provided.

Another initiative that harked back to the 1980s Sanctuary Movement was the struggle against local implementation of provision 287(g) of the 1996 immigration law, which authorizes police departments to apprehend and hand over undocumented or criminal aliens to ICE. Many towns and cities have signed on to the program. But activists in more than 30 localities that passed sanctuary laws or resolutions to protect Central American asylum seekers in the 1980s have tried to prevent city councils from allowing their police to enforce federal immigration laws.[1]

In 2007 the city council of Takoma Park, Maryland, just outside Washington, D.C., held a public hearing at which the police chief asked for permission to participate in 287(g), whose implementation would violate the town's sanctuary law, passed in 1985. The chief described meeting with representatives of a local advocacy group founded by Central American exiles, "whose objections focused on the reported unreliability of the federal crime database and with the importance of not fraying the immigrant community's trust in the police" (*The Washington Post* 2007b: B1). The city council unanimously voted to uphold the local sanctuary law after 25 of 28 local residents spoke against the police chief's proposal. (One of the speakers who supported the chief was a longtime Somali resident of the town, who worried about criminal activity by foreigners.) One of the local residents commented that Takoma Park was "a sanctuary for *me* against what is going on in this country. I have always been proud of the fact that our city is a place where I can feel not just physically safe but politically safe."

The supporters of sanctuary laws do not represent majority opinion in the United States, however. Opinion polls often report that most Americans see immigration as a problem, want to restrict all kinds of immigration, and do not distinguish among the various categories of legal and illegal migrants.[2] In 2007 an online anti-immigrant group called Numbers USA claimed 447,000 members, up from 50,000 in 2004. The group has lobbied Congress for years to reduce the number of immigrants admitted to the United States. In 2006 its website transmitted more than a million faxes opposing the immigration reform bill that then failed in the U.S. Senate. Other groups seek the denial of medical care, education, social services, driver's licenses, and housing to undocumented migrants, because they entered the country without authorization; they also call for the expulsion of some 12 million illegal aliens from the United States.

Sanctuary continues to be a controversial practice in the USA. Arizona's notorious immigration law SB 1070, passed in 2010, included a provision that criminalized aiding and abetting the entry of illegal aliens into the state. Eerily reminiscent of the charges against the members of the 1980s Sanctuary Movement, the provision was not overturned by a federal judge who struck down most other parts of the law. Then sanctuary became a national political issue when Republican Senate candidate Carly Fiorina of California called for the federal government to outlaw local ordinances protecting undocumented migrants in so-called sanctuary cities such as San Francisco and Takoma Park, MD (Garofoli and Joseph 2010: A1).

Americans' conception of the United States as a nation of immigrants mixes uneasily with strong traditional strains of nativism, racism, and intolerance. On the one hand, every year the United States resettles more refugees than any other country; on the other hand, ICE oversees the detention of thousands of asylum seekers under harsh, prison-like conditions. The underlying reasons for these contradictory policies, attitudes, and actions are not only political, economic, and social but profoundly human. Under cover of national security they express the seemingly inescapable, overwhelming fear and hatred of the unknown Other. Yet official expressions of meanness are countered by irrepressible acts of hospitality, as ordinary citizens protest and lobby on behalf of strangers and give refuge to them. It seems inevitable that the might of government will prevail and expel the stranger. But in American society as in so many others, sanctuary maintains its quiet strength, buttressed by ordinary people whose convictions impel them to take action.

CHAPTER ELEVEN

Does Asylum Have a Future?

*But the stranger that dwelleth with you shall be unto
you as one born among you, and thou shalt love him as
thyself; for ye were strangers in the land of Egypt.*

LEVITICUS 19:34

Everywhere capital encounters no obstacles but the free movement
of human beings is blocked. Even if they manage to cross deserts,
oceans, and fortified borders, people fleeing persecution, poverty,
and conflict can find no sure welcome or refuge. The structures of
humanitarian protection have corroded and failed over time. The
legal framework of asylum perversely serves to exclude, imprison,
and segregate the stranger. Even in the era of globalization, borders
undermine the sense of moral obligation and human dignity that
the Universal Declaration of Human Rights and other instruments
of international law are supposed to uphold for all members of our
species. Their promise of rescue, shelter, and safety has been broken,
especially for the weak and vulnerable. In contrast, sanctuary seems
to open an escape valve that asylum fails to provide.

Underlying asylum is the principle of "a universal moral/legal
order as the source of just norms" (Stastny 1987: 288). This principle
emerged from religious beliefs and practices to become part of the
secular political culture over the past 400 years. However, for various
political and economic reasons governments have repeatedly sought
and found ways to undermine or overrule international agreements
guaranteeing the availability of asylum. As government support for

asylum has degenerated into lip service, public opinion has turned against the institution. In response sanctuary movements have become the "self-appointed instrument striving to close the gap between the needs for a safe haven and the official grants of political asylum" (Stastny 1987: 294).

Looking back to the development and decline of the institution of sanctuary from the 7th to the 17th century c.e., we can see that it gradually became corrupted and discredited as the church lost its power and influence vis-à-vis the state. Meanwhile, secular authorities came to use asylum as an instrument of foreign policy, giving the state, rather than the church, the right to grant asylum and deny extradition. An early example of the role of asylum in politics is the case of Martin Luther. In 1521 the Elector of Saxony gave Luther sanctuary in Wartburg Castle in defiance of the Holy Roman Emperor Charles V, who had declared Luther an outlaw, made it a crime to give him food or shelter, and called for him to be killed because of his heretical pronouncements. With the long-term support of the Elector of Saxony and other secular political leaders, Luther survived and flourished— unlike Jan Hus, Giordano Bruno, and other religious reformers, who lacked such protection.

Even at its height in the late Middle Ages sanctuary was usually temporary and limited. Accused criminals could stay in British churches for only a few weeks, and then they had to decide whether to surrender to legal authorities or abjure the realm and go into exile. When it became possible for thieves and debtors to remain permanently in sanctuary, the institution lost its moral authority. It seemed wrong for the church to provide immunity from prosecution to those who ventured out to commit more crimes and then returned to their haven. Along with the state's increasingly effective claim to a monopoly over legal authority and coercive force, this unintended consequence fatally compromised church sanctuary.

In our time the pendulum has swung: Asylum has become corrupted and discredited while sanctuary has regained its moral authority. For example, despite the lack of protection for sanctuary in U.S. law, in recent years federal officials have made it known that they will not raid churches, schools, or hospitals to apprehend undocumented migrants. (They have arrested undocumented people as soon as they left the church or hospital or on their way to or from school, however.) When Congressman James Sensenbrenner proposed criminalizing those who would give sanctuary or assistance to undocumented migrants in 2005, he had to back down in the face of outraged opposition by nonprofit and faith-based organizations. Police who raided St. Bernard Church in Paris and brutally expelled Sans-Papiers occupiers in 1997 sparked mass public protests on behalf of undocumented workers and influenced Catholic bishops to support them. Although the German public disapproves of immigrants and asylum seekers according to opinion polls, a movement has grown to shelter undocumented migrants in churches and homes. When Canadian authorities seek to deport unsuccessful asylum seekers, again and again local communities give them sanctuary.

Perhaps it was inevitable that asylum would lose legitimacy over time. Every limitation of entry into receiving countries over the past 20 years by governments and international agreements has led to the increase of human smuggling, fraudulent asylum claims, overstaying, and the destitution underground. Whether for political or economic reasons desperate people find ways to migrate, no matter what obstacles they may encounter on the way. It is now impracticable for governments in the United States, Britain, and the European Union to remove all the undocumented migrants living in those countries. They have reacted by trying to prevent individuals from seeking asylum, but their methods have proven to be futile in stopping smuggling, fraud, overstaying, and destitution. On the contrary, these problems are likely to worsen with each turn of the screw. In the meantime hundreds of thousands of vulnerable people, many with legitimate asylum claims, suffer harm at the hands of those who are supposed to give them refuge, simply because they present themselves to the authorities and are therefore the easiest to apprehend, detain, and deport.

Yet, despite their continuing attempts to make migration more difficult, governments have established and maintained formal resettlement programs for asylees and refugees. Thus they acknowledge their obligation to protect those fleeing persecution, as well as the possibility of providing permanent sanctuary in the form of integration into national society.[1] These programs may be underfunded, inefficient, and inadequate, but at least they exist. With all their limitations, they embody the commitment nation states have made to the principle of refuge.

In the United States, Britain, and other countries, NGOs and advocacy groups have made detailed recommendations for reform of the asylum system, to make it adhere to the Refugee Convention, other international agreements, and national laws. However, these agreements and laws have serious shortcomings. Genuine reform is likely to be obstructed by the system's entrenched nature, the privatization of detention, and politicians' unwillingness to abandon the political advantages of scapegoating the powerless, alien Other. And the treatment of asylum seekers is only a small part of a much larger immigration system, in which they can get lost all too easily. Policymakers and lawmakers must consider what to do about asylum in the context of overriding concerns about national security, terrorism, economic crisis, and political gridlock.

The world may need a new refugee convention that reflects both post-Cold War realities and changing human aspirations. But even if a new convention were created, it would soon need an overhaul. Without serious reconsideration of the unintended consequences of reform and rededication to protection of basic human rights, any law, regulation, or policy governing asylum is likely to fail sooner or later.

In the meantime it makes sense to monitor and replicate asylum systems that combine legal efficiency and humanitarian treatment. The recently changed Australian and Dutch systems and the relatively liberal Swedish system could provide models for other nations. A certain amount of political courage is also necessary to reform punitive, inefficient, and inhumane policies that create more problems than they solve. If they are to abide by their legal obligations to refugees, political leaders must be ready to tell the public some home truths about the important contributions migrants make to the national economy, the difficulty and expense of removing undocumented workers, and the benefits of integrating strangers into national society. They must resist the temptation to scapegoat the most vulnerable outsiders for their own policy failures, and they must defend the human rights of noncitizens they have a legal and moral obligation to protect. These are difficult and demanding tasks. If political leaders make an honest effort to carry them out, they will encounter strong opposition, not only from reactionary and racist elements but also from progressive activists who worry about overpopulation, environmental degradation, crime, and other compelling problems that they associate with the unrestricted entry and long-term presence of immigrants. Consequently fostering public debate and education about immigration and asylum must be ongoing priorities for political, economic, and social leaders.

It is often said that the solution to the problems of immigration can be found in advancing social, political, and economic justice in the countries from which people flee. Then, the argument goes, they would have fewer reasons to leave and more reasons to stay to improve their own societies. If progressive land reform were implemented in the Philippines, the daughters of small farmers would not have to leave home to take nursing jobs overseas. If Mexican youth could farm in or near their own village or find jobs in the city, they would not feel compelled to cross the Sonoran Desert to mow lawns in southern California. If minority-group members had freedom of speech or religion in Cameroon, Sudan, or Nigeria, they would not petition for asylum in France, Britain, or Australia. If women had equal rights in Iran, they would not seek refuge with relatives in North Dakota.

To solve these and many other problems significant, long-term, social, economic, and political change is necessary in those countries. Generous and effective development assistance from First World nations could help to a modest extent. And change is taking place, however precariously and incrementally. But people from all walks of life still leave their homes for better, safer lives in other countries, undeterred by border patrols, indefinite detention, entry quotas, or any other bureaucratic obstacles from starting on their way. Recognition of these facts by politicians and the public might make a difference in the conception and implementation of asylum and immigration policies.

One issue that most politicians are reluctant to question or even address is the unassailability of borders as the first line of defense of countries and their populations against all manner of interlopers. Borders and sovereignty are sacred categories in modern political discourse, the very foundations of nationalism, even though galloping globalization threatens them. A few utopian theorists and critics have questioned the viability of fortress states by pointing to the possibility of opening borders in a world where the Internet links everybody and everything almost instantaneously. Open Borders proponents "pose a significant moral challenge. . . . they help us to think about the central dilemma of the global world order, the role of the sovereign state in an increasingly interconnected world," Gibney and Hansen pointed out (2005: 459).

The Open Borders theorists do not tend to focus on asylum but rather on immigration in general. They base their arguments on several basic ideas:

- "Freedom of movement ought to be regarded as a fundamental individual right" for all, regardless of "arbitrary" criteria such as nationality.
- All human beings are free and equal and of equal moral worth.
- One's labor is one's private property, to be disposed of as one chooses.
- Inequality of wealth among nations should be redressed by the right of individuals to move where there is more opportunity.
- No one way of life or culture is superior over others; therefore people should be able to choose which society they live in. (Gibney and Hansen 2005 II: 457f)

These ideas are very attractive to libertarians, capitalists, and some human rights advocates, but other theorists point out that states also have the "right to exclude." For example, political philosopher Michael Walzer believes in the universal equality of human beings, who are all "culture-producing creatures" (Gibney and Hansen 2005 II: 458). He acknowledges that states must give aid to strangers when it is urgently needed and the costs of providing it are low. But the obligation to help is not absolute, he points out. For Gibney and Hansen the broader underlying question that Walzer raises is "how to reconcile the moral obligations we owe to any individual human being, simply on the basis of our equal moral dignity, with the special duties we acquire toward particular people and groups on the basis of particular relationships and attachments" (2005 II: 458). Politicians are almost never elected with a mandate to protect all humankind but rather to advance the interests and rights of the people who elected them (and perhaps even people who did not vote for them—but not people in far-off countries who might need help).

Tazreiter quoted Immanuel Kant (1724–1804) to make a human rights and international law-based argument for open borders: "The peoples of the earth have . . . entered in varying degrees into a universal community, and it has developed to the point where a violation of laws in one part of the world is felt everywhere. The idea of a cosmopolitan law is therefore not fantastic and overstrained; it is a necessary complement to the unwritten code of political and international law, transforming it into a universal law of humanity" (2004: 23).

Tazreiter admitted that "there are cogent arguments to defend the actions of a state in ensuring its sovereignty is not threatened, and the economic and social well-being of its citizens is safeguarded. This does not, however, relieve the state of obligations to noncitizens in their territories" (2004: 13). She raised but did not answer the question of how to strike "a balance between local needs and interests and those which are held universally" (2005: 15). Policymakers face these dilemmas when they try to craft asylum policies that uphold international agreements while protecting both citizens and strangers.

Teresa Hayter took a more radical position in reacting against exclusionary immigration and asylum policies (2004). She argued that immigration controls do not work, restrictions do not keep migrants from entering countries, detention and deportation cause much suffering, and deportation en masse is not feasible. Economic migrants come to receiving countries because of economic conditions in their own country, and they come to work, not to sponge off the welfare system. Aging populations make it likely that young migrants will keep coming to fill job places and to care for the elderly in coming years. The current immigration system works for the benefit of employers who hire illegal workers. These workers drive down the cost of labor and can be fired with a telephone call to the police if they try to organize other workers. Detention and deportation are extremely expensive and not cost effective. For practical as well as moral reasons, therefore, borders should be open, and workers should be able to come and go as they need to, Hayter insisted.

Khalid Koser responded to Open Borders theorists in a sober and measured way by pointing to the recalcitrant realities of migration in the post-Cold War world:

> It has become clear that control measures such as border fences, biometric testing and visas are in isolation unlikely to reduce irregular migration in the long term. They probably need to be combined with more proactive measures that address the causes of irregular migration, including achieving development targets to increase security and improve livelihoods in origin countries, as well as expanding opportunities to move legally. At the same time, it is unrealistic to expect states to dismantle controls altogether and open their borders, as is sometimes advocated. Most

commentators now acknowledge that irregular migration will continue for the foreseeable future. (2007: 119)

Hayter and other writers stress morality in calling for generous and humane asylum policies. Hugo Gryn, an Auschwitz survivor who became a rabbi in London, told the British Refugee Council in 1996: "It is imperative that we proclaim that asylum issues are an index of our spiritual and moral civilization. . . . I believe that the line our society will take in this matter on how you are to people to whom you owe nothing is a signal. . . . I hope and pray it is a test we shall not fail" (Kushner 2006: 234). Gryn seemed to be following Walzer's line of reasoning in saying that British people owed nothing to asylum seekers. In trying to characterize granting asylum as a test of virtue, he seemed to contradict the universalistic values of reciprocal altruism and equality underlying both human rights law and Open Borders theory.

It seems likely that a sanctuarian would operate out of a broad sense of moral obligation to *anyone* who needed help, not only members of his or her family, neighborhood, city, state, or country. How else can one explain the actions of Sanctuary Movement activists, Holocaust rescuers, and Underground Railroad conductors, who saved the most stigmatized people in their society or outsiders with no apparent relation to themselves? They reinvented sanctuary in response to life-threatening realities, without taking time to theorize about systemic change. They did not challenge the idea of borders, but they transgressed them whenever they believed it necessary.

In the 20th century people had to redefine and expand the meaning of sanctuary to respond to the realities of total war and its aftermath. Demilitarized zones, nuclear-free zones, weapons-free zones, humanitarian relief corridors, and refugee camps acquired the status of sanctuaries under international treaties and agreements. The organizations that maintained them struggled to keep them safe in the midst of violent conflict.

For example, Zones of Peace were first established in the Philippines in 1988, after the overthrow of Ferdinand Marcos by a people's revolution. A Zone of Peace is "a geographical area that community residents themselves declare to be off-limits to war and other forms of armed hostility" (Hancock and Mitchell 2004: 11). The Catholic Church has been instrumental in setting up and maintaining these sanctuaries. In 2000, when the Filipino government was waging war on the Moro

Islamic Liberation Front (MLF), officials tried to take over existing Zones of Peace and use them as bases to expel the MLF. The military then tried to forcibly relocate residents. Communities had to defy the government to establish and maintain their own zones.

In Colombia, which has millions of internally displaced people as a result of more than 50 years of civil conflict, local communities have set up 100 Zones of Peace that practice "active neutrality." Participants include Catholic clergy, indigenous groups, nongovernmental organizations, local officials, peasant organizations, and educators' groups. Associations of Zones of Peace "use their combined power to attempt to educate one another and influence the process of the conflict and peacemaking on a larger scale" (Hancock and Mitchell 2004: 11). These associations meet with guerilla leaders to gain the release of abducted officials and set up safe passage for peasants to pass through roadblocks on their way to market. National organizations, such as the Network of Initiatives for Peace and against War (REDEPAZ), support the local zones and help them communicate with one another. REDEPAZ received a grant from the European Initiative for Democracy to set up the zones in the late 1990s.

Usually peace communities try to solve local disputes without violence. In this context their activities consist of "almost invisible processes of people building peace in the midst of a civil war" on the local level, from the bottom up (Hancock and Mitchell 2004: 25). Maintaining the zones under these circumstances has not been easy. Peace communities have started in areas "characterized by being historically abandoned by the state," where armed insurgents have stepped in to fill the vacuum (Hancock and Mitchell 2004: 24). Local residents resist their control at great risk. In one of many similar incidents, peace leaders in San Pablo, Colombia, had to flee, and local supporting organizations had to discontinue their activities under attack by guerilla forces in 2002–03. To avoid such incidents the peace communities have sought outside and international support, "so that any decision to undertake an attack or perpetrate a massacre on a Zone of Peace will involve a high political cost for the perpetrators" (Hancock and Mitchell 2004: 22).

Other countries with Zones of Peace include El Salvador and Guatemala, where violence has continued even after the end of long-running civil wars. These homemade sanctuary communities "are responses generated by peoples to ensure that they overcome the helplessness and hopelessness they suffer" as a result of endemic violence (Hancock and Mitchell 2004: 39). Zones of Peace in all these places were established during civil wars by the victims, during peace negotiations by the warring parties, or after wars by survivors seeking to recuperate and develop communities. They may be established to provide relief and rescue, to administer health care, to protect sacred or historic sites, to observe festivals and other events, or to protect vulnerable groups, such as children. The International Center for the Study and Promotion of Zones of Peace and other groups support and keep information on the zones.

The Zones of Peace are notable because they are grassroots efforts, usually unsupported or unacknowledged by the state, to establish and maintain havens without force of arms in the midst of conflict. Fragile though it may be, sanctuary in this context is a dynamic process that operates autonomously, beyond the polar antagonisms of war, in the small space where people can achieve the evanescent freedom to govern themselves by their own rules. Sanctuary may not last, but while it does it satisfies a deep human longing. It defies the supremacy of arbitrary authority, coercion, and punishment. For as long as it lasts, it provides surcease to those who flee the imposition of brute power and a sense of accomplishment to those who shelter them. If the powers that be refuse to give sanctuary, then people make their own. If the persecuted cannot find refuge outside their home territory, they create it where they live.

A venerable and sacred institution, sanctuary is also malleable and responsive to current conditions. Human beings in almost every time and place keep reinventing it as they go along. As Rabbi Gryn pointed out, asylum defines our level of moral and spiritual development; but sanctuary has a much more basic—and life-saving—significance to those who seek and give it. The legal institution of asylum may flourish or decline, but sanctuary—a spontaneous, voluntary, unregulated act of reciprocal altruism—is in our DNA and will survive in some form as long as we do.

Many incidents reported in this book show that as governments try to limit or undermine asylum, ordinary citizens provide or promote sanctuary, either secretly or openly. Each person must decide if he or she will defy the legal authorities for conscience's sake by offering refuge outside the law to persecuted strangers. Some sanctuarians, such as the activists of Humane Borders in Tucson, go right to the edge of legality but not over it. Most people do not feel compelled or able to take such actions, which often occur in extreme situations such as the run-up to the American Civil War, occupied Europe during World War II, and the Central American wars of the 1980s. They may, however, support sanctuarians in a variety of ways, from contributing funds to demonstrating against official policies and lobbying for changes in restrictive laws.

Individuals and organizations in many countries have loudly or quietly expressed their opposition to anti-asylum measures. In some instances grassroots sanctuary efforts have led to positive changes in government policies vis-à-vis asylum seekers, although they often take years to make any impact. Powerful xenophobic forces get much more public attention and seem to have considerable political clout and influence over government decision making. One can see numerous examples of the negative consequences of anti-immigrant sentiment and agitation on asylum policies in dozens of countries, including Australia, Britain, France, Germany, and the United States. Even so, persistent public support for sanctuary and the actions of sanctuary movements have helped asylum seekers in those and other countries.

Time and time again, when governments have failed to abide by international law and their own laws, ordinary citizens have stepped in to enforce and advance human rights, even at great personal risk. Consider the example of Paul Rusesabagina, the Rwandan who saved about 1,200 people during the 1994 genocide by giving them sanctuary in the hotel he managed in Kigali. An unassuming man, Rusesabagina did what he had to do, including cheat, lie, and steal, to protect his own family and everyone else who sought his help in the midst of monstrous government-sponsored crimes and social chaos.

Thousands of other ordinary people have taken much less risky but modestly effective actions to give refuge to strangers or support those who did. If you donate money to pro-asylum groups, write letters to the editor on behalf of asylum seekers, teach English to refugees, hire an unemployed asylee, or volunteer to help torture survivors, you are a sanctuarian. Hundreds of organizations can use whatever help you choose to give. Through such actions you, too, can know the pleasures of rescue. As a universal human right and an intrinsic part of our species' heritage, sanctuary belongs to everyone.

Organizations That Help or Advocate for Asylum Seekers, Refugees, and Immigrants

A Partial List

Australia

Actors for Refugees
Asylum Seekers Resource Centre
Australian Catholic Migrant and Refugee office
Australian Lutheran World Service
Australian National Committee on Refugee Women
Centre for Advocacy, Support and Education for Refugees
ChilOut
Coalition Assisting Refugees after Detention
Ecumenical Migration Centre
Immigrant Women's Speakout
Jesuit Refugee Service
National Council of Churches
Oxfam Australia
Red Cross of Australia
Refugee Action Collective
Refugee Advice and Casework Service
Refugee Council of Australia
Refugee Rights Action Network
Sanctuary Refugee Foundation
YWCA

Canada

Amnesty International
Asylum Seekers Centre
Canadian Council for Refugees
Jesuit Refugee and Migrant Service
Romero House

France

ANAFE (Association nationale d'assistance aux frontières pour les étrangers)
CIMADE (Comité inter-mouvements auprès des evacués)
Forum Réfugiés
France Terre d'Asile
GISTI (Groupe d'information e de soutien des immigrés)

Germany

Amnesty International
Arbeiterwohlfahrt–AWO Bundesverband e.V.
Borderline-Europe
Caritas
Diakonie
German Red Cross
Ökumenische *Bundesarbeitsgemeinschaft* Asyl in der Kirche e.V.
Pro Asyl
Raphaels-Werk

International

European Council on Refugees and Exiles
International Catholic Migration Commission
International Detention Coalition
International Rehabilitation Council for Torture Victims
United Nations High Commissioner for Refugees

United Kingdom

Amnesty International
Asylum Aid

Asylum Support Appeals Project
Bail for Immigration Detainees
Black Women against Rape
British Refugee Council
Campaign to Close Campsfield
Crossroads Women's Centre
Education Action International
Immigration Advisory Service
Immigration Law Practitioners Association
Kalayaan
London Citizens
Medical Foundation for the Care of Victims of Torture
Medical Justice
Refugee Action
Scholar Rescue Fund
South London Refugees Association
UNISON

United States

Advocates for Survivors of Torture and Trauma, Baltimore
American Civil Liberties Union
American Friends Service Committee
American Immigration Law Association
Amnesty International
Annunciation House
Arab Community Center for Economic and Social Services
Boston Center for Refugee Health and Human Rights
Capital Area Immigrant Rights Coalition
Catholic Legal Immigration Network (CLINIC)
Center for Victims of Torture, Minneapolis
Chaldean Federation of America
Church World Service
Detention Watch Network
Episcopal Migration Ministries
Ethiopian Community Development Council
Hebrew Immigrant Aid Society
Human Rights First
Human Rights Watch
Interfaith Refugee and Immigration Ministries

International Rescue Committee
Iowa Bureau of Refugee Services
Jesuit Refugee Service
Jewish Family Service
Karen American Communities Foundation
Kurdish Human Rights Watch
Lutheran Immigration and Refugee Service
Lutheran Social Services
National Immigrant Solidarity Network
Refugee Council USA
Refugee Works
Southeast Asia Resource and Action Center
Upwardly Global
U.S. Committee on Refugees and Immigrants
U.S. Conference of Catholic Bishops/Migration and Refugee Services
Welcome Back Initiative
Women's Initiative for Self-Improvement
Women's Refugee Commission
World Relief

And Many, Many More.

NOTES

Introduction

1. For a review of the decades-long debate over Darwinian and neo-Darwinian explanations of human altruism and the "selfish gene," see Markowitz (2010).
2. For a recent history of refugees by an anthropologist, see Haines (2010).
3. According to a UN report published in March 2010, "the number of people seeking asylum in western countries is not rising, contrary to popular belief. Around 377,200 people applied for asylum in 2009. . . . Most people sought asylum in the European Union, where 246,200 claims were registered" (Panos Institute 2010). The estimated population of the 27 EU states is about 501 million, according to the EU's statistical commission (Eurostat 2010).

Chapter One

1. "In recent years 72% of the world's refugees have found asylum in developing countries" (Student Action for Refugees n.d.).
2. A refugee has fled across international boundaries, often as part of a group, and has officially obtained temporary or permanent sanctuary from a receiving government before entering the country of refuge. An asylum seeker applies to a foreign government on his or her own initiative after arriving in the receiving

country for temporary or permanent refuge from persecution in the home country. A successful asylum seeker, or asylee, is classified as a refugee and may be eligible for various kinds of resettlement assistance. In the United States asylees constitute a small proportion of refugees, and relatively few people seek asylum; but in the UK and Europe entering asylum seekers vastly outnumber entering refugees. Many receiving countries establish annual quotas of refugees, depending on varying (sometimes arbitrary) criteria. A person who flees persecution and finds refuge inside his or her own country is designated as internally displaced. According to the UN High Commissioner for Refugees, in 2008 there were many more internally displaced persons (26 million) than refugees (15.2 million) in the world. Some 800,000 people applied for asylum around the world in 2008.

3. For an anthropologist's perspective of the way the UK government's asylum system works, see Good (2007).

4. Mary's story is based on the author's interview with an asylum seeker who requested anonymity, Providence, RI, August 2006.

5. Leah's story is based on the author's interview with an asylum seeker who requested anonymity, London, June 2007.

6. A report by academics and NGOs on conditions at the Immigration and Nationality Directorate headquarters outside London estimated that the Home Office had lost documents related to more than 2,500 out of 42,000 asylum appeals in a two-year period (2001–02). "The proportion of lost documents may be small but the effects on the cases of a large number of individuals may be serious. There can be long delays and it may not be possible for the asylum seeker to replace the documents lost. . . . The absence of such clear evidence can result in appeals being lost" (Back, Farrell, and Vandermaas 2005: 121).

7. Jason's story is based on Bernstein (2008).

8. The slave's story is based on proceedings of a hearing the author attended at the Independent Asylum Tribunal, Taylor House, London, May 16, 2007.

9. An estimated 250 children are trafficked into the UK each month (Stevens 2004: 232).

10. Aisha's story is based on proceedings of a hearing the author attended at the Independent Asylum Tribunal, Taylor House, London, May 4, 2007.

11. Jeff's story is based on Kenney and Schrag (2008).

12. After ICE reported some 70 deaths of immigrant detainees in re-cent years and families attempted to sue the government in some of those cases, U.S. Rep. Zoe Lofgren and Sen. Robert Menendez introduced the Detainee Basic Medical Care Act (HR5950) in May 2008. By 2010 more than 100 immigration detainees, includ-ing asylum seekers, were estimated to have died in custody in U.S. facilities (Bernstein 2010).

13. According to the British Refugee Council, 50% of women claim-ing asylum in the UK have been raped (Kofman, Raghuram, and Merefield 2005).

14. For a detailed and indignant account of another such case, see Merjian (2009).

15. "A kind of schizophrenia seems to pervade Western responses to asylum seekers and refugees' great importance is attached to the principle of asylum but enormous efforts are made to ensure that refugees . . . never reach the territory of the state where they could receive its protection" (Gibney 2004: 2).

Chapter Two

1. I am indebted to Prof. Josiah Heyman for encouraging me to reach these conclusions.

Chapter Five

1. The states were Connecticut, Delaware, Illinois, Indiana, Iowa, Maryland, Michigan, Massachusetts, New Jersey, New Hampshire, New York, North Carolina, Ohio, Pennsylvania, Rhode Island, Vermont, and Wisconsin, according to Siebert.

2. According to Larson (2004), Tubman rescued about 70 slaves.

3. Slavery was formally abolished in the British Empire starting in 1833.

Chapter Six

1. Historian Gérard Bollon collected the names of 3,458 refugees who were sheltered in Le Chambon and its environs.

Chapter Seven

1. By Rabbi Hugo Gryn, as quoted by Kushner (2006: 232).

2. Bau (1985: 43). In 1965 the McCarran-Walter Act was amended, and national quotas were abolished. Priority was given to entry of close relatives of U.S. citizens and those with special skills.

3. *The Independent* of London reported in 2001 that the concert had raised only 1 million.

4. Cunningham wrote: "Church sanctuary was first declared publicly in the United States on October 16, 1967, by the Arlington Street Unitarian Church in Boston, Mass., when it claimed [*sic*] asylum for nearly 300 Vietnam War draft resisters" (1995: 84).

5. According to MacEoin (1985), support for the Sanctuary Movement came from mainline churches and organizations, including the General Assembly, Presbyterian Church (USA), Clergy and Laity Concerned, Church of the Brethren General Board, National Assembly of Religious Women, Mennonite Central Committee, National Coalition of American Nuns, United Methodist Board of Church and Society, Unitarian-Universalist Service Committee, United Church of Christ Office for Church and Society, Pax Christi, Board of National Ministries of American Baptist Church, Methodist Federation for Social Action, Commission on Home Ministries of the General Conference, Mennonite Church, Lutheran Immigration and Refugee Service, National Federal of Priests' Councils, National Bishops of the Lutheran Church of America, and Association of Evangelical Lutheran Churches. From 1981 to 1986 Tucson groups raised $725,000 to pay bonds and legal expenses for asylum seekers.

Chapter Eight

1. In 21 of the 36 incidents Lippert recorded, migrants gained legal status.

2. Statistics are approximate, because the U.S. government has been slow to provide complete data.

3. Rev. Dantica's story is from Danticat (2007).

4. Tam Tran's story is from Watanabe (2007).

5. The 10 VOLAGs operating in 2010 were Church World Service, Episcopal Migration Ministries, Ethiopian Community Development Council, Hebrew Immigration Aid Society, Kurdish Human Rights Watch, International Rescue Committee,

Lutheran Immigration and Refugee Services, U.S. Conference of Catholic Bishops, U.S. Committee on Refugees and Immigrants, and World Relief.

Chapter Nine

1. In 2006 the Democratic Republic of Congo, Eritrea, Iran, Sudan, and Zimbabwe refused to issue travel documents to refused asylum seekers in the UK.
2. For a recent account by a gay Iranian asylee of his experience in the UK, see Anonymous (2010).
3. The railings were still outside Lunar House when I visited the building in February 2008. In 2009 the UKBA announced it would turn the reception area into a Welcome Centre.
4. According to the Global Detention Project, eight of 11 asylum detention centers in the UK are privatized.
5. Anonymous, handwritten note, June 27, 2007. I have corrected numerous spelling and grammatical errors.
6. In 2009–10 the UK government reportedly paid £12 million in compensation to migrants traumatized by detention or detained illegally. In one case, "a Ugandan who had been tortured was awarded £110,000 after the court ruled he had been unlawfully detained in the UK for 10 months" (Taylor 2010: 14).
7. In October 2010 an Angolan deportee died after being forcibly restrained by private security guards on a British commercial flight.
8. Ten British cities have joined the City of Sanctuary movement, which started in Sheffield in 2005. These local communities offer hospitality and help to asylum seekers. In 2009 Movement members published a guide, *Becoming a City of Sanctuary: A Practical Handbook with Inspiring Examples*, available online at www.cityofsanctuary.org/book.

Chapter Ten

1. The cities included New York, Berkeley, Chicago, Seattle, San Francisco, Albuquerque, Austin, Los Angeles, and St. Paul, Minnesota.
2. See, for example, the surveys by the Pew Research Center for the People and the Press.

Chapter Eleven

1. However, in 2005 the British government stopped providing indefinite leave to remain to asylum seekers granted refugee status. Since then "successful applicants have been granted . . . [only] five years limited leave to remain in the UK" in an apparent attempt to circumvent international law (Crawley and Crimes 2009: 5).

Abrams, Fran. 2007. "Fees Rules Hurt Refugees," *Guardian*, June 19.

Abramsky, Sasha. 2008. "Gimme Shelter. What the New Sanctuary Movement Offers, Beyond a Safe Space, for the Undocumented," *The Nation*, February 25: 24–28.

"Accelerated Removals: A Study of the Human Cost of EU Deportation Policies, 2009–2010." 2010. European Race Audit. Briefing Paper No. 4, October. London: Institute of Race Relations.

Acer, Eleanor, and Jessica Chicco. 2009. "U.S. Detention of Asylum Seekers. Seeking Protection, Finding Prison." New York: Human Rights First.

"Action Alert in Support of Women in Yarl's Wood Removal Center on Hunger Strike Protesting against SERCO's Draconian Regime." N.d. (2007?). Pamphlet.

Alaya, Flavia, et al., eds. 2007. "Voices of the Disappeared: An Investigative Report of New Jersey Immigration Detention." Piscataway, NJ: New Jersey Civil Rights Defense Committee.

Allman, W. 1994. *The Stone Age Present*. New York: Simon and Shuster.

Alston, Philip. 2008. "Statement of the UN Special Rapporteur," June 30. Detention Watch Network listserv, July 1, 2008.

Amadiume, Ifi. 1987. *Male Daughters, Female Husbands: Gender and Sex in an African Society*. London: Zed Books.

American Friends Service Committee. 1940–44. Archives, RG-67.007. Series I, Perpignan; Series II, Vichy France; Series VIII, Marseille; Series IX, Montauban. Washington, D.C.: Holocaust Museum Library.

Amnesty International. 2005. "United Kingdom: Seeking Asylum Is Not a Crime: Detention of People Who Have Sought Asylum," EUR45/015, June 20.

Amnesty International UK. 2006. "Down and Out in London. The Road to Destitution for Rejected Asylum Seekers." London: Amnesty International UK.

Amnesty International USA. 2009. "Jailed without Justice. Immigration Detention in the USA." New York: AIUSA, www.amnestyusa.org/uploads/ JailedWithoutJustice.pdf.

An-Na'im, Abdullahi Ahmed. 1990. *Toward an Islamic Reformation. Civil Liberties, Human Rights and International Law*. Syracuse: Syracuse University Press.

Anonymous. 2010. "As a Gay Asylum Seeker, I Was Lucky," *Guardian*, May 22, www.guardian.co.uk.

Archibold, Randal S. 2007. "Illegal Immigration Advocate for Families is Deported," *The New York Times*, August 21.

Ashton, Rosemary. 1986. *Little Germany. Exile and Asylum in Victorian London*. Oxford: Oxford University Press.

Associated Press. 2007. "Dutch Government Approves Amnesty for 25,000 Rejected Asylum Seekers," *International Herald Tribune*, May 26, www.iht. com/bin/print.php?id = 5876291, accessed June 4.

Asylum Aid. 2007? *Annual Report 2006*.

Asylum Support Appeals Project. 2007. "Failing the Failed? How NASS Decision Making Is Letting Down Destitute Rejected Asylum Seekers."

Aynsley-Green, Al. 2010. "The Arrest and Detention of Children Subject to Immigration Control." London: 11 Million.

Back, Les, Bernadette Farrell, and Erin Vandermaas. 2005. "Report on the South London Citizens Enquiry into Service Provision by the Immigration and Nationality Directorate at Lunar House." London: South London Citizens.

Bacon, Christine. 2005. "The Evolution of Immigration Detention in the UK: The Involvement of Private Prison Companies." Oxford: Refugee Studies Centre, Working Paper No. 27.

Bacon, David. 2008. *Illegal People. How Globalization Creates Migration and Criminalizes Immigrants*. Boston: Beacon Press.

Bade, Klaus J. 2003. *Migration in European History*. Oxford: Blackwell.

Bail for Immigration Detainees (BID). 2005. "NASS Accommodation for Those at the End of an Asylum Case," May 4.

———. 2006? "Working against the Clock: Inadequacy and Injustice in the Fast-Track System."

———. 2007. Letter to Liam Byrne, Minister of State for Immigration, Nationality and Citizenship, June 4.

———. 2009a. Briefing Paper on Access to Immigration Bail.

———. 2009b. Briefing Paper on Children and Immigration Detention.

———. 2009c. Briefing Paper on the Detained Fast Track.

———. 2009d. Briefing Paper on Immigration Detention in London.

———. N.d. General Information Sheet.

———. N.d. *Annual Report 2005–2006. Challenging Immigration Detention in the United Kingdom*.

Bakhash, Shaul. 1989. *Historical Setting* [Iran]. Washington, D.C.: Library of Congress.

Barkow, Jerome, ed. 2006. *Missing the Revolution: Darwinism for Social Scientists*. New York: Oxford University Press.

Barnett, Ruth. 2004. "The Acculturation of the Kindertransport Children: Intergenerational Dialogue on the Kindertransport Experience," *Shofar* 23, no. 1: 100–08.

Barry, Tom. 2009. "The Expanding Immigration Enforcement Apparatus," *Border Lines*, May 23, http://borderlinesblog.blogspot.com/2009/05/expanding-immigration-enforcement.html. Washington, D.C.: Center for International Policy.

Bau, Ignatius. 1985. *This Ground Is Holy. Church Sanctuary and Central American Refugees*. New York: Paulist Press.

Bellamy, John. 1973. *Crime and Public Order in England in the Later Middle Ages*. London: Routledge and Kegan Paul.

Bernstein, Nina. 2008. "Ill and in Pain, Detainee Dies in U.S. Hands," *The New York Times*, August 13.

———. 2010. "Officials Hid Truth of Immigration Deaths in Jail," *The New York Times*, January 9.

Bernstein, Richard. 2010. "A Very Superior 'Chinaman,'" *The New York Review of Books* LVII, no. 16 (October 28).

Bettex, André. 2005? "Un juste parmi les nations," CD.

Bevan, Vaughn. 1986. *The Development of British Immigration Law*. London: Croom Helm.

Black Womens' Rape Action Project (BWRAP). 2006. *Misjudging Rape. Breaching Gender Guidelines and International Law in Asylum Appeals*. London: Crossroad Books.

———. 2007. "Threatened Removal Friday 1 June of Breastfeeding Mother with Two Babies," www.asylum-seekers-defence.org.uk/wiki/index.php?title = Threatened–removal, accessed June 4.

Blight, David W. 2004. *Passages to Freedom. The Underground Railroad in History and Memory*. Washington, D.C.: Smithsonian Books.

Boehm, Christopher. 1984. *Blood Revenge: The Anthropology of Feuding in Montenegro and Other Tribal Societies*. Lawrence: University of Kansas Press.

Boismorand, Pierre. 2007. *Magda et André Trocmé, figures de resistances*. Paris: Éditions du Cerf.

Bolle, Pierre, ed. 1992. *Le Plateau Vivarais-Lignon. Accueil et résistance 1939–1944*. Le-Chambon-sur-Lignon: Société d'Histoire de la Montagne.

Bollon, Gérard. 2002. "La Montagne Protestante, terre d'accueil et de résistance pendant la seconde guerre mondiale (1939–1945)," *Cahiers du Mézenc* 14 (July), 25–32.

———. 2004. "Femmes militantes et résistantes de la Montagne," *Cahiers du Mézenc* 16 (July), 57–68.

Borderlines. 2001. "Activists: Deaths in Arizona Desert Could Have Been Avoided," www.americaspolicy.org/borderlines/2001/bl79/bl79deaths/body.html.

Bordewich, Fergus M. 2005. *Bound for Canaan: The Underground Railroad and the War for the Soul of America*. New York: HarperCollins.

Borjas, George J., and Jeff Crisp, eds. 2005. *Poverty, International Migration and Asylum*. New York: Palgrave Macmillan.

Bowcott, Owen. 2007. "From Asylum Seeker to Ireland's First Black Mayor in Seven Years," *Guardian*, June 30.

Brané, Michelle. 2007. "Locking Up Family Values: The Detention of Immigrant Families." Washington, D.C.: Women's Refugee Commission.

British Broadcasting Corporation. 2007a. "Group Wants Asylum Seeker Stories." http://newsvote.bbc.co.uk/1/hi/scotland/glasgow, accessed June 8.

————. 2007b. "Food Protest by Asylum Detainees," http://news.bbc.co.uk/go/or/fr/-/1/hi/scotland/6339135.stm, accessed June 11.

Buckley, Cara. 2007. "Fleeing Hitler and Meeting a Reluctant Miss Liberty," *The New York Times*, July 8.

Burnett, Jon, et al. 2010. "State-Sponsored Cruelty. Children in Immigration Detention." London: Medical Justice.

Butt, Audrey. 1952. *The Nilotes of the Anglo-Egyptian Sudan and Uganda*. London: International African Institute.

Campbell, Duncan. 2007. "Number Fleeing Homeland Starts to Rise," *Guardian*, June 20.

Carter, Helen. 2009. "Congolese Primary Pupil Tony Lola Wins Deportation Battle," *Guardian*, April 21, www.guardian.co.uk, accessed April 28.

Ceneda, Sophia, and Clare Palmer. 2006. "Lip Service or Implementation? The Home Office Gender Guidance and Women's Asylum Claims in the UK." London: Asylum Aid.

Center for the Study of Human Rights. 1992. *Twenty-Four Human Rights Documents*. New York: Columbia University.

Chapais, Bernard, and Carol M. Berman, eds. 2004. *Kinship and Behavior in Primates*. Oxford: Oxford University Press.

Cissé, Madjiguene. 1997. "The Sans-Papiers: A Woman Draws the First Lessons," samizdat@ecn.org, April 24. Also published as *The Sans-Papiers: A Woman Draws the First Lessons*. London: Crossroads Books.

Community Care. 2008. "End to a Draconian System," November 13. www.communitycare.co.uk, accessed April 2009.

Connery, William. 2002. "Proud Lion of Baltimore: The Life and Legacy of Frederick Douglass," *World and I*, www.worldandi.com/newhome, accessed December 19, 2008.

Constable, Pamela. 2007. "Persecuted Gays Seek Refuge in US," *The Washington Post*, July 10.

Cook, Maria Lorena. 2007. "Advocacy on the Frontlines: Defending Migrant Rights in Southern Arizona," unpublished paper delivered at Latin American Studies Association, September.

Corbett, Jim. 1988. "Sanctuary, Basic Rights and Humanity's Fault Lines," *Weber Studies* 5, no. 1.

Corbett, Jim. 1991. *Goatwalking*. New York: Viking.

Council for Assisting Refugee Academics. 2006. Untitled brochure. London.

Courlander, Harold. 1987. *The Fourth World of the Hopis*. Albuquerque: University of New Mexico Press.

Cox, John Charles. 1911. *The Sanctuaries and Sanctuary Seekers of Mediaeval England*. London: George Allen and Sons.

Crawley, Heaven. 2007. "When Is a Child Not a Child? Asylum, Age Disputes and the Process of Age Assessments." London: Immigration Law Practitioners Association.

Crawley, Heaven, and Tina Crimes. 2009. "Refugees Living in Wales: A Survey of Skills, Experiences and Barriers to Inclusion." Swansea, UK: Centre for Migration Policy Research.

Crittenden, Ann. 1988. *Sanctuary: A Story of American Conscience and Law in Collision*. New York: Weidenfeld and Nicolson.

Cunningham, Hilary. 1995. *God and Caesar at the Rio Grande: Sanctuary and the Politics of Religion*. Minneapolis: University of Minnesota Press.

———. 2002. "Transitional Social Movements and Sovereignties in Transition: Charting New Interfaces of Power at the US-Mexican Border," *Anthropologica* 44: 185–96.

Curio, Claudia. 2004. "'Invisible' Children: The Selection and Integration Strategies of Relief Organizations," *Shofar* 23, no. 1: 41–56.

da Silva, Milton Manuel. 1972. *The Basque Nationalist Movement: A Case Study in Modernization and Ethnic Conflict*. Ann Arbor, MI: University Microfilms.

Danticat, Edwidge. 2007. *Brother, I'm Dying*. New York: Knopf.

Davidson, Miriam. 1988. *Convictions of the Heart. Jim Corbett and the Sanctuary Movement*. Tucson: University of Arizona Press.

———. 2001. "Appreciation. Corbett Offered Sanctuary to Refugees," *National Catholic Reporter Online*, September 14, www.natcath.com/NCR_Online/archives/0911401/091401j.htm, accessed December 7, 2006.

"Dawn Raids, Detention and Deportation. Statement of Pupils, Drumchapel High School." 2007. Typescript.

De Chickera, Amal. 2010. "Unravelling Anomaly. Detention, Discrimination and the Protection Needs of Stateless Persons." London: Equal Rights Trust.

de Waal, Frans B. M. 1996. *Good Natured. The Origins of Right and Wrong in Humans and Other Animals*. Cambridge: Harvard University Press.

———. 1998. *Chimpanzee Politics: Power and Sex among Apes*. Baltimore: Johns Hopkins Press.

———. 2001. *Tree of Origin. What Primate Behavior Can Tell Us about Human Social Evolution*. Cambridge: Harvard University Press.

———. 2009. *The Age of Empathy. Nature's Lessons for a Kinder Society*. New York: Harmony Books.

Deardoff, Merle H. 1951. *The Religion of Handsome Lake: Its Origin and Development*. Washington, D.C.: Smithsonian Institution.

DeSaix, Deborah D., and Karen G. Ruelle. 2007. *Hidden on the Mountain. Stories of Children Sheltered from the Nazis in Le Chambon.* New York: Holiday House.

Dobbs, Michael. 2007. "When 'Sanctuary' Becomes a Dirty Word," *The Washington Post*, November 30, A2.

Douglass, Frederick. 1971. *Narrative of the Life of Frederick Douglass an American Slave, Written by Himself.* Cambridge, MA: Belknap Press.

Dow, Mark. 2004. *American Gulag: Inside U.S. Immigration Prisons.* Berkeley and Los Angeles: University of California Press.

Doward, Jarnie. 2007. "Self-Harm Soars among Detainees," *Observer* [London], May 20, 24.

Dumper, Hildegard. 2008. "Navigation Guide: Women Refugees and Asylum Seekers in the UK." London: Information Center about Asylum and Refugees.

Dunn, Jean. 2008. "Albanian Muslims Who Sheltered Jews Honored at Program," International Raoul Wallenberg Foundation, www.raoulwallen berg.net, May 7.

European Council on Refugees and Exiles (ECRE). 2009. www.ecre.org/ members, accessed May 16.

Eurostat. 2010. "EU27 Population 501 Million at 1 January 2010," 110/2010, July 27, http://epp.eurostat.ec.europa.eu/cache/ITY_PUBLIC/3-27072010-AP/ EN/3-27072010-AP-EN.PDF.

Evangelical Lutheran Church in America (ELCA). 1998. "A Message on Immigration," November.

Farley, Jonathan. 2002. "Asylum Seekers in Britain," *Contemporary Review*. May.

Fiske, Lucy. 2006. "Politics of Exclusion, Practice of Inclusion: Australia's Response to Refugees and the Case for Community Based Human Rights Work," *International Journal of Human Rights* 10, no. 3: 219–29.

Florida Immigrant Advocacy Center. 2009. "Dying for Decent Care: Bad Medicine in Immigration Custody." Miami: FIAC.

Fogelman, Eva. 1994. *Conscience and Courage: Rescuers of Jews during the Holocaust.* New York: Anchor Doubleday.

Franz, Barbara. 2003. "Bosnian Refugees and Socioeconomic Realities: Changes in Refugee and Settlement Policies in Austria and the United States," *Journal of Ethnic and Migration Studies* 29, no. 1: 5–25.

Friedman, Edie, and Reva Klein. 2008. *Reluctant Refuge. The Story of Asylum in Britain.* London: The British Library.

Frontex. 2007. "European Patrols Network," www.frontex.europa.eu/news room/news_releases/art25.html, accessed June 4.

Garofoli, Joe, and Drew Joseph. 2010. "Immigration Adds Heat to State Races. Feds Should Challenge Sanctuary Cities, Fiorina Says," *San Francisco Chronicle*, July 31, A1; A7.

Gerety, Tom. 1986. "Sanctuary: A Comment on the Ironic Relation between Law and Morality," in *The New Asylum Seekers: Refugee Law in the 1980s*, David A. Martin, ed. Dordrecht: Martinus Nijhoff Publications, 159–80.

Gershon, Karen, ed. 1966. *We Came as Children. A Collective Autobiography.* New York: Harcourt, Brace and World.

Gibney, Matthew J. 2004. *The Ethics and Politics of Asylum. Liberal Democracy and the Response to Refugees.* Cambridge: Cambridge University Press.

Gibney, Matthew J., and Randall Hansen, eds. 2005. *Immigration and Asylum. From 1900 to the Present.* 3 vols. Santa Barbara, CA: ABC-Clio.

Gilbert, Martin. 2003. *The Righteous. The Unsung Heroes of the Holocaust.* New York: Henry Holt.

Global Detention Project. 2009. "Sweden Detention Profile." Geneva: Programme for the Study of Global Migration, the Graduate Institute, www.globaldetentionproject.org.

Golden, Renny, and Michael McConnell. 1986. *Sanctuary: The New Underground Railroad.* New York: Orbis Books.

Good, Anthony. 2007. *Anthropology and Expertise in the Asylum Courts.* New York: Routledge-Cavendish.

Goodstein, Laurie. 2001. "Church Group Provides Oasis for Illegal Migrants to US," *The New York Times*, June 10, 1, 20.

Gopfert, Rebekka. 2004. "Kindertransport: History and Memory," *Shofar* 23, no. 1: 21–27.

Government Accountability Office. 2008. "U.S. Asylum System. Significant Variation Existed in Asylum Outcomes across Immigration Courts and Judges," GAO-08-940. Washington, D.C.: GAO.

Grahl-Madsen, Atle. 1980. *Territorial Asylum.* New York: Oceana.

Greenslade, Roy. 2005. "Seeking Scapegoats. The Coverage of Asylum in the UK Press." Asylum and Migration Working Paper 5. London: Institute for Public Policy Research.

Guardian. 2006. "'Everything in My life Has Crumbled,'" December 6: 16–17.

———. 2010. "Asylum Seeker Takes His Own Life after Losing Legal Aid," August 2: 7.

Haines, David W. 2010. *Safe Haven? A History of Refugees in America.* Sterling, VA: Kumarian Press.

Hainey, Raymond. 2007. "Asylum Seekers Stage Hunger Strike amid Claims of Brutality," *Scotsman*, http://news.scotsman.com/glasgow.cfm?id=910002007&format=print, accessed June 22.

Hallie, Philip P. 1979. *Lest Innocent Blood Be Shed. The Story of the Village of Le Chambon and How Goodness Happened There.* New York: Harper and Row.

Halter, Marek. 1998. *Stories of Deliverance. Speaking with Men and Women Who Rescued Jews from the Holocaust.* Chicago: Open Court.

Hancock, Landon, and Christopher Mitchell. 2004. *The Construction of Sanctuary: Local Zones of Peace amid Protracted Conflict.* Arlington, VA: George Mason University Institute for Conflict Analysis and Resolution.

Harcourt, Alexander H., and Frans B. M. de Waal, eds. 1992. *Coalitions and Alliances in Humans and Other Animals.* Oxford: Oxford University Press.

Harris, Mark, dir. 2000. *Into the Arms of Strangers: Stories of the Kindertransport.* DVD.

Hasegawa, Toshipazu. 1989. "Sexual Behavior of Immigrant and Resident Female Chimpanzees at Mahale," in *Understanding Chimpanzees*, Paul Heltne and Linda Marquardt, eds. Cambridge, MA: Harvard University Press, 90–103.

Hatton, T. J. 2005. "European Asylum Policy," *National Institute Economic Review* no. 194 (October): 108–19.

Hayter, Teresa. 2004. *Open Borders: The Case against Immigration Controls.* London: Pluto, 2nd ed.

Heartland Alliance et al. 2010. "United States of America. Submission to the United Nations Universal Periodic Review. Ninth Session of the Working Group on the UPR Human Rights Council, 2 November–3 December 2010. Human Rights Violations in the Immigration Detention System," www.scribd.com/doc/30181709, accessed October 10.

Henry, Patrick. 2001. "Banishing the Coercion of Despair: Le Chambon-sur-Lignon and the Holocaust Today," http://people.whitman.edu/~henrypg/banishing.htm.

Hewett, Nelly Trocmé. 2007. Interview, St. Paul, MN, November 9–12.

Heyman, Josiah. 1998. *Finding a Moral Heart for U.S. Immigration Policy: An Anthropological Perspective.* American Ethnological Society, Monographs in Human Policy Issues. Washington, D.C.: American Anthropological Association.

Hobson, Chris, Jonathan Cox, and Nicholas Sagovsky. 2008a. "Fit for Purpose Yet? The Independent Asylum Commission's Interim Findings." London: Independent Asylum Commission.

———. 2008b. "Saving Sanctuary. The Independent Asylum Commission's First Report of Conclusions and Recommendations." London: Independent Asylum Commission.

———. 2008c. "Safe Return. How to Improve What Happens When We Refuse People Sanctuary. The Independent Asylum Commission's Second Report of Conclusions and Recommendations." London: Independent Asylum Commission.

———. 2008d. "Deserving Dignity. The Independent Asylum Commission's Third Report of Conclusions and Recommendations." London: Independent Asylum Commission.

Home Office. 2008. "Control of Immigration: Quarterly Statistical Summary, United Kingdom," April 2008–June 2008, www.homeoffice.gov.uk/rds/pdfs08/coiq208.pdf, accessed April 24, 2009.

Hornsey and Crouch End Journal. 2007. Council Needs £3m More to Cover Cost of Asylum Seekers, www.hornseyjournal.co.uk/content/haringey/hornseyjournal/news/story.aspx?br, accessed June 4.

Houston Catholic Worker. 2008. "Bishops Resist Anti-Immigration Laws," January–February: 1.

Human Relations Area Files. "Sanctuary."

Human Rights First. 2008a. "Challenges to Legal Representation at Pearsall Detention Center," May 20, www.humanrightsfirst.org/blog/rpp/2008/05/challenges-to-legal-representation-at.html.

———. 2008b. "How to Repair the U.S. Asylum System. Blueprint for the Next Administration," December. Washington, D.C.: Human Rights First.

Human Rights Watch. 2008. "Stuck in a Revolving Door. Iraqis and Other Asylum Seekers and Migrants at the Greece-Turkey Entrance to the European Union." New York: Human Rights Watch.

———. 2009. "Detained and Dismissed. Women's Struggles to Obtain Health Care in United States Immigration Detention." New York: Human Rights Watch.

ICORN. International Cities of Refuge Network. www.icorn.org.

Immigration Law Practitioners Association [UK]. 2007. "Update on Asylum."

Independent Asylum Commission [UK]. 2007. "About the Commission."

Information Center about Asylum and Refugees. 2007a. "Asylum Support and Destitution."

———. 2007b. "Detention of Asylum Seekers in the United Kingdom."

———. 2007c. "The Operation of the Asylum Determination Process," thematic briefing for Independent Asylum Commission.

———. 2007d. "Removals."

———. 2007e. "Vulnerable Groups in the Asylum Determination Process. Thematic Briefing Prepared for the Independent Asylum Commission."

———. 2007f. "Women Refugees and Asylum Seekers in the UK."

Integrating Toryglen Community Ltd. 2007? "Integration and Orientation Programme. Information Pack." Glasgow.

Ira, Kumaran, and Antoine Lerougetel. 2008. "Undocumented Workers Occupy CGT Union Hall in Paris," May 6, www.wsws.org/articles/2008/may2008/immi-m06.shtml.

Isbell, Lynne. 2004. "Is There No Place like Home? Ecological Bases of Female Dispersal and Philopatry and their Consequences for the Formation of Kin Groups," in Bernard Chapais and Carol M. Berman, *Kinship and Behavior in Primates*. Oxford: Oxford University Press, 71–108.

Iyer, Pushpa, and Christopher Mitchell. 2004. "The Collapse of Peace Zones in Aceh: Problems of Incorporating Local Peace Zones into Settlement Processes," in Landon Hancock and Christopher Mitchell, *The Construction of Sanctuary: Local Zones of Peace amid Protracted Conflict*. Arlington, VA: George Mason University Institute for Conflict Analysis and Resolution, 26–38.

James, Harry C. 1974. *Pages from Hopi History*. Tucson: University of Arizona Press.

Jasinsky, Agnes. 2007. "Takoma Park 'Sanctuary City' Ordinance Discussed Monday in Closed Session," *Montgomery Gazette*, July 18: A-14.

Johnson, Christopher. 2007. "Ageing UK Needs 7m Immigrants to Survive," *Observer* [London], May 13: 6.

"Joint Parliamentary Briefing from the British Refugee Council, the Scottish Refugee Council and the Welsh Refugee Council. Borders, Citizenship and Immigration Bill 2009. House of Lords Second Reading, 11th February 2009." 2009. London: British Refugee Council.

Jones, William R. 1994. "Sanctuary, Exile and Law: The Fugitive and Public Authority in Medieval England and Modern America," in *Essays on English Law and the American Experience*, Elisabeth A. Cawthom and David E. Narrett, eds. College Station: Texas A&M University Press.

Joutard, Philippe, Jacques Poujol, and Patrick Cabanel. 1987. *Cévennes, Terre de Refuge 1940–1944*. N.p.: Presses du Languedoc/Club Cévenol.

Kassindja, Fauziya, and Layli Miller Bashir. 1998. *Do They Hear You When You Cry*. New York: Delacorte Press.

Kelly, Annie. 2007. "Frank Stevens Is an Iranian Table Tennis Champion and Asylum Seeker," *Guardian*. April 18.

Keneally, Thomas. 1982. *Schindler's List*. New York: Touchstone.

Kennedy, Stephanie. 2009. "Sweden Sending Iraqi Asylum Seekers Home," Australian Broadcasting Corporation, September 25, www.abc.net.au.

Kenney, David Ngaruri, and Philip G. Schrag. 2008. *Asylum Denied: A Refugee's Struggle for Safety in America*. Berkeley and Los Angeles: University of California Press.

Kennon, Kenneth. 2001. *Prisoner of Conscience: A Memoir*. N.p.: Xlibris.

Kesselring, Krista. 1999. "Abjuration and Its Demise: The Changing Face of Royal Justice in the Tudor Period," *Canadian Journal of History* 34: 345–58.

Kleinman, Susan, and Chana Moshenka. 2004. "Class as a Factor in the Social Adaptation of the Kindertransport Kinder," *Shofar* 23, no. 1: 28–40.

Klempner, Mark. 2006. *The Heart Has Reasons: Holocaust Rescuers and Their Stories of Courage*. Cleveland, OH: Pilgrim Press.

Kofman, Eleonore, Parvati Raghuram, and Matt Merefield. 2005. *Gendered Migrations. Towards Gender Sensitive Policies in the UK*. Asylum and Migration Working Paper 6. London: Institute for Public Policy Research.

Koser, Khalid. 2007. *International Migration: A Very Short Introduction*. Oxford: Oxford University Press.

Kroeger, Alix. 2007. "Europe Considers Single Asylum Policy," BBC News, Brussels, June 6, http://newsvote.bbc.co.uk/mpapps/pagetools/print/news.bbc.co.uk/1/hi/world/europe.

Kuper, Adam. 1994. *The Chosen Primate. Human Nature and Cultural Diversity*. Cambridge, MA: Harvard University Press.

Kushner, Tony. 2006. *Remembering Refugees. Then and Now*. Manchester: Manchester University Press.

Kushner, Tony, and Katharine Knox. 1999. *Refugees in an Age of Genocide. Global, National and Local Perspectives during the Twentieth Century*. London: Frank Cass.

Larson, Kate Clifford. 2004. *Bound for the Promised Land*. New York: Ballantine.

Liberty. N.d. "Defending the Human Rights Act." Pamphlet.

Lindisfarme, Nancy. 1981. *Direct Exchange and Brideprice: Alternative Forms in a Complex Marriage System*. London: Royal Anthropological Institute.

Lippert, Randy K. 2005. *Sanctuary, Sovereignty, Sacrifice: Canadian Sanctuary Incidents, Power, and Law*. Vancouver: University of British Columbia Press.

Lorentzen, Robin. 1991. *Women in the Sanctuary Movement*. Philadelphia: Temple University Press.

Louden, Eveline. 2008. Interview, Glasgow, February 20.

Lutheran Imigration and Refugee Service. 2006. Statement of Mark S. Hanson, Presiding Bishop, ELCA, and Ralston H. Deffenbaugh Jr., President, LIRS.

Lynch, M. 2004. "Forced Back." Washington, D.C.: Refugees International, May.

MacEoin, Gary, ed. 1985. *Sanctuary: A Resource Guide for Understanding and Participating in the Central American Refugees' Struggle*. San Francisco: Harper and Row.

Mackay, Neil, and Rachelle Money. 2008. "SNP Accused of Betraying Refugees," *Sunday Herald* (Edinburgh), May 24. www.sunday.herald.com/search/display.var.2295694.0.snp, accessed August 28.

MacMichael, N. H. 1970. "Sanctuary at Westminster," Westminster Abbey Occasional Paper No. 27. London: Westminster Abbey.

Maillebouis, Christian. 2005. *La Montagne Protestante. Pratiques chrétiennes sociales dans la region du Mazet-St.-Voy 1920–1940*. Lyon: Editions Olivétan.

Maltby, Edward. 2008. "Parisian Migrant Workers Strike," May 12, www.workersliberty.org.

Marino, Andy. 1999. *A Quiet American: The Secret War of Varian Fry*. New York: St. Martin's Press.

Markowitz, Miriam. 2010. "The Group," *The Nation*, October 11: 25–34.

Martin, Susan, and Andrew I. Schoenholtz. 2006. "Promoting the Human Rights of Forced Migrants," in *Human Rights and Conflict. Exploring the Links between Rights, Law, and Peacebuilding*. Washington, D.C.: United States Institute of Peace Press.

Masters, William Murray. 1953. *Rowanduz: A Kurdish Administrative and Mercantile Center*. N.p.: n.p.

Mazzinghi, Thomas John de. 1887. *Sanctuaries*. Stafford, UK: Halden and Son.

McConnell, Michael. 2007. Interview, Takoma Park, MD, January 28.

McDaid, Brendan. 2007. "Abused Asylum Seeker to Meet with Deputy First Minister," *Belfast Telegraph*, www.belfasttelegraph.co.uk/news/politics/article2647097.ece, accessed June 22.

McGlynn, Rev. Moyna. 2008. Interview, Glasgow, February 18.

McKenna, Helen. 2007. "What Happened to . . . Asylum-for-Sex Whistleblower," *Observer*, May 27.

Mead, Margaret. 1956. *New Lives for Old: Cultural Transformation—Manus 1928–1953*. New York: Morrow.

Medical Foundation for the Care of Victims of Torture. 2007. "Medical Foundation Warns Asylum Child Care Reforms Could Be Damaging," www.torturecare.org.uk/node/1038/print, accessed June 12.

Medical Justice Network. 2007. Pamphlet.

Mendelsohn, Daniel. 2006. *The Lost. A Search for Six of Six Million*. New York: Harper Collins.

Merjian, Armen H. 2009. "A Guinean Refugee's Odyssey: In Re Jarno, the Biggest Asylum Case in U.S. History and What It Tells Us about Our Broken System," *Georgetown Immigration Law Journal* 23 (Summer): 649–90.

Miller, Scott, and Sarah Ogilvie. 2006. *Refuge Denied: The* St. Louis *Passengers and the Holocaust*. Madison: University of Wisconsin Press.

Miroff, Nick. 2007. "Questions Remain on Illegal-Immigrant Measure," *The Washington Post*, July 12: B2.

Mitchell, Grant. 2009. "Case Management as an Alternative to Immigration Detention: The Australian Experience." Carlton, Australia: International Detention Coalition.

Montgomery Gazette. 2007. "Takoma Park Council Keeps Sanctuary Law," October 31, A-21.

Moorehead, Caroline. 2005. *Human Cargo*. New York: Holt.

———. 2007. "Women and Children for Sale," *The New York Review of Books* 54, no. 15 (October 11): 15–18.

Musson, Anthony, ed. 2005. *Boundaries of the Law. Geography, Gender and Jurisdiction in Medieval and Early Modern Europe*. Aldershot, UK: Ashgate.

Nan, Susan A., and Christopher Mitchell. 2004. "Local Zones of Peace as a Form of Institutionalized Conflict: Some Introductory Thoughts," in Landon Hancock and Christopher Mitchell, *The Construction of Sanctuary: Local Zones of Peace amid Protracted Conflict*. Arlington, VA: George Mason University Institute for Conflict Analysis and Resolution, 3–15.

New Londoners. 2007. "British . . . But Illegal." June 1.

New Sanctuary Movement of Philadelphia. 2010. www.sanctuaryphiladelphia.org, accessed October 19.

New York City New Sanctuary Coalition. 2010. www.newsanctuarynyc.org, accessed October 19.

Nguyen, Tram. 2005. *We Are All Suspects Now. Untold Stories from Immigrant Communities after 9/11*. Boston: Beacon Press.

No More Deaths. 2010. "'Littering' Conviction of Border Volunteer Overturned by Appeals Court," September 2, www.nomoredeaths.org, accessed October 9.

Noll, Gregor, and Joanne van Selm. 2003. "Rediscovering Resettlement," *MPI Insight*, No. 3 (December).

Obermeyer, Gerald J. 1969. *Structure and Authority in a Bedouin Tribe: The 'Aishabit of the Western Desert of Egypt*. Ann Arbor: University Microfilms.

Oldfield, Sybil. 2004. "'It Is Usually She': The Role of British Women in the Rescue and Care of the Kindertransport Kinder," *Shofar* 23, no. 1: 57–70.

Olson, Trisha. 2004. "Of the Worshipful Warrior: Sanctuary and Punishment in the Middle Ages," *St. Thomas Law Review* 16.

———. 2005. "Sanctuary and Penitential Rebirth in the Central Middle Ages," in Anthony Musson, ed., *Boundaries of the Law. Geography, Gender and*

Jurisdiction in Medieval and Early Modern Europe. Aldershot, UK: Ashgate, 38–52.

Panos Institute. 2008. "Australia Ends Asylum Lock-ups," July 29, www.panos. org.uk.

———. 2010. "Asylum Seekers Number Is Stable, Says UN," March 24, www. panos.org.uk.

Patel, Sunita, and Tom Jawetz. 2007. "Conditions of Confinement in Immigration Detention Facilities." Washington, D.C.: American Civil Liberties Union National Prison Project.

Pear, Robert. 2007. "A Million Faxes Later, A Little-Known Group Claims a Victory on Immigration," *The New York Times*, July 15: 13.

Pedley, John. 2005. *Sanctuaries and the Sacred in the Ancient Greek World.* Cambridge: Cambridge University Press.

Pew Global Attitudes Project. 2007. "World Publics Welcome Global Trade— But Not Immigration," October 4. Washington, D.C.: Pew Research Center.

Phelps, Jerome, et al. 2009. "Detained Lives. The Real Cost of Indefinite Immigration Detention." London: London Detainee Support Group.

Pirouet, Louise. 2001. *Whatever Happened to Asylum in Britain? A Tale of Two Walls.* New York: Berghahn Books.

Plaut, W. Gunther. 1995. *Asylum: A Moral Dilemma.* Westport, CT: Praeger.

Pres, Terrence des. 1979. "Goodness Incarnate. Sheltering Jews in Vichy France," *Harper's*, May: 83–86.

Price, Jonathan. 2007. "History of Asylum in London," Researching Asylum in London, www.researchasylum.org.uk/?lid = 282, accessed June 6.

Pro-Asylum Working Group. 2008. "Protecting the Persecuted: Closing the Gaps in the U.S. Asylum System Submitted to the Obama-Biden Immigration and Asylum Policy Transition Team by the Pro-Asylum Working Group," December 22.

Qazi, Zubaida. 2008. "Canadian Federal Court: US Is Not a Safe Third Country for Refugees," *International Law News*, Spring: 19.

Rabben, Linda. 1997. "Conditions of Asylum Seekers in INS Detention Centers and Contract Prison Facilities," *Immigration Policy Report No. 34.* Washington, D.C.: American Immigration Law Foundation, June.

Refugee Assessment and Guidance Unit. 2006. "Refugees and Asylum Seekers. An Education, Training and Employment Guide." London: London Metropolitan University.

Refugee Council [London]. 2006? "Update. Newsletter for the Supporters of the Refugee Council."

———. 2006. "The Truth about Asylum." Pamphlet, June.

———. 2007a. "How Can the Refugee Council in London Help You?" Brochure.

———. 2007b. "Still Human Still Here. The Campaign to End Destitution of Refused Asylum Seekers," June.

Religionlink.com. 2008. "The New Sanctuary Movement: Protecting and Welcoming," www.religionlink.com/tip_081208.php, December 12, accessed May 6, 2009.

Riggs, Charles H., Jr. 1963. *Criminal Asylum in Anglo-Saxon Law*. University of Florida Monographs, Social Sciences, no.18, Spring 1963. Gainesville: University of Florida Press.

Rittner, Carol, and Sondia Myers, eds. 1986. *The Courage to Care. Rescuers of Jews during the Holocaust*. New York: New York University Press.

Robinson, J. Armitage. 1907. "An Unrecognized Westminster Chronicler, 1381–1394." London: British Academy.

Rodseth, Lars, and Richard Wrangham. 2004. "Human Kinship: A Continuation of Politics by Other Means?" in *Kinship and Behavior in Primates*, Bernard Chapais and Carol M. Berman, eds. Oxford: Oxford University Press, 389–419.

Rojas, Catalina. 2004. "The People's Peace Processes: Local Resistance Processes and the Development of Zones of Peace in Colombia," in *The Construction of Sanctuary: Local Zones of Peace amid Protracted Conflict*, Landon Hancock and Christopher Mitchell. Arlington, VA: George Mason University Institute for Conflict Analysis and Resolution, 16–25.

Rosser, Gervase. 1989. *Medieval Westminster, 1200–1540*. Oxford: Clarendon Press.

———. 1996. "Sanctuary and Social Negotiation in Medieval England," in *The Cloister and the World. Essays in Medieval History in Honour of Barbara Harvey*, John Blair and Brian Golding, eds. Oxford: Clarendon Press, 57–79.

Saint Paul Pioneer Press. 2007. "Reunited, after US Does the Math, Then the Right Thing," November 11: 1–3B.

Sartain, Dorthea M. 2002. *Sanctuary in the Reign of Henry VII, with Particular Reference to Beverley and Durham*. Ph.D. thesis, Cambridge University.

Sauvage, Pierre. 1989. *Weapons of the Spirit*. DVD.

Scottish Executive Equality Unit. 2006. "Scottish Refugee Integration Forum, Action Plan 2006."

Shaw, Jan, and Rachel Witkin. 2004. *Get It Right. How Home Office Decision Making Fails Refugees*. London: Amnesty International UK.

Shoeb, Marwa, Harvey M. Weinstein, and Jodi Halpern. 2007. "Living in Religious Time and Space: Iraqi Refugees in Dearborn, Michigan," *Journal of Refugee Studies* 20, no. 3: 441–60.

Siebert, Wilbur H. 1968 [1898]. *The Underground Railroad from Slavery to Freedom*. New York: Arno Press/The New York Times.

Siebold, Martin. 1937. "Sanctuary," in Edwin Seligman, *Encyclopaedia of the Social Sciences*. New York: Macmillan, 534–37.

Smith, Christian. 1996. *Resisting Reagan. The U.S. Central America Peace Movement*. Chicago: University of Chicago Press.

Somerville, Will, Dhananjayan Sriskanadarajah, and Maria Latorre. 2009. "United Kingdom: A Reluctant Country of Immigration." Washington, D.C.: Migration Policy Institute, www.migrationpolicy.org.

Souidi, Ahlam. 2008. Interview, Glasgow, February 19.

Spicer, Andrew. 2005. "'A Place of Refuge and a Sanctuary of a Holy Temple': Exile Communities and the Stranger Churches," in *Immigrants in Tudor and Early Stuart England*, Nigel Goose and Lien Luu, eds. Brighton, UK: Academic Press.

Stastny, Charles. 1987. "Sanctuary and the State," *Contemporary Crises* 11: 279–301.

Stevens, Dallal. 2004. *UK Asylum Law and Policy. Historical and Contemporary Perspectives.* London: Sweet and Maxwell.

Still Human Still Here. 2007a. "The Campaign to End Destitution of Refused Asylum Seekers," May.

———. 2007b. "Amendment to UK Borders Bill 2007. Lords Report Briefing."

———. 2009. "Briefing Paper on Destitute Refused Asylum Seekers," www. stillhumanstillhere.wordpress.com/resources, accessed April 25.

Stowe, Harriet Beecher. 1952 [1852]. *Uncle Tom's Cabin*. New York: Dodd, Mead.

Strangers into Citizens. 2007. "National Day of Action and Celebration." London.

Stringer, Eleanor, and Tris Lumley. 2006. "A Long Way to Go: Young Refugees and Asylum Seekers in the UK. A Guide for Donors and Funders." London: New Philanthropy Capital.

Student Action for Refugees. N.d. "Refugee Loyalty Card." Pamphlet.

Switala, William J. 2004. *Underground Railroad in Delaware, Maryland and West Virginia*. Mechanicsburg, PA: Stackpole Books.

Sydney Morning Herald. 2007. "Dutch Amnesty for 30,000 Asylum Seekers," May 26. www.smh.com.au.

Symonds, Steve. 2007. Experiences of the UK Immigration Service: Report Launch and Information Day, Refugee and Migrants' Forum, May 14. London: ILPA.

Talbot, Margaret. 2008. "The Lost Children. What Do Tougher Detention Policies Mean for Illegal Immigrant Families?" *The New Yorker*, February: 58–67.

Taylor, Diane. 2009. "Underground Lives. An Investigation into the Living Conditions and Survival Strategies of Destitute Asylum Seekers in the UK." Leeds: Positive Action for Refugees and Asylum Seekers.

Taylor, Matthew. 2010. "Millions Paid in Compensation to Migrants Locked up in UK," *Guardian*, September 27: 14.

Tazreiter, Claudia. 2004. *Asylum Seekers and the State: The Politics of Protection in a Security-Conscious World*. Aldershot, UK: Ashgate.

The New York Times. 2007. "Johtje Vos, Who Saved Wartime Jews, Dies at 97," November 4: 27.

The Washington Post. 2007a. "American Immigration Basic. Broad Reform May Have to Wait. Decent Treatment at Detention Centers Does Not," July 7.

———. 2007b. "Takoma Park Stays Immigrant 'Sanctuary,'" October 31: B1.

———. 2008. "Mount Rainier Council to Vote on Becoming 'Sanctuary' City," January 25.

Thornley, Isobel. 1924. "The Destruction of Sanctuary," in R.W. Seton-Watson, ed., *Tudor Studies*. London: Longmans, Green, 182–207.

Tickle, Louise. 2007. "I Thought They'd Have a Nice House but They Don't. Schoolchildren Lose Their Preconceptions as They Listen to the Personal Stories of Asylum Seekers," *Guardian*, May 29: 6.

Tobin, Jacqueline, with Hettie Jones. 2007. *From Midnight to Dawn: The Last Tracks of the Underground Railroad*. New York: Doubleday.

Tomsho, Robert. 1987. *The American Sanctuary Movement*. Austin: University of Texas Press.

Tram, Nguyen. 2005. *We Are All Suspects Now. Untold Stories from Immigrant Communities after 9/11*. Boston: Beacon Press.

Trauner, Helene. 2005. "Dimensions of West African Immigration to France: Malian Immigrant Women in Paris," *Stichproben: Wiener Zeitschrift für kritische Afrikastudien* 8: 221–35.

Travis, Alan. 2007. "Rescued Trafficking Victims Liable to Face Deportation," *Guardian*, October 12: 15.

———. 2010. "Home Office Bids to Restrict Jobs for Asylum Seekers," *Guardian*, July 29, www.guardian.co.uk.

Trocmé, André. 1940. "This Is My Will and Testament," typescript, Trocmé Collection, Peace Collection, Swarthmore College, Pennsylvania.

———. 2004. *Jesus and the Nonviolent Revolution*. Farmington, PA: Bruderhof Foundation.

———. N.d. "Autobiographie," typescript, Trocmé Collection, Peace Collection, Swarthmore College, Pennsylvania.

Tsangarides, Natasha. 2010. "The Refugee Roulette: The Role of Country Information in Refugee Status Determination." London: Immigration Advisory Service.

UNISON. N.d. "Networking Migrant Workers."

United States Department of Homeland Security. 2003. "Detention and Removal Strategy 2003–2012. Detention and Removal Strategy for a Secure Homeland." Washington, D.C.: DHS Office of Detention and Removal, www.thenyic.org/uploads/ICE_Endgame_Strategic_Plan.pdf, accessed October 8, 2010.

Varian Fry Foundation. 2008. www.almondseed.com.

Walzer, Michael. 1983. *Spheres of Justice: A Defense of Pluralism and Equality*. New York: Basic Books.

Watanabe, Teresa. 2007. "Vietnamese Refugee Family in Limbo," *Los Angeles Times*, October 19.

Webber, Frances. 2010. "Asylum Battles: Two Victories and One Setback," London: Institute of Race Relations, August 12, www.irr.org.uk/2010/august/ha000013.html.

Welch, Michael. 2002. *Detained: Immigration Laws and the Expanding INS Jail Complex*. Philadelphia: Temple University Press.

———. 2007. "Deadly Consequences: Crime-Control Discourse and Unwelcome Migrants," *Criminology and Public Policy* 6, no. 2: 275–82.

Welch, Michael, and Liza Schuster. 2005a. "Detention of Asylum Seekers in the United States, United Kingdom, France, Germany and Italy: A Critical View of the Globalizing Culture of Control," *Criminal Justice* 5, no. 4: 331–55.

———. 2005b. "Detention of Asylum Seekers in the UK and USA. Deciphering Noisy and Quiet Constructions," *Punishment and Society* 7 (4): 397–417.

Westermarck, Edward. 1909. "Asylum," in J. Hastings, ed., *Encyclopaedia of Religion and Ethics*, vol. II: 161–64.

Winder, Robert. 2004. *Bloody Foreigners. The Story of Immigration to Britain.* London: Little Brown.

Woolf, Maria. 2007. "Blears Sparks Race Row over Immigrants 'Undercutting Wages,'" *Independent* [London], http://news.independent.co.uk/uk/politics/article2640423.ece, accessed June 12.

Yarl's Wood Detainees. 2007. Letter to Gordon Brown MP from Detainees at Yarl's Wood, May 28. Typescript.

"Yarl's Wood Detention Centre's Family Wing to Be Shut Down." 2010. *Guardian*, July 21, www.guardian.co.uk.

INDEX

257

For more than 20 years Linda Rabben has worked on human rights issues as a researcher, editor, writer, and advocate for nonprofit organizations, print media, a public radio program, a refugee resettlement agency, and colleges and universities.

After doing field research in Brazil and receiving a Ph.D. in anthropology and Latin American studies from Cornell University, she returned to Brazil many times in the 1980s and 1990s to carry out research on social movements and to represent nongovernmental organizations.

For her writing on Brazil she received the Spann Memorial Essay Prize and a Catholic Press Association award. Her articles have appeared in numerous periodicals, and she has spoken on Brazil and human rights in the United States, Brazil, the UK, and Europe. She served on the American Anthropological Association's Committee for Human Rights and the Brazilian Studies Association's human rights task force.

Her books include *Unnatural Selection: The Yanomami, the Kayapó and the Onslaught of Civilization* (1998); a second edition, *Brazil's Indians and the Onslaught of Civilization*, appeared in 2004. *Fierce Legion of Friends: A History of Human Rights Campaigns and Campaigners* was published in 2002. Her translation of *Walking the Forest with Chico Mendes*, by Gomercindo Rodrigues, appeared in 2007.

She has worked on immigration issues since 1996. In 2007–08 she studied asylum policy as a visiting fellow at London School of Economics' Centre for the Study of Human Rights.